Together Forever?

TOGETHER FOREVER?

The Gay Guide to Good Relationships

Andrew Marshall

PAN BOOKS

First published 1995 by Pan Books

an imprint of Macmillan General Books
Cavaye Place London SW10 9PG
and Basingstoke

Associated companies throughout the world

ISBN 0-330-33688-6

Copyright © Andrew Marshall 1995

The right of Andrew Marshall to be identified as the
author of this work has been asserted by him in accordance
with the Copyright, Designs and Patents Act 1988.

1 3 5 7 9 8 6 4 2

A CIP catalogue record for this book is available from
the British Library

Typeset by CentraCet Limited, Cambridge
Printed and bound in Great Britain by
Cox & Wyman Ltd, Reading

Dedicated to my partner Thom
(my sweetest research)

CONTENTS

ACKNOWLEDGEMENTS

Thanks to: Gary Grant (for being a wonderful sounding-board), Ingrid Connell, my editor (for believing in me), Hazel Orme, Alan Goodall, Nick Kirby Turner, Donald Duggan, Jean Lockett . . . and Connie 'Comma' Cashmere.

Not forgetting the couples who shared their experiences with me.

1

HOW TO USE
THIS BOOK:

Introduction to the Stages of Gay Relationships

Most heterosexuals expect to fall in love with someone, get married, have children and remain faithful to each other happily ever after. We know this is a myth from the number of divorces, single-parent families and all the step-parenting, but it has such a strong pull on the imagination that it is felt by the majority to be the ideal way to live. Heterosexuals have a role model for how their relationship should be conducted. Movies, plays, books and television all explore how boy meets girl and lives happily ever after. They also have their own families as laboratories for how to conduct their relationships; their parents, brothers and sisters, aunts and uncles have all given examples of either how or how not to fall in love.

Gay people are free of the straitjacket of expectations but they have fewer clues to work out what happens after boy meets boy or girl meets girl. Gays and lesbians seldom feature in popular entertainment except as the celibate best friend of one of the leading characters, an axe murderer, or comedy sideline playing a mincing queen or a bull-dyke. We have no road map given us by our childhood experiences, schools or the media. To make matters worse, gay relationships are often kept invisible through fear and homophobia. However, thousands of gay and lesbian couples are negotiating their own individual ways of living. In this book we will celebrate their successes, chronicle their diversity and look at the pleasures and pitfalls of gay relationships. The featured couples were mainly recruited through letters and advertisements in the gay press but some were found through personal contacts. I have also drawn on my own relationship experiences and ten years of counselling – mainly heterosexual – couples for Relate, the marriage guidance service.

I have used the interview format for this book for three reasons. First, gay people have always had to learn from each other: when many of us were growing up there were no books about being gay (or the few that existed were deeply negative), which has made gay history an oral tradition. When we first 'come out' or explore the gay world, we have to ask questions: it is our only way of learning and making sense of it. Second, I wanted to provide possible role models and to explore in depth the reality of gay relationships. The interview format allows other couples to pick and choose the structures and ideas that make sense to them for their own relationships. Third, I wanted to give a wide variety of perspectives, to further the debate about gay relationships rather than provide tablets of stone. Therefore I have let the couples speak for themselves and followed up with my own interpretations and explanations. You can choose to agree or disagree with both the couples' and my ideas but I hope it starts you thinking.

Relationships progress and change over time. A couple who have been together for ten years have different problems from one just starting out. In this book I set out a theory about the stages that gay relationships pass through.

Some of the problems that couples might put down to 'something wrong with us' can be the natural issues of that period of the partnership. I have arranged the interviews in an order that reflects these gay-relationship developmental stages. Therefore I would recommend that you start at Chapter One and work through the book rather than leap to those that seem most relevant to you.

I have called the book *Together Forever?* with a question mark because when I started researching I wanted to know if it was possible for two men to forge a rewarding long-standing relationship. I also hope to challenge the myth that 'gay relationships never last' and find out what makes the enduring partnership work. If you also want the answers to these questions this book is for you. I hope that *Together Forever?* will change lives – *your* life!

2

FINDING A PARTNER

Many gay men complain that they can easily make sexual contacts but that it is far more difficult to find someone special and fall in love. What makes the difference between a lasting relationship and a passing affair?

Bill and Jamey contradict one of the major myths that gay men cannot cope with commitment. They are an attractive couple in their early forties: Bill is a businessman involved in importing and exporting, while Jamey is a freelance design consultant. They live together in a pleasant part of South London, and their relationship has lasted over twenty years. They have strong views about the secret of their success.

How did you meet?

JAMEY We were both at the same school together in 1966 – we met in the PE class. There were lots of gay students, but nobody talked about it. It was three years before Stonewall and everything was still innuendo – everybody made jokes about it but nobody was out.

How old were you?

BILL We were thirteen and fourteen. It wasn't the age when you were thinking about sex. Subconsciously yes, but it wasn't the first thing on your mind. But we were friends, not close friends.

JAMEY   I had a heavy crush on another boy during those three years of school, but we were part of the same group. We also grew up in the same area.

How did it change from schoolboy friends into something different?

JAMEY   We went to separate colleges, but neither of us moved away. We became interested in the same hobby, collecting old records. We used to go out at weekends to junk shops.

BILL   And other things as well. I think we just naturally knew, although I wasn't out yet, that our interests and outlooks were similar. Different from the kids playing football down the street.

Had you started fooling around in a schoolboy way?

BILL   No, not me.

JAMEY   Not me either. There was no pressure to date girls – my parents never brought the subject up. Around sixteen, I started to realize I was gay, and I wasn't frightened by it but I didn't deal with it on a conscious level. At eighteen, one weekend we were in my parents' house – they'd gone away.

BILL   There were vibes going on.

JAMEY   There had been vibes going on for about a year before that. We knew it was there. We had gone out and bought a batch of new records while they were away, and something just happened. That was it, it just happened, and we've been together ever since.

BILL   We pulled each other out of the closet in one afternoon, and that was the end of the discussion.

What was your reaction to each other the next day? Was there any awkwardness?

BILL   Not with each other, with the situation.

JAMEY   No, there was an awkwardness with each other as well, because we both felt that we were the only two in the world. I remember feeling sick, though not guilty about it. When I was growing up, I was a very camp child, very outrageous, so I never cared what other people thought, but I just didn't know how to handle this. I was still living at home, my parents were close and hawk-eyed. They knew everything I was doing. We lived in a small flat and I shared a bedroom with my brother, who was a typical macho boy. I didn't know what to do with it. But I remember the feeling of terrific release, relief, thank God now it's out.

BILL   I didn't feel guilty – awkward in the sense I was only eighteen. How do I deal with this? What do I do? Where do I go? I can't tell anybody. You can't tell anybody – that was the initial reaction.

JAMEY   It was about how do you tell your parents, or not to tell your parents.

So how important do you feel it was that you knew each other as people before you had the sexual contact?

JAMEY   Looking back, I think that's what's kept us together until this day, because we didn't get together as a sexual kick in a bar and then find out six months later we had nothing in common. We had already built a social interaction and structure together before the sex happened.

BILL   No, I disagree. Fate just happened to bring the two of us into the same room at the same time. It could have been somebody else. I don't think I would ever have started this by picking someone up in a bar. I don't think I would have realized to do it. If it hadn't been him I would most probably have found somebody else at school — unlike today's kids, they wake up and say, 'I'm gay', and the next day they're on Compton Street.

JAMEY But there was no Compton Street, there was nothing like that then.

BILL I was nineteen, he was eighteen and we were both so desperate to have sex. That was a lot of the driving force.

JAMEY That was the driving force behind the sex but it wasn't behind us spending so much time together, and enjoying so many different things together. We had already established a good rapport and a relationship, so the sex was secondary, but it is usually the other way round.

BILL We always tell our friends now who pick up people in bars that it never works out. I have a friend who is a cellist and I say, for heaven's sake join a music club, go to night school, meet someone that way. You have a much better chance of finding the right person. You might find someone in a bar, but it will take you a hundred times to find someone who has your interests.

What happened next?

BILL We lived in our own little closet, we had no friends, we didn't know what to do.

JAMEY Even though we were living in a major city with the rumblings of the gay movements beginning, and we knew all about it. I remember the day after we had had sex for the first time, I said, 'Well, it's going to improve, there's all this talk about gay lib,' but we were not part of it. And for the first couple of years we lived about fifteen miles apart and the only time we could see each other was weekends. We had no time for any other people. All our free time we spent with each other, and we became extremely cocooned and isolated.

BILL   Looking back on it, it was totally unhealthy.

JAMEY   It wasn't very good at all. After three years we finally got a flat together.

BILL   For about a year we were still living in our own world. We found a gay bar and, like everybody, we were petrified, walked around the block fifteen times. We finally went in and it was no big deal. After that, it all just fell into place.

When did you tell your parents the true nature of your relationship?

JAMEY   Shortly after we got a nice two-bedroom flat I went over to my parents for lunch one afternoon. My grandparents were there and my mother just flat out asked me if I was gay.

BILL   We decided to get brave about it. We were comfortable about it. We had made an adjustment. I guess everybody does. We were not militant, but just a little more cocky about it.

JAMEY   No, I think that when you are living on your own you can begin to build your own identity. You're no longer in the shadow of your parents.

BILL   We were both working, so if they decided to tell us to jump in the lake we didn't care.

JAMEY   I suppose, really, I had been dropping hints. Wanting to goad them into asking me, because I felt that once they asked they already knew. My mother asked, 'Why is it that you never go out with women?' Now my parents had never brought that subject up, all the years I had lived at home. I said, 'Because I'm gay and Bill is my lover.' My mother feigned a sort of temper tantrum and she started to cry and went into the bedroom and locked the door. My grandparents looked at me and said, 'We've always known.' So my grandmother went to my mother and said, 'Don't be so ridiculous, you've always known. What did you think when he used to wear your clothes?'

Were both of your parents supportive?

JAMEY   I told my mother, 'You can either accept it or not. I'm completely comfortable. As far as I'm concerned, it's the same as being left- or right handed.' From that moment, no problems. Not even one second.

BILL   I told my sister first and she called up and told my mother. My mother rang back and said, 'Why don't you come up and we'll have a talk about it?' which we did for an hour and that was the end of it.

Do your in-laws treat you like the partner of one of their heterosexual children?

JAMEY   No. My mother hates my sister-in-law and she loves Bill. He can do no wrong.

BILL   My sister is divorced now, but my parents hated her husband. Jamey's mother is a typical victim of what heterosexuals always fall into: you must be this way, this way, this way. Therefore when his brother had an affair, that was like the end of the world to her. He got a divorce from his first wife and Jamey's mother had a nervous breakdown for six months. When he had an affair with the second wife she went to pieces again.

JAMEY   It's also that my mother feels betrayed, because . . . that's not the right word . . . but that she's lost my brother to another woman. She hasn't lost me to another woman.

BILL We are immediately outside the conventions of society, and that makes it easier. We do not have to follow the rules.

JAMEY I've always had my parents' support. We never felt guilty about being gay, so they never saw us in that light. They never saw us doing something wrong because we did not project that kind of feeling or image. To us it is the most natural thing in the world and to them the same.

You say that heterosexual people are expected to get married and be faithful. You seem to be suggesting that you are not faithful to one another.

JAMEY Emotionally, we are.

BILL Not sexually.

How long was it before you decided not to be sexually faithful to each other?

JAMEY It was not exactly a decision. Three years into the relationship we had a big row over it because I found out that he had been sleeping with one of our friends. I was very jealous and wanted complete monogamy. It was in November, I'll never forget it, and he said, 'We can't apply the rules of straight marriage to our relationship. If you're going to insist on that, it's not going to work.' From that time onwards we have not had a problem.

BILL Our initial house-keeping together is what I call suburban, we were, like, basically straight. His parents and his grandparents lived a three-minute walk away. I just realized it was wrong.

JAMEY But once we had that argument, we made a conscious decision that we would not lie to each other.

You had just this one bad argument?

BILL I told him everything I had been doing, everything I had been thinking. I told him the reason I hadn't told him was because he had kept saying that he wanted a monogamous relationship. I did not feel that way. So I did it behind his back for a while but then it came out as it does inevitably.

So did you negotiate where you were going to go?

JAMEY No. We never discussed it again. We never set ground rules. It was never a problem again.

BILL It happened very naturally, we slipped into the threesome story. The ground rules have changed as the need has.

How have the ground rules changed?

BILL Initially we were much closer sexually. Initially we had a strong sexual relationship. So the natural thing at that point was to introduce a third person.

JAMEY And for Bill and me to share the outside sexual experiences.

BILL It all happened very naturally. A friend came to visit, we all felt comfortable about it. We had a queen-sized bed and one thing led to another. We stayed friends with this person for years. Unfortunately he died last year.

JAMEY We continued our sexual relationship. Was there any jealousy between the two of us? No, never.

BILL Then we became a little more professional – we'd go out cruising together as a couple.

JAMEY You must remember this was the age before Aids.

How many years had you been together at this stage?

JAMEY We had been living together for five years in suburbia before we moved into the heart of the gay community.

It would always be threesomes. You were not allowed to have sex on your own with somebody else?

JAMEY We did occasionally have sex with somebody else. It wasn't important, I honestly can't remember.

BILL Actually I do know how the progression came along. We went out as this unit, buzzing around, dragging people back. Then a brand new bar opened – it was 1980 – and we went for the opening and we each met somebody different and we did something very daring – we brought them both back. But we had separate two and two, and that kind of opened up a new little thing.

No problems with this?

JAMEY None whatsoever. We were friends with them for years. If one would go out with somebody else, we would tell each other and we found it quite erotic the discussions of those things.

It became part of your love-making to tell each other about the things you were doing with the other person?

BILL Not while we were having sex, but as part of our sexuality.

What was the next stage?

BILL Sometimes he would spend a few days away with somebody else and I would join them later. If he was at his mother's I would go back with somebody else for a couple of hours.

JAMEY   We used to joke about it.

BILL   After a while it became a bodily function. It never really meant much.

Has either of you ever had an affair with somebody else?

BILL   I never had. He gets infatuated.

JAMEY   I got infatuated with an architect. He came down for a birthday party and it started off as a threesome and then Bill left on a business trip and the guy stayed on. We had an affair and I was infatuated to the point of obsession. It ended up quite embarrassingly. I went up to visit him and he had a boyfriend, but we've been friends ever since. It's not been a problem.

How did you feel when he was infatuated with somebody else?

BILL   I used to say it will run the course. Two years from now it will happen again and it will run the course. I know perfectly well that he ain't going to run off with somebody else, that's for sure.

Is it trust that stops you from worrying what the other person is doing?

BILL   I don't think it's trust. We have such an established relationship that I know in a hundred billion years he would never meet anybody and consciously say to himself this person is for me.

JAMEY   But that is trust, you're trusting the other person's emotional fidelity. Bill is ferociously independent as a person, but he's just not the type to get emotionally involved with anybody.

Do you still have sex together?

13

JAMEY   No. We stopped about five years ago. We both realized it was just not working any more sexually.

Why wasn't it working sexually?

BILL   I think we've gone past it.

JAMEY   I think we're too close. For me there has to be a little bit of distance to make that work.

BILL   I feel that I can separate sexual enjoyment from the emotional side of a relationship. To me sex is, like, totally physical. In fact, the more anonymous the better.

JAMEY   I don't agree with his view on that. I've made a lot of friends that way. For me, it can be anything you want it to be. Sex can be an expression of love, violence, power, hate, friendship, bonding with somebody for a few moments. Anything that talking can be – it's the same thing only it's done physically. It's a means of communication.

Do you miss the sexual contact with each other?

JAMEY   I don't, no.

BILL   No, we always sleep together and have a lot of physical contact.

JAMEY   We do have one little rule. We come home for the night, we don't spend it in other people's houses. This is our home and we're together for that.

There seems to be a bit of sadness. The atmosphere in the room has changed.

JAMEY   No no. A lot of people force themselves to have sex, force each other to have sex, when it's not working any more. It's making them miserable, because they think that they have to, that they're expected to do it. If it doesn't work, why bother? We share everything else – we sleep together, we cuddle every morning – so why force something that doesn't work? If anything, it's going to cause problems that just don't need to be caused.

BILL   You find this strange? I have sadness in my feelings, but it's nothing to do with that.

What's it about, then?

BILL   We're both getting older. When we were talking about our twenties, of course my eyes were bright. I don't miss having a sexual relationship with him, but I miss the fact that I'm not twenty-five any more.

JAMEY   We haven't had sex with each other for a long time – this isn't something new. Once in a great while, sometimes while we travel, we do, but it's really not successful. I don't think that either of us is satisfied by it.

What do you mean by not successful?

BILL   Just more mechanical.

JAMEY   Like if we've been away travelling for two months and we haven't had sex and we're really horny, it's a release. I think sex between two people in our situation, if it is to work, should be more than release, and if it doesn't work beyond that level, it really isn't the right thing to do.

Does one of you have more success than the other? Do you ever feel a tinge of jealousy?

JAMEY   Have we ever been jealous of each other? I don't think even for one second.

BILL   Our approach is totally different. Jamey is a talker, he likes to be with people. If I go away on a trip for one night he goes out of his mind. He has to be with people. He's great going into a bar, going to a restaurant, going into a café, chatting, *chatting* for eight hours and then maybe something might happen. I'm great – you just give me the towel, open the sauna door, in I go, wonderful. I don't want to know the person's name, I don't want to talk to them.

JAMEY   I think of sex as communication. I like to talk.

Do you think that is one of the reasons why you don't feel jealous, because sex means different things to each of you?

JAMEY   That could be, but we never felt jealous except at the beginning of the relationship. His way of having sex – going to a sauna or a wanky cinema – is a bodily function, like going to the loo.

But the way that you organize your sexual affairs is more like a relationship.

JAMEY   Which is why from time to time I've got infatuated with people – because I've spoken to them, I've got to know them.

BILL   I consciously avoid it. There have been occasions when it could have happened but I put a stop to it.

I'm trying to understand why you don't feel jealous of him, Bill.

BILL   Jamey will tell you why I don't feel jealous. The reason is, it lets me off the hook.

JAMEY   I'm very emotionally demanding.

BILL   Jamey demands your time eighty-four hours a day. I haven't got that much time, and I also feel that one person can't supply you with everything, emotionally, sexually or friendship. If he can collect a group of people who can help take care of his emotional needs, that's great to me.

It lets you off the hook.

16

BILL   Yes. It's tiring, sometimes you just want to sit and read a book or watch a TV programme, fart around and be left alone – he needs people.

JAMEY   He's very independent, I'm not. If anything has been the one problem in our relationship, that's the recurrent theme that's caused trouble. Never money and never sex.

BILL   It's not just his infatuations. He has close relationships with other people, not even sexual – one of them has been going on for years.

JAMEY   I've always had somebody like a soulmate.

BILL   Not to compare us with straights, but my sister has a best girlfriend and she can do certain things with her that her husband can't be bothered with. I think that's common in any kind of relationship.

How has Aids affected the sexual relationship?

JAMEY   This is the big story. I'm absolutely terrified, paranoid about Aids to the point that a lot of people consider it unreasonable. As soon as we heard about Aids, we made a very strong ground rule, that any form of unsafe sex was absolutely forbidden. That we did discuss.

BILL   Basically we were good little children and we followed the rules.

JAMEY   Bill's been tested and I haven't, also some of the people I had unprotected sex with before 1982 subsequently died. So I'm sort of suspicious that I might have it, which is the reason why I'm extremely careful – I wouldn't want to be responsible for spreading it to anybody else. I use condoms for oral sex as well. A lot of other people don't believe in it and think that's going too far.

BILL   Aids hasn't changed what I want out of the sexual side – it just makes me careful of what I do.

Has it made you closer?

JAMEY   It has made a big difference emotionally to me. I think I appreciate him more as a person. I appreciate having a relationship more than I think I would otherwise. Not that I'm saying that us staying together is just a reaction to Aids. Yet things I might have got upset about I don't, because they're small in comparison with Aids. That doesn't mean that we don't have rows over stupid things because we do. We went to a funeral recently – our two friends had been together for eleven or twelve years and one of them died, and that's sobering. We've lost an unusually high proportion of our friends. I suppose it's our age – we're right in the thick of it. One of the big problems in our relationship is that Bill won't talk about Aids and that I do find difficult.

What stops you from talking about Aids?

BILL   I talk about it all the time.

JAMEY   No, you don't, you don't talk about it.

BILL   I don't know what I'm supposed to be talking about.

JAMEY   You're not supportive emotionally on that subject, you avoid it. You run away intellectually.

BILL   Jamey thinks I'm not obsessed enough with it. But you need a balance between concern and awareness of Aids and getting on with your life. If you become obsessed with it, you'll turn around and say, 'What have I done with the last twenty years of my life? I haven't done anything with it, just sat around fretting all the time.'

JAMEY   But that's not what I mean. When friends have died he hasn't been terribly supportive and I think he has blocked it out. We lost a very close friend last April, who lived just over the road, and he was one of our oldest friends and I felt that Bill blurred the whole thing, to make it less painful.

What are you asking for?

JAMEY Crying, maybe. Just an expression of grief, an expression of regret, maybe anger, but some emotion. Bill was unemotional about the whole thing. He treated it as if nothing had happened, like this person has just disappeared.

BILL That's not true.

JAMEY Well, that's how you acted.

BILL I don't know what you want from me.

JAMEY This is one subject we do argue about frequently. The reaction to Aids is an issue.

BILL It does not affect our relationship.

Perhaps in a way it's part of the larger argument, about emotions and independence.

BILL I'm much more two feet on the ground and I can analyse anything that's going on, and say all right this is what has happened, and this I can deal with.

JAMEY But at the funeral Bill didn't hug me, didn't offer any kind of emotional support and it was extremely painful for me. Often I've had to turn to other people for that emotional support, which is a problem. Frankly I think it's something we should seek counselling for because it does disturb me greatly. In the last two years I have found that there's this void, which is making me a little bit uncomfortable.

The two of you are emotional opposites.

BILL   I say thank heavens for it. If we were both the way he is we would be living in the street by now – the electricity wouldn't have been paid for twenty years.

JAMEY   And if we were both the way he is, the electricity bill would have been paid right on time but we would have no friends. He hates making telephone calls, he hates writing letters. We have friends all over the world and it requires a lot of letter-writing, card-writing to keep in touch with them. He's never written once. But I don't chastise him for that.

BILL   I think we're a good balance in a way.

We all need emotion and we all need stability in our lives. You've separated it out: one of you represents one, and one represents the other.

JAMEY   Maybe it's a good chemistry – apparently it is. We're together and I think we have a good relationship.

BILL   I think it's a good chemistry because he can be on the phone crying to a friend about something I consider dealt with or not necessarily that important, and I'll be in here paying the bills.

JAMEY   I can deal with it on every issue except Aids, and that's where it's a real problem because I find it so devastating and so horrific. For me the biggest pressure on our lives is Aids. If that was removed as an issue, not only from us, but also from our friends, everybody in the community, everything would be more fulfilling, brighter. But it's a very pressing issue for me, not so for him. There's a bit of a rub there.

Once again the difference between you is that Bill knows he is not positive and you don't know whether you are or not.

JAMEY I've wrestled with the idea of taking the test, but I haven't been able to get up the courage to do it. I went once and walked out before my name was called at the clinic, I was just too terrified. They would never have gone through with it because I was literally shaking, so I don't think I would have been a very good candidate anyway. I think if that issue were removed there would be a lot less pressure on the two of us.

You've been with each other all this time, have you ever thought how one of you would cope without the other?

JAMEY No, we've never discussed it.

BILL No, because I know in my heart that there is nothing the matter with him.

BILL I think the reason why, is that both of our sets of parents are still alive. So we're still children in a way. I think that until your parents are gone, not that I'm wishing them away, you're not really an adult on your own two feet.

JAMEY I'm very concerned about my parents. They haven't planned for their future – my mother is very fragile emotionally.

Have you, Jamey, re-created your parents' marriage with Bill? Are the dynamics of your relationship the same as the dynamics of your parents' relationship?

JAMEY Not at all, completely different. My mother was allowed to be virtually a child. She can't do anything.

BILL I'll tell you the truth of the matter. When we first started out he was much more like her. He wouldn't travel, he hadn't been anywhere in his life and I'd already been all over Europe. I was much more aware that there was something out there that I wanted to investigate.

JAMEY I wanted to, but he had to pull a little.

BILL We're all like our parents – you've grown up in their house.

But both of you have a different relationship from that of your parents.

JAMEY I'm not so terribly sure. He's very much like his parents – they're unemotional people. Very efficient, planned for the future.

BILL My big concern at the moment is that I'm planning my retirement fund.

In a way the relationship has helped you grow?

JAMEY I think it has, for both of us. Bill was terribly introverted, never had any friends, terribly shy.

BILL Part of that was being a gay teenager.

JAMEY I was a gay teenager in the closet and I never felt that way. But when we were first out on the gay scene in the seventies you didn't make friends easily. You still don't, which I find annoying at times.

Do you think that one of the reasons your relationship has worked, is not only do you complement each other, but that you've become more like each other? You've learned from each other?

JAMEY Definitely. I'm more like him. I was a complete and utter household slob before I met him and now I'm reasonably organized. He's more sociable than he was fifteen years ago.

BILL Jamey is much more worldly than he was.

JAMEY A little of him has rubbed off on me and vice versa.

Do you still share the same hobbies that brought you together?

BILL It's not a question of specific hobbies but a general outlook on life – politically, socially, music, culture, travel, art, we have the same temperament.

What's the difference between your relationship and a friendship?

BILL We're committed to spending and sharing the rest of our lives together. Friendship means that if you had a job offer in Timbuktu you'd take it. Now, if I had a job offer, we'd have to sit and discuss it and say, 'Are you interested in coming along or are you not?'

JAMEY We don't live as just two flatmates sharing the house. It's not quite that, we have a life together. Not sexually, and we don't care, but in every other sense, yes.

If people ask you the secret of your success, what do you say?

JAMEY Having got together as people first, before a sexual relationship began. Sex was not the most important component, even at the beginning.

I agree with Jamey and Bill that knowing each other outside the sexual environment first is one of the main reasons why their relationship has lasted so long. This is the lynchpin of their success. However, there are other reasons which support and are born from this.

There has been flexibility in their relationship: they have allowed each other to grow and change. This has been possible because they implicitly trust each other through having got to know each other first as friends and then as exclusive lovers. They are secure in themselves, they feel secure in the relationship. All too often we are afraid that if our partner does something new, it will lead him away and we will lose him. Yet over a long period we change as people, and our needs change. A good relationship has to be dynamic and flexible. If it remains static when our outlook has changed we may feel trapped.

Jamey and Bill have not only allowed the relationship to change, but as individuals they have been changed by it. Jamey could have become the weak emotional creature he portrayed his mother as, but Bill has widened his horizons and helped him become more self-reliant. In his turn Jamey has shown Bill the importance of emotions and given him a more rewarding relationship than the unemotional efficiency of his parents' marriage. Bill and Jamey are also realistic about their relationship: they do not expect it to fulfil all their needs. They share interests and hobbies with others.

How do we choose our partners?

If you ask long-term couples they find it difficult to explain. They often say something like 'I thought he was very attractive', or 'I liked his sense of humour.' However, we meet lots of handsome people and people who make us laugh, so what makes one so special that we want to spend the rest of our life with him? Henry Dicks was one of the pioneers of marital therapy in the fifties, and he found that couples chose each other for three reasons. The first was social pressure, that someone came from the same class, race or religion. The second were conscious reasons, the ones that couples normally give when answering this question, good looks or shared interests. The third were unconscious reasons, the ones of which we are often unaware. It is what we would call *chemistry*, and is by far the most important factor in explaining why we fall in love.

Robin Skynner is a pioneer in group and family psychological treatment; he founded the Institute of Family Therapy and with John Cleese wrote the best-selling *Families and How to Survive Them*. He believes that we are attracted to people because they are like us in some deep psychological sense, and they complement our own personality in some hidden way. This is the buzz you sometimes get when you meet somebody, start exchanging information and find a million similarities and coincidences.

The evidence for what makes lovers pick each other is supplied by the 'Family Systems Exercise', which is often used in the training of counsellors. When the course starts and the trainees are strangers to each other, they are asked to walk around the room and look at the other people without talking until they find someone with whom they wish to pair off – not unlike a gay bar on a Saturday night! When they have done so they are asked to compare their family backgrounds. What is amazing is that they discover how alike they are, that the families they come from both functioned in a similar way. Perhaps both families had trouble with showing emotions, or becoming angry; and those whose fathers were absent in some way chose each other, as did the families of alcoholics. The circumstances are not always the same but the patterns are.

We choose people for a reason, which is nearly always subconscious. The reasons why the trainees choose someone out of the group of strangers relates to how we fall in love. It is like a play that is waiting to be cast: we search for other factors to re-create the people and issues that are important to us, because we have been unable to sort them out when we were children. Our partners have to speak the same language and want to play the same scenes as we do, or there is no connection.

Jamey's mother falls apart if something goes wrong for her while his father is the opposite. Jamey needed to learn how to be emotional without letting his feelings overwhelm him – in other words, to solve the dilemma his parents set him. Bill's parents are practical, they did not show their feelings easily, which may have made their child feel not truly loved. Bill learnt how to be practical, but the dilemma his parents set him was how to integrate emotions and feelings into a relationship. Bill and Jamey were not aware of these needs when they met but, like the trainee counsellors in the Family Systems Exercise, it explains their initial attraction. Their relationship has been successful because it has allowed them to find *accommodation* for the issues of emotions versus rationality.

However, a central dilemma is never settled to the complete satisfaction of both partners: new circumstances can appear which test the compromise. Bill and Jamey are still arguing about feelings and rationality. I do not want to belittle the tragedy of Aids and Jamey's heartfelt recollection of his friends' death, but the Aids debate is another way of playing out the dilemma of a feelings/emotional response versus the practical/rationalized approach. Jamey and Bill felt so strongly when we discussed Aids because they were debating Aids *and* continuing to solve the dilemma that brought them together in the first place.

To find a partner, it is important that we search beyond the attraction of a good-looking face and a great body: to relate properly to someone, our subconscious should be talking to their subconscious and finding out if there is anything in common. This is one of the reasons why cruisy bars are not a good place to meet prospective partners. Sex is such a strong feeling it can overwhelm the more complex factors that are going on when you meet someone in the more neutral way that Bill and Jamey suggests. First, talk to that interesting new man you have just met. However gorgeous and sexy he is, get to know him a little *before* you make love so that your relationship has a sounder basis than just physical attraction.

Where do I find a partner?

The best way to find someone to love is to stop looking! How many times have you been out searching for a lover and come home alone? Somehow we appear too desperate, too needy and unconsciously we give off signals that turn other people off. I met all the men who have been important in my life when I was least expecting to. Therefore, I was relaxed and able to be myself without worrying what the other person was thinking, how I measured up to his ideals and how he measured up to mine. The couples in this book all found that love 'took them by surprise', their defences were down and they were open with their feelings.

If you have now decided to stop looking for Mr Right, how could you, too, be ambushed by love? The best places to meet a partner are:

(1) **In a gay organization.** It does not matter what kind of group it is as long as you are all there to do something beyond meet men and have sex. It could be fund-raising for the local gay switchboard, volunteering to help an Aids organization or joining the gay outdoors club. The choice depends on your own interests, but while you are enjoying yourself or helping others you will begin to relate to the people you meet, rather than just lining up a sexual partner. Even if you do not find anyone special you'll make friends, raise money, help others and have wonderful thighs from all the long country walks.

(2) **Any kind of group!** It doesn't have to be gay. If you are 'out' it is amazing how many gay people you find in the

most unlikely settings. The oldest and most hackneyed piece of advice that agony aunts give their readers is to take up a new interest, or join an evening class – with good reason for you will meet plenty of new people, some of whom will be gay.

(3) **Through friends.** I am not suggesting that you ask your friends to matchmake for you, but let them know you would like to meet some new people. You are more likely to get on with your friends' friends than a complete stranger. You will probably have shared values and attitudes as well as the shared friend.

(4) **Through courage.** How many times have you been going to work or out shopping, with sex the last thing on your mind, when you suddenly spotted somebody really cute? He smiled at you and you smiled back but neither of you did anything about it. To judge by the personal columns, it happens all the time: 'Number 2 bus in Dulwich. You, brown leather jacket, red jeans; me, purple coat, white jeans, sat next to me. Smiled as I got off. Get in touch.' This is just one example from four columns of adverts. Next time you are in a similar position say hello, be courageous, who knows what will happen? I once interviewed a couple who met in a traffic jam on the M25! The crucial difference between chance meetings and being out cruising is that when you are out looking for sex the subtle connections I have described in this chapter are overwhelmed.

There are other well-known routes for finding men. Bars and clubs are less neutral and you are therefore less likely to find someone who shares your interests and attitudes. Cottages and saunas are the places you are least likely to meet a long-term partner. In some small rural areas, a cottage might be one of the few places to go, but the people hanging around are most likely to be married or looking for some quick anonymous sex, which is fine if that's all you want.

Contact ads and telephone dating are popular and lots of people advertise for someone special: 'Ruggedly handsome sailor/swimmer seeks first mate for much more than a one-night cruise.' Once again I have friends who have found lovers in this way, but my experience is that most enjoy a boost to their ego from receiving the letters and having plenty of fun dates but nothing seems to come of it. This is because you find out enough about your potential 'first mate' to start fantasizing, but not enough to get to know them. I can almost picture the golden sunset as the couple in the advert skim over the ocean to happy-ever-after, and I expect everyone who replied to the advertisement could, too. The danger with contact adverts is that you build a mountain of expectations that prevent you from communicating properly when you meet.

The new nineties way of meeting people is through computer networking. Sitting at your keyboard you can use special bulletin boards or electronic mail to flirt with other computer owners all over the world. There is even a special language of symbols to communicate different feelings. If you have exotic tastes, having the whole universe of gay men to explore your fantasies with is a great idea. However, computer networking has severe limitations: it is easy for your Romeo to put on a false personality to please you. Conversing with you on his PC he does not have to deal with the ex-lover he is still sharing a house with, who is as jealous as hell of any new man. He can subtract years from his age and add them to his height without your being any the wiser!

How do you know if you have found the right person?

Gay men start so many relationships it is sometimes difficult to tell which is special and which just a diversion. It is all too easy to be carried away on a cloud of fantasy: within two minutes of meeting someone your mind is conjuring up a gay version of the Kodak advert family, and you have not only decided what kind of dog you'll buy, but you're picking out names for its puppies. The danger with such fantasies is that more often than not you end up disappointed and bitter – two of the least attractive human qualities. I doubt this contact advertiser had many replies: 'Is it a crime to love? Does it necessarily constitute an invasion of privacy? Is it naïve to want to be loved? Did I ask too much? Anybody? Any answers?' If you are giving off these vibrations I doubt you will meet many interesting men either. It is important to balance the optimism and excitement of a new relationship with a pinch of realism.

In Victorian times, a man would ask a girl's parents for her hand in marriage. Her father or guardian would want to find out if the suitor's intentions were honourable. Your new lover might be making encouraging noises but here are a few questions that will allow you to be your own guardian.

(1) How 'out' is he? A relationship is a public phenomenon and until someone is out and honest about his sexuality, it is difficult for him to have a successful relationship. If his mother does not know he is gay, do you really want to have to move out all your clothes and possessions and hide every time she visits? I had a friend who had not told his parents that he was gay and was secretive about his boyfriend. It reached farce-like proportions after my friend

30

invited his lover to move into his home. If this 'unofficial partner' was alone in the house he was not allowed to answer the phone in case he was discovered. I had to let the phone ring three times, hang up and then call back before the boyfriend was permitted to pick up the phone. Needless to say, they are no longer together. On a deeper level, being secretive about your sexuality is being ashamed and even hating yourself. Not a recipe for love.

(2) Does he already have a boyfriend/partner? Many men in steady relationships cheat on the side. He might be economical with the truth because he is ashamed of what he is doing, or because he wants to keep you interested. Even if he is upfront and tells you he is in an open relationship, just like a married man he is unlikely to leave his partner and settle down with you.

(3) When did his last relationship end? The break-up of an affair is like a bereavement. We need to mourn the loss and we need time to recover from the pain. You might feel that you are helping him put his life back together, but if you become involved on the rebound, if he has not worked through all the issues from his previous relationship he will dump them into your new one.

(4) Are you closing your eyes to anything? We are good at avoiding anything that might spoil the pictures of roses round the door. Another friend told me about the wonderful new man in his life and proudly showed me a collage of photos he had made. It sounded extremely promising but it was only weeks later when he was about to rip the pictures out of their frame that he confessed the whole story: the ex-lover had abused drink and had a wife who lived in the flat upstairs. He admitted that he had known this all along but had chosen to ignore it.

(5) What does he want out of the relationship? This is the most important question to ask yourself. Is he looking to settle down, or is he still playing the field? Why has there

never been anybody serious in his life? Do you have similar values? Are you both home birds? Do you both enjoy exotic holidays? Do not expect to have similar ideas on all the major issues, but the more you agree on the better the chance of the relationship working.

(6) How well do you communicate with each other? If you find yourself telling him things you have never told anybody before you know you're on to a winner.

Even if your new man fails one of the 'guardian' tests, it is still possible to have a successful relationship but it is less probable. Your love could help him come out of the closet, or he might split up with his lover and sell their gorgeous home. I have met people who defy the odds and win through. It is also possible to communicate fantastically well but discover that you have met a new friend rather than a lover. There are no hard and fast rules for relationships – think of my six guardian questions as indicators.

You do not have to engage in a long courtship to have a successful partnership, although it could be fun! Allow time, at least, for the two of you to get to know each other, even if it's just a couple of hours of talking, before you go to bed. This provides space for the more complex process of falling in love to begin, which has a deeper emotional level than falling in lust – which is mainly physical.

STAGE 1 OF A GAY RELATIONSHIP
Blending

Bill and Jamey's interview shows how a relationship alters through the years. The issues that are important when you first meet are different from those you face twenty years later. Just as gay couples have no role models on how to conduct their relationships, they also lack any on how gay relationships develop and change. By contrast, a heterosexual couple move through various well-defined stages: having babies, coping with teenagers, the empty nest syndrome, etc. Until recently there has been little research into the dynamics of gay relationships, which has meant that couples do not know whether what they are experiencing is 'normal' for two people who have been together for that length of time or caused by a problem unique to them.

To date, the most comprehensive study on gay couples has been completed by the American researchers, McWhirter and Mattison, *The Male Couple: How Relationships Develop*. Over a period of five years they conducted interviews with 156 gay couples living in California who were not in therapy, and aged between twenty and sixty-nine. The length of the relationships ranged from one to thirty-seven years, a similar range to those featured in this book. McWhirter and Mattison's key finding was that a pattern of developmental stages could be identified. My research leads me to believe that the model is also applicable outside the United States and I have adapted their ideas to create my own model for how gay relationships change. This developmental model allows us to move away from anxieties about our own inadequacies and gives a wider picture of hurdles hat we have to get over at each life-stage: some people leap over with no problem, others have to take several runs at them, while others trip over them and are injured.

The Blending stage is a magical time when neither partner has eyes or time for anybody or anything beyond their new love. You do not just want to be together, you want to merge into each other. This stage normally lasts for about a year. The couple are two forces joining to create a third one – the relationship. Love and 'limerence' are at their the strongest. This term was coined by Dorothy Tennov, in her book *Love and Limerence: The Experience of Being In Love*, to distinguish between the overwhelming romantic feelings when you first meet and the long-term qualities of being in love. Limerence is the period of strong sexual attraction and long nights of sweaty passion, the feelings of falling in love are at their height; when you are away from your lover you ache to be together again. You count the hours and minutes until you are reunited and when it finally happens you are swept away by a huge wave of emotion. Everyone will recognize these feelings from romantic movies and novels, as well as from their own experience of the heady early days of an affair. There is intense togetherness, all the cares in the world go when you are with each other. It does not matter that you are deeply in debt because you are in love! You are almost permanently floating several feet above the ground with a look on your face that other people can find infuriating. All the differences between you and your new love are ignored in the intense bonding process that is going on. Not only are potential problems ignored, they are sometimes seen as a positive: it doesn't matter that he drinks because I can sober him up.

Arguments seem terrible because you are terrified that your feelings of longing will not be returned or that your partner's love could be withdrawn. When you have been together for ten years, you know that you will overcome a temporary falling out and that everything will return to normal. When you are starting out you do not have this experience to fall back on. In the early days, when you are in limerence, you might know intellectually that it is possible to argue and still love each other but you have no emotional proof. Therefore, differences feel scary and need to be minimized to the point where the relationship seems not to be made up of two individuals but one blended unit.

Problems may emerge in the Blending stage if one partner holds back or is frightened of losing his own identity

– particularly if he has been hurt before. This can prevent the couple from merging properly to create a relationship.

Limerence normally lasts for only a year when people commonly panic as reality begins to set in. They think that they are falling out of love, but the truth is that they are just moving on to the next stage in their relationship. It is a necessary move because we cannot remain tied at the hip to our partner: we are different people with different needs. One of the problems for gay men is that they have often had more relationships than heterosexuals. Therefore we have more experience of limerence and can become addicted. It is a strong, exhilarating feeling and, like a drink, drugs or sex, can be used temporarily to soothe or solve our problems. However, it is important to stick with your relationship and work through the problems. You will come out the other side and find new joys with your lover. I remember feeling cheated when I was told that these feelings could not last for ever, that coming out of limerence is only natural. It felt like I was being told it is all downhill from here. The good news, though, is that these feelings come back if you learn to sort out your differences. They are reawakened with a shared memory from that period or, for no reason, an intense feeling of togetherness will suddenly pop up again and you are bound tighter than ever to your partner.

It is natural to move out of the 'Blending' period and each stage has its own rewards and pleasures. If you have just recognized the problems of coming out of limerence in your relationship, don't worry. You are just starting the journey and, as we will see through the book, love changes, develops and deepens at each of a gay relationship's stages.

3

THE IMPORTANCE OF COMING OUT

A relationship is a public phenomenon and until a gay man is out and honest about his homosexuality, it is difficult for him to have a successful relationship. Unfortunately many gays are still partially in the closet: if the only people who know you are gay are the people you are gaying with, you are still in the closet. These men divide their lives into different compartments: they have anonymous, casual sex in a backroom or cottage and lead a different life with their workmates, neighbours and family. It takes courage to come out of the saunas and bars and live openly with another man. Yet being secretive and therefore ashamed is not a recipe for a successful partnership – there is no half-way house.

Ian and Andy have been lovers for two years. They live together with Ian's father, who does not know they are gay. Ian is thirty-three, a fifteen-stone bodybuilder and a delivery driver. He is extremely out-going and, on the surface, very confident. He has a high sex drive – claiming to have had sex with eighteen people in the last four weeks! He dominates the room with his large physical presence. Andy is more thoughtful. At twenty-three he has been to university, enjoys cinema and books, and has just started a new job giving quotes over the phone for car insurance. Andy has recently grown a small moustache because in the past he was sometimes mistaken for a lesbian. They live in a two-up, two-down terraced house in a large northern city.

ANDY I didn't have a particularly wonderful life before I met Ian. I had just been made redundant, dumped by the guy I was going out with and was living in a bedsit. I was on the dole, still paying off my overdraft from being a student and was bored and lonely. Most of my graduate friends had left the city to do other things. A lesbian couple were keeping my spirits up and took me to the local bisexual-group meeting because they knew a man they thought I would be interested in. I have a predilection for older-brother figures, who are hairy, 'tached and bearded. When I got there, I thought he looked a nice bloke but I didn't fancy him, but while I was there I saw a gorgeous guy standing at the bar. I thought, Wow, and was even more surprised when I discovered he was involved with the group.

IAN The bisexual meeting was held in a local pub. As the evening progressed I thought, There's something up here.

Are you both bisexual then?

IAN I would say there's more of me gay than straight, about 70 per cent and 30 per cent straight.

ANDY I would say 99 per cent gay. I've never had a sexual experience with a woman. I went out with a girl when I was fourteen for about three days and that was only because I felt pressured into it by my peers. I didn't want to do it at all.

IAN I've had one or two girlfriends. The last one I slept with was my best friend's wife. He was straight; they'd got married because she was pregnant. About two years later as the marriage started breaking up, they both turned to me. I ended up sleeping with her and losing a best mate. That was the last girl I slept with and that was three years ago.

ANDY   I had never considered having a bisexual man for a boyfriend. My previous lover used to let a room to a straight couple. The girl didn't know that her boyfriend was sleeping with the landlord to get money and privileges. Because the man involved was a bit sleazy I didn't have a good picture of bisexual men. There were so many lies. I didn't want to get involved with that sort of thing.

IAN   He hasn't mentioned that he was bouncing about from person to person because he was emotionally down at the time. Lots of people just used him for his body. Quite a few of them were very sleazy.

How did you come to live here?

ANDY   I invited Ian back for coffee that night because I needed a lift, it was quite late and I wanted to save the bus fares. I dragged him in.

IAN   Tell him what you'd done that week.

ANDY   On Wednesday a guy who I'd contacted through a personal advert had come over and I slept with him. On Friday a man who I'd been friends with for quite a while arranged to come over because I was depressed. He took me out and I ended up having sex with him as well. On Sunday Ian came round again, he brought lots of books and a computer game for me.

IAN   I thought, This is not right because it's not getting him anywhere. He's not got a job, he's not got a life, he's just bouncing around. We got to know each other properly and I thought, This one's all right. I'd never really had a boyfriend before. The one that I had before him lasted about four weeks. He was a bodybuilder and, being the direct person I am, I asked him three times if he wanted a boyfriend and three times he said no. So I thought, Bugger this.

ANDY   So I got him instead.

IAN   The first thing I stated when we started going out was that we would have an open relationship. I dislike lies and hiding anything. I'm so highly sexed that I tend to cottage or cruise or whatever. But I do it safely, of course, and I have had the test.

ANDY   Under duress, I must add.

Ian, you'd reached your thirties without having a boyfriend?

IAN   I was having a problem accepting that I am basically gay. Growing up in the eighties, you had the Conservatives and the Clause 28 bit. Gay was a bit weird and a bit naughty. When I was five or six I knew I was never going to get married, but my gay feelings didn't come out until I was about thirteen. My wet dreams would usually involve girls, then they started involving boys and girls and then boys on their own. I still do have dreams about girls but not very often.

How did you feel about Andy moving in here with your father living here too?

IAN   It was my idea. I thought, I like him, we get on well, he's the boyfriend. I just said, 'You're going to come and live at our house' or something similar. He was quite gobsmacked. I said, 'It's OK, you can have a room all to yourself.' Before that my dad had met him and they were getting on all right, although Andy was a bit nervous of him. I told him just to talk to him, treat him as a person. My father's like me, very forward and direct.

ANDY   It's understandable why I had reservations at first about moving in. How many gay relationships do you come across where they end up living with the father as well?

What were you anxious about?

ANDY   I'd had bad experiences. I moved in with a man just after I'd graduated and I thought it was all going to work out really well. However, I split up with him after two weeks but couldn't afford to move out of the house until six weeks later. I was sleeping in the same bed, and still having sex with him occasionally even though he'd sent me a 'Dear John' letter. I was worried that as soon as I moved in with Ian the same thing would happen and I'd end up back at square one.

IAN   But I'm not that sort of person, because if I'd thought it wasn't going to work I wouldn't have brought him over. The strange thing is that, sexually, he's not my type – my type is usually bodybuilders, or like on the calendars. I go for big men. I'm a man's man. But me and Andy get on very well – there's something very strong. If anybody harmed him I'd probably kill them. It does work in a negative way too. He sees somebody gay who he fancies, they take one look at me and run off. Because of my size I tend to terrify them, which I don't mean to do.

ANDY   It's also because lots of gay men don't trust an open relationship. Normally if one party says it's open the other doesn't know anything about it! So when they see Ian, they don't want to tangle with him and you don't see them for dust after that.

IAN   I'm not like typical gay men. I don't have their insecurity. I have other ones, but not the usual ones.

What's the insecurity of gay men?

IAN   Being gay! Most gay men are, I suppose, regarded as shifty and not to be trusted. They have their friends in the straight world who think that gays are like that. So they tend to bring that back into their own lives. Most gay men are quiet and shy round me. I'm bouncy and drive them up the wall within half an hour.

But when Andy moved in your father didn't know you were moving your boyfriend in!

IAN   Er, probably not, but I think it dawned after a few weeks or so. The rest of the family know. They worked it out for themselves.

ANDY   It's not a question of either of us being all lovey-dovey and calling each other darling. If we do it's probably as a joke because we think it's a bit naff and tacky, all that sentimentality towards each other. We've been talking about opening a joint cheque account, so we're bonding in ways that two men wouldn't usually do unless they have a relationship that went deeper than normal friends.

But your father didn't know you were gay or the nature of your relationship.

IAN   From what I can work out, over the years my family must have known something. I've never had a serious girlfriend and when my mother was alive she used to say, 'Are you gay?' I would say, 'No', because I couldn't accept being gay. Now if anybody asks I'll say yes, but I don't know what I'd do if my dad asked me now – whether I'd actually say it. I think he may have suspected it over the years.

What impact does it have on the relationship between you and Andy that your father doesn't know you're a couple?

ANDY   We had some trouble when somebody we thought was a friend tried to split us up so he could get his hands on me. He sent a solicitor's letter to Ian threatening action unless he sent a series of photos which he had joked about taking. They didn't exist. Ian was very upset about the letter so he discussed what to do with his father. After we had resolved it, the three of us were talking about it . . .

IAN My father said, 'Was he trying to break you and Andy up?' Mentally my jaw dropped. I thought, He must know. He just came out with it. I thought, Does he know? I think he does!

Why didn't you say anything to him then?

IAN I have never felt the need to. It's like being in a comfortable chair – you tend not to play around with it. If he said, 'Are you gay? Are you a couple?' I'd say yes, but he's never asked so I leave it as is. The rest of the family know, so he must know from them. I've got nieces and nephews who are all OK round me – I flirt with the lot. My dad's there sometimes when I'm flirting with them, so he must know something.

What do you think his reaction would be if you did tell him?

IAN As he's nearly seventy-four, and considering the period when he was brought up, he'll think negative towards it. He obviously doesn't want to know about sex or the lovey-dovey or the kissing that goes on behind closed doors, but he's not worried as long as he doesn't have to see it.

What's it like, Andy, living with your father-in-law without him knowing that you're his son-in-law?

ANDY It's worked really well. This might sound a bit weak or wimpish but it doesn't seem necessary to go around flaunting that we're a couple, especially at home, because it's not as if we've got anything particularly to prove. Why rock the boat? We all work well together, we've all got our tasks within the house. Ian's dad does the cooking, Ian does the hoovering and cleaning, and I do the washing and ironing.

You've got separate bedrooms. How did you feel, Andy, about being asked to move in, but for there to be no official marital bed?

ANDY I've always found it difficult to get any sleep in the same bed as someone else. Not because I was constantly being leapt on, it's just difficult. I don't understand how married couples can stand it.

IAN I don't believe in it. I want someone to have their own space. My room is my room, anything that goes on there is what I get up to. It's like being two separate people but being married. We're not under each other's feet all the time. I don't believe that if you're a couple you have to do everything together.

ANDY We both prefer the independence of a den each where we can do our own thing. My bed is the one used for guests, friends and sex. We both use the bed for sex with other people – Ian especially for his cottaging and cruising pick-ups. Ian's dad's room is below mine, so we have to be careful how much noise we make.

Have you ever wanted to be intimate with each other but have felt inhibited because Father's here?

ANDY I had quite a problem with that. After a while I was beginning to resent it. I wanted to be affectionate towards Ian but I couldn't because his father would object. It all got mixed up with the fact that I like living in the house with his father. We all get on well and because I knew that Ian's father wouldn't like it, it felt unfair for me to want to do it anyway! That all got tangled up and I got all stressed. I went to talk to a friend about it.

IAN I was slightly resentful because he didn't tell me.

ANDY I also felt I couldn't talk to you because it could sound like I don't like living with your father. You could have been terribly annoyed with me and think I was being selfish. I needed an outside opinion. The strange thing is that once I had talked about it, nothing got resolved, nothing changed, but I accepted the way that I felt.

IAN I'm not one that goes around touching all the time. I'm not a hand-holder – I can do it occasionally. I like hugging as this tattoo shows. [*They each reveal their bear tattoos.*]

Aren't the matching tattoos a bit of a give-away for your father?

IAN I suppose it's like a secret way of saying we're a gay couple.

ANDY It's a way of being blatant without being blatant.

IAN I don't mind him occasionally playing with my hair or my ear because it's a good stress release. But I don't like it all the time because I can go standoffish. I'm very independent. I couldn't have stood a relationship where we lay on the sofa together. I'd have gone straight to the other corner and sat on a chair.

So your father is a convenient chaperone for you?

IAN Yes, in some ways he is. It's good to have him around because we can both talk to him and he's there.

ANDY It's almost like having a peer even though he's related to Ian.

IAN If there's any problems, he'll come straight out and say, 'I think you're both being pillocks.' It's a good way of keeping us both on our toes.

There seems to be a discrepancy, Ian. You say you're up front and tell everybody about everything, yet you don't tell your father that you're gay. This seems to be two sides to your character.

IAN I suppose it is. I've never been comfortable telling him anything personal about myself. It's hard to show emotion towards my father. I'd love to, but it's always been hard. I've never really wanted to tell him I'm gay — maybe something subconsciously in me is ashamed about what I am. But now I'm more comfortable I'm not so ashamed of it.

Do you think Andy has helped you be less ashamed?

IAN In some ways, yes, he has brought me out. I'm more open and honest towards my own sexuality. Years ago, I would have denied vehemently that I was gay. I would then go out cottaging. It's like this Tory MP. Everybody thought he was respectable and normal, then suddenly they found him dead in stockings with a satsuma in his mouth. Everybody is suddenly shocked. 'Oh, my God, this is not the person I knew.' In some ways I'm like that. I used to have a sub-world, a secret world that people never knew about. I'm now more open about it. Another way my father will have worked it out is because I am the chairman of the Bisexual Group. The mail comes here, addressed to the Bisexual Group, and he obviously knows what bisexual is. I do bring men home occasionally while he's here. So he must know something, he's not stupid.

So why can't you be open and have it over and done with?

45

ANDY   Just in case he does react badly. It could cause too much bad feeling in the house to be worth it.

IAN   Also I don't believe in telling people 'I'm gay'. It's like someone saying, 'I'm straight, Mummy.'

You're very involved with the bisexual group here. Yet you said it's three years since you've had sex with a woman although you've had sex with eighteen men in the past month.

IAN   Since my sexuality has come on stream I think I've gone through about three and a half thousand men.

And about how many women?

IAN   Four, but I am attracted to women.

It does seem to be rather an imbalance!

IAN   Oh, yes, I agree. But there are three types of bisexual. The true bisexual probably has a boyfriend and a girlfriend. The straight bisexual occasionally has flings with men but goes home to the wife he loves, has kids and is happy that way. Finally there's the ones like me who have the boyfriend but occasionally the odd fling with a woman. I haven't done it in years and I don't feel I need to. Maybe I'm turning completely gay. Being bisexual can be a bit of a transitory thing – sometimes you can feel that you're straight and sometimes you can feel that you're gay. For years I'd felt different from everybody else but I didn't feel gay.

Andy, how would you feel if Ian had sex with a woman? Would it feel any different from when he has sex with other men?

ANDY   It might feel a little bit strange, but as long as I knew what was happening I wouldn't resent it. Across the back street from us there's a sixteen-year-old girl. For the past month or so we've realized that she has a fixation with Ian. But all the time I've known him he hasn't slept with any women. It's something in our relationship we haven't come across before.

IAN It's a crush. If I asked her to drop her knickers she would. I could have sex. I've had wet dreams about her – but I'm at the stage in my life where I won't use people. Years ago I would have taken her to bed and that would have been it. Now I think this is wrong because I don't want to take the humanity away from that person. I treat them as people. The other reason why I don't sleep with girls at the moment is because they are brought up to believe that if you sleep with them you're going out with them. She would think that we would get married, have kids, get a house – which would be wrong. If I was going out with a girl, I would also treat it as an open relationship.

You've said you don't want to sleep with girls because you'd be using them but aren't you using the eighteen men you had sex with?

IAN Yes. It's a two-way street – they're using me as much as I'm using them. They know the rules – if you cottage, you know the rules. You are there for sex. That's all it is, it's not emotional entanglements or anything. It's just quick convenient sex.

ANDY One of those eighteen men is me! He wouldn't be using me either.

IAN I don't use people. I try not to – I mean I have done in the past. Some gay men think it's filthy and it does have its dirty element. Standing by the toilets, waiting for somebody to come in, it's a bit like being a prostitute. I regard it as being a healthy part of myself. I've come to terms with what I do. I do it for a reason, I do it either because I'm getting tense about something or because I'm in a randy mood and I don't want to bother him. Our sex life is good, but it isn't rampant by any means. The last time we had sex was last week and the last time before then was about two months ago.

ANDY   It's by no means regular and by no means often. To be honest, my sex drive always went up when I wasn't going out with someone. I've been in this relationship for almost two years now, and it hasn't disappeared completely – I do have sexual relations with people, it's a matter of calming down. I wanted sex with people when I was single because it was a means to an end of bonding with someone. Now that I've got someone I don't feel the need. I still masturbate quite often.

IAN   Which I do as well.

ANDY   You do it much more often than I do.

IAN   We've discussed why we don't have sex. We've come to an understanding, we're good round each other. I don't like using the term lovers, we're boyfriends. We don't have to have mechanical sex, we have sex when we want sex. It just spontaneously happens as it did last weekend.

Ian, you say that you don't want to trouble him when you're randy. Would you mind if he troubled you more, Andy?

ANDY   I can't cope with it. He's much much more sexually active than I am. If I don't want to have sex and he does and he's harassing me about it, it doesn't feel like rape but it might as well be.

On an average week, Ian, what sex would you have?

IAN   I would masturbate fourteen times, that's an average, it can be more than that. I go cottaging most days, some-times twice. I come at least twenty times a week. When I was younger, it used to be to thirty or forty times a week. I'm slowing up but I can still come back after having sex in under an hour and enjoy sex again. I'm randy constantly. Occasionally I do shut down for repairs, a quiet rest.

ANDY It's like having a Chinese, he wants another after half an hour.

It sounds like you're addicted to sex?

IAN I suppose I am in some ways. I describe myself as a predator. It's a habit I've had since eleven or twelve when it started. I know it's there, you have to accept that it's part of me. I will always discuss sex or flirt with somebody. I flirt with everybody at work. I'm chasing them all over the place, or goosing them, or being terribly camp, hugging them or chatting them up. They get it constantly.

The men and the women?

IAN I don't get very sexual with the women because it's wrong, but I treat the men at work the same way that they treat the women. I tell this to the girls and they quite like it. I treat the men as sex objects.

Do you have any success with straight men?

IAN No. I terrify them.

I find it strange that you're chatting up straight men at work, but you won't tell your father! Wouldn't it make life easier between the two of you? You wouldn't have to hide everything.

ANDY It's surprising how families can react. My mum found out that I was gay when I was sixteen because she read a letter to me from an agony aunt. My stepfather, her new husband, found out about a year later after my first sexual rendezvous. It's taken some time for my mum to get used to it and she's not overly keen now. She knows I'm happy, which was one thing she worried about – she's met Ian and trusts him. Because I haven't told any other member of the family, I've always wondered if they were talking about it – whether they knew. I got my answer the Christmas before last. I don't often see my father, my parents are divorced and remarried, and he arranged to come over and see me and spend some time with me. We're not particularly close, never have been. He asked if he could talk about something personal and I said, 'Yes', and he said, 'Are you gay?' I was gobsmacked because I'd worried for years about him finding out. He's very macho – so when he asked me outright I was quite shocked. I admitted it and he just nodded as if it was confirming something. I asked him why he had suddenly asked me, and it turned out that, as a taxi driver, he has been doing quite a lot of business in the gay village in Manchester. His attitude to homosexuality has changed, from what I recognized as a kid, so I had to update a lot of information about what my father was like. It turned out that he had had an argument with his brother. My father made a joke about one of my little cousins being a bit of a sissy and my uncle took umbrage and shot back with me being exactly the same. Apparently my father threatened to knock his teeth out unless he retracted what he said. Even if my dad doesn't particularly like what I am, he's still prepared to defend me.

Why would you want to be defended? Does it bother you that somebody calls you a sissy?

ANDY A few years ago, if he had called me it to my face I would have been pissed off. Now I feel like Harvey Fierstein in *Torch Song Trilogy*. If people are going to give me shit about being gay, when it's got nothing to do with them anyway, I've got no time for them. What's the point in being involved with anybody who's not going to treat you the way you've been taught to treat them? I had the same trouble with my friends. One found out through rather underhand means and then told everybody else. I plucked up the courage to come out to more of my friends but they already knew. I was livid when I found out. I was upset in case they reacted badly but they wouldn't be proper friends if they *had* reacted badly. When I went to university, I made an unconscious pact with myself to stop leading a double life. I tried to be as honest as I possibly could.

So you've wanted to be as honest as you possibly could, but you haven't been honest here.

ANDY   When I moved in it was more important to sort out my life. It doesn't seem necessary to tell Ian's father. Other people will feel differently, but it's just a matter of personal choice.

When you moved in, Andy, what sort of state had these two bachelor boys got into?

ANDY   I was not very impressed by the state of the house. When I moved in my room's walls and woodwork were bright orange, there were bits of mankey carpet on the floor, the rest was bare boards and lino, and it was full of junk. One of the ways we complement each other is that Ian is impulsive and chaotic, while I am far more organized. I like sorting things out. Mentally I rubbed my hands together and thought, A challenge, get this place shipshape.

How did you feel about trying to impose something of yourself on the house? On one hand, you are partners while on the other hand you are officially a lodger?

ANDY   The last other person who had been living in the house was Ian's mum, who died five years ago, and the place had run to seed a bit. Ian stressed when I moved in that it would not just be as his boyfriend but as part of the household.

IAN I treat people as family if I get to know them well enough.

ANDY I thought that gave me permission to talk if I thought something was wrong and get it changed. As much as we all knew it was necessary, I agonized over the cleaning up – I thought that Ian's father might think I was trying to take over and wipe out traces of their past.

IAN I knew this was going to happen. He couldn't just come into the house and have his quarter and that would be it. You have relationships that grow. He's part of us and we've absorbed part of him.

What do you think makes your relationship work?

IAN This is something we've always wondered about but we've tried not to go into or pull it apart – in case we do it any harm. I suppose we're just compatible. We complement each other. He's got strengths where I've got weaknesses and he's got weaknesses where I've got strengths.

ANDY To use a phrase that Ian likes, I'm the brains and he's the brawn.

IAN We're like a body, he's the head and I'm the motive power. I do have street smarts and things like that.

ANDY And I haven't, and I have no wisdom at all. I might be intelligent but I can be incredibly thick when it comes to practical things.

IAN I'm a good watcher of people, I can work them out quickly. As I said, it's strange, he's not my ideal type. Andy's the wallflower and I'm the show-off. I don't deliberately do this. I don't like him being in my shadow. Sometimes I try to force him out in front of me as much as possible. He hates it but I will put myself in the shadows.

Do you see yourself committed to each other for ever?

IAN It's an open-ended relationship. One day we may break up. We don't know. I can't say that we're here for ever and ever amen, because that would be wrong.

ANDY I'd like to be but I know it's unrealistic.

IAN It's unrealistic to say we'll be here in twenty years' time because it's unrealistic to predict what will happen in twenty years.

ANDY I'm not amazed that it's still going on but before I went out with Ian the longest relationship I had was two months. Hopefully we'll be going on holiday next year. We are also going to Pride together this year.

Ian and Andy's relationship shows many positive elements. They complement each other, and although Ian has sex with a lot of other people he cares deeply about Andy. I could feel a strong sense of protection: when it was time to leave Ian warned me to lock my car door as I drove through certain parts of the city and it felt much more than a casual piece of advice. However, the secrecy causes problems and is stopping their relationship from reaching its true potential. While I was interviewing Andy and Ian, the father was visiting his daughter. Although we had finished and were just chatting generally, when Ian's father returned I instantly felt as though we were all teenagers again. The conversation became stilted and we had to be careful not to mention genders.

Ian bought the house from his father, who is almost a

lodger and Ian has no reason to fear that he could be evicted if the truth comes out yet he seems to have chosen every way except directly of telling his father that he is gay. Among the videos in the living room are soft porn tapes of beautiful men cavorting in the surf; in Ian's bedroom is a huge collection of pornography and on the walls thousands of pictures of naked and semi-naked men, including one of Ian having sex with another man! Although parents can be blind if they are determined to believe that their son is straight, we can safely assume that Ian's father knows everything. My favourite coming-out story is from a friend whose mother was stunned when he finally told her he was gay. He said, 'But, Mother, what did you think all those nights that you sat up sewing sequins on my ballgowns?'

The closet can shut out the light on a potential relation-ship, denying it the support and cultivation it needs. Despite all the positive elements, this couple are the least committed I interviewed. While the others expect to spend the rest of their lives together, Ian and Andy can think no further ahead than their next holiday and Pride. Relationships need the support of other people: they need to be acknowledged. If they are conducted in secret they feel less real and therefore less stable.

It took me a long time to tell my parents that I was gay. I rationalized this to myself by saying that they lived a long way away and therefore did not need to know. In the meantime, I had series of boyfriends who were in some way 'unavailable'. One lived in America and the other was too busy breeding and looking after his cats to play a role in my life. I moaned that I could not see more of them, but they fulfilled my conscious need for a relationship *and* what I wanted subconsciously – no complications and no need for my parents to know. An old proverb says, 'God protect us from getting what we want.' Ian's secret means that he can avoid the touching and intimacy he finds uncomfortable.

His father's official ignorance allows him to have a relationship but keep Andy at arm's length.

Sometimes we subconsciously sabotage what we say we desire, because we are not ready to cope with the reality. It's easier to mourn the perfect but broken relationship, wallowing over our albums of torch songs, and choosing more inappropriate boyfriends rather than deal with the mundane reality of a day-to-day partnership. When I felt comfortable with my sexuality, within six months of telling my parents I met my partner.

What stops men from coming out

(1) *Society's attitudes.* I do not need to repeat the barrage of negative images and words that gay men face every day – we are all too familiar with the ignorance and lies. The psychological violence directed against young gays means that we can only grow up as balanced and happy individuals through a combination of luck, inner strength and support when we discover the gay community. It is always difficult to be different, be it through colour, ethnic background or disablement, but these groups can find support from their families. Gays often have to struggle on their own, which makes the first step always the hardest.

(2) *Internalized homophobia.* This is sometimes so deep that we are not aware of having put on our attacker's clothes. If negatives are repeated often enough you may take some of them on board: if everyone thinks you're sick you may begin to believe that you are. This is far less of a problem than it used to be. If you watch Mart Crowley's 1960s play/film *Boys in the Band* it feels like a period piece. However, it was the first time that homosexuality was approached openly in mainstream entertainment. Today we

feel more comfortable about our sexuality, but the climax of the film still rings true. Michael, the host of a birthday party at which the guests end by attacking each other, sobs, 'If we could just not hate ourselves so much – that's it, you know – if we could just learn not to hate ourselves quite so much.'

(3) *Projected homophobia*. This is the 'kick the cat' syndrome: something we dislike about ourselves is taken out on other people. Ian is a good example of this: he feels that he is not like typical gays whom he describes as insecure. Rather than deal with his insecurity about his sexuality he pushes it on to others and distances himself from the feelings. (Queer-bashers punish us for what they cannot cope with about themselves.) Many gay men are uncomfortable around effeminate men; when they claim they hate drag queens, they are saying that they do not like their own more feminine side. Gay men who are comfortable with their sexuality do not give a damn how much somebody minces.

(4) *Is it really necessary?* Many gays keep quiet because, after all, 'Heterosexuals don't announce – "I'm straight".' Next time you meet a heterosexual try this simple test: time how long it takes for their wife/husband, girlfriend/boyfriend or children to come into the conversation. Just a simple question like, 'What did you do last weekend?' will suffice. I bet you cannot chat with them for ten minutes without them announcing somehow that they are straight. Gay celebrities are also criticized for 'flaunting their sexuality', while it is forgotten that heterosexual stars sell their wedding photos to the highest bidder and use photo-spreads of their children to promote their latest movie, record or TV series.

(5) *The relationship with your parents*. This is an important stumbling block. If, like Ian, you do not talk about feelings it is doubly difficult to tell them you are gay. You are breaking two sets of taboos: the first that you are

not going to marry a girl, and the second in discussing your inner feelings. If the weather and the garden are the usual topics in your family, it is because the real issues are too threatening. This may be something that has passed down from generation to generation so that no one has learnt, or been given permission, to discuss intimate matters. It can also spring from knowing at a young age that our instincts are 'different' and unacceptable – often long before we understand about sex and being gay. Therefore we learn from an early age to edit our lives, making it difficult to discuss our feelings when we grow up.

If you are finding it difficult to come out to your parents, it is important to analyse and understand your relationship with them. In my own case, I was able to tell them after I had acknowledged a deep-seated need to be their 'perfect child'. It was tied in with my ambitious mother giving up work to have children (the done thing in the late fifties) so that she concentrated her considerable energies into raising me and my sister. I felt that I had to repay her by always being the best and rising to the top of my profession. I had to mourn this 'perfect child', and wept buckets of tears, before I could truly be myself.

Reasons to come out

(1) *If you do not tell your parents and family, someone else will.* Andy lost control of when he came out and what was said, because somebody else beat him to it. If you tell people yourself you can set the agenda, choose the moment and prepare yourself for it.

(2) *Society's attitudes are changing.* This has a trickle-down effect, even on parents. Andy discovered that his image of his father needed updating.

(3) *People will admire your openness.* It shows a strength of character that people warm to and if you treat being gay as normal others will take their cue from you.

(4) *Honesty will improve your relationship with your parents.* It is difficult to be close to somebody if you spend half your life lying to them. Although it can cause short-term problems I have yet to meet a gay man who regretted telling his parents.

(5) *You will feel better.* It wil make you feel more 'whole'. You no longer have to be different people in different circumstances.

The coming-out ladder

When we become more confident we climb up the 'coming-out ladder'; when we feel threatened we may slip down again. Some men get stuck and are unable to move up another rung. The first two rungs are still in the closet, but by the third you are breathing the fresh air of freedom.

(1) *Coming out to yourself.* This can happen before or after you start having sex with other men.

(2) *Coming out to other gay men.* At a basic level, this can mean that you no longer ignore your sexual partners if you see them on the street, and at a more advanced level, that you have a circle of gay friends.

(3) *Coming out to straight friends.* The good friends will be supportive so who needs the other kind?

(4) *Coming out to family.* Whether you choose to start with your siblings, just one parent or both at the same time, this is the most important and difficult rung.

(5) *Coming out to the world.* I now tell complete strangers about my partner in the same way that they talk

about their loved ones. It is not a grand declaration, just part of normal conversation.

The further up the coming-out ladder you climb, the easier it becomes. However, it is not a one-off battle, more a continuous campaign. Your parents need to climb an 'acceptance ladder'. As I discuss in Chapter Seven on families, it is one thing for them to cope with the theory of your being gay, and another to confront the reality and let you and your partner sleep together in their spare bedroom.

Ian and Andy are good examples of how hard it is to come out of the closet. If people who are as direct as Ian claims to be find it impossible to tell their father, what hope is there for the shy and introverted? I sometimes feel that people who insist on selling something to me, in this case 'forward and direct', are trying to prove something; perhaps these are qualities to which Ian aspires rather than has achieved. However, I am sure he will one day tell his father about his sexuality and become truly 'forward and direct'.

It is vital to progress up the coming-out ladder – the more open you are, the more support you will discover and the better your relationship will become. When I explain to my heterosexual friends the theory that you cannot have a good relationship until you are fully open, they see it as self-evident. They are so used to having the support of society, family and friends and cannot imagine how they could survive without it. We can tap into this by coming out. We feel better for it and it has the knock-on effect of providing positive role models for other gays. Also, heterosexuals who personally know gays have fewer prejudices, which results in a less-prejudiced society and makes it easier for others to be honest about their sexuality, creating a positive circle of advancement.

4

SETTING UP
HOME TOGETHER

It is only when two people move in together that they begin
to know each other intimately. They will fight or negotiate
about the practical side of life together – who does the
laundry, the cooking, the washing-up – and it's a million
miles away from the romantic candlelit meals when they
were wooing each other. In the past, each was a guest in the
other's flat or house where the rules are different from
setting up home together.

This is also a time of discovery for heterosexual couples.
It is often the first time that they recognize how different
their family is from other families. Without thinking, the
man will expect his wife to perform the role his mother did
and the woman will expect her husband to undertake her
father's jobs. Each family will have their own arrangements
and what is natural to one partner is strange to another.
Often the couple will not realize why they argue and why
they feel so strongly.

The traditional role models are useless for gay couples,
who have to start from scratch in dividing up the jobs. The
process of integrating the traditional male and female roles
into one same-sex household throws up the issues of gender

identity: do real men wear Marigold washing-up gloves? We have to make adjustments in our own attitudes, masculinity, and what it means to be a man, before we can bond effectively in a gay relationship. Although these issues arise when you are single, they are thrown into stark contrast when you become half of a couple.

The next stage of a gay relationship is sometimes difficult to reach as each partner must be able to trust the other and be confident of the relationship before they can move in together. Although many younger guys will welcome the chance to share bills and save money, older men, who already have their own flats or houses, gain fewer financial benefits. Instead, there is disruption and they fear losing their material security. Set against the background assumption that 'all gay relationships fail', gay couples find it hard to feel secure and settled. On a superficial level, the assignment of day-to-day household tasks seems petty but it is important if you are going to live together in harmony.

Trevor and Ian have been living together for eighteen months and are still in the process of making a home together. They would like to buy a house, but Trevor has just ended an eighteen-year marriage and his money is tied up with his ex-wife and his three children. He has a daughter of eighteen and two sons, fifteen and six. Trevor is thirty-eight and works in graphic design while Ian is twenty-two and is in customer relations. Until recently, both would have described themselves as either heterosexual or bisexual. Trevor, in particular, is in a good position to talk about the issues of gender identity and the differences between setting up home as a gay man and a heterosexual one.

TREVOR When you're married you take lots of things for granted, like ironing or cooking meals. Cooking was something I'd never done but now I'm enjoying it. In a heterosexual relationship, you come home to a wife. I'm coming home to a relationship. You forget the relationship when you're married. Now I'm working at my gay relationship as soon as I come through the door. You're on a one-to-one basis. Before the house was clean and everything was done nicely

IAN I think you've mentioned on a few occasions that having kids tends to alter the relationship anyway. The relationship takes a back seat, whereas in a gay relationship there's only two people involved. It's more intense, and you tend to work at it a lot harder and literally be into each other a lot more. When you've got kids about, the norm of a heterosexual relationship, it tends to be quite bland.

Describe a typical day when you were married, Trevor, and then a typical day with Ian.

TREVOR Before, I was getting up and not taking notice of the kids, not interested in what they'd done. Since I've been in a gay relationship, I've taken more notice of them – when they're with me I give them undivided attention. In the morning the shirts would already be ironed and the wife would get the children off to school – occasionally I took them. I'd be at work and perhaps not even contact the wife during the day. She was at home, a housewife. She'd know the time I'd be home and dinner would be cooked. I'd take the dog for a walk for an hour or so – I always needed that time outside to myself. It was nice to get out and just be on my own for an hour or so, away from family life with the kids running around.

IAN Now, one of us will get up and make a cup of tea, come back to bed for a cuddle for about quarter or half an hour. Trevor drops me off at work and then goes on to wherever he's going. He contacts me about five times during the day.

What do you talk about?

TREVOR Anything, it's a pick-me-up. In my job, it's a lonely life on the road, which is something that a wife doesn't realize. Ian's in an office – I call it his ivory tower. If he's feeling low he will phone me and vice versa, just have a chat, which is the difference between being married and being in a gay relationship.

IAN We take it in turns cooking the dinner and doing the dishes. Sometimes we go out socializing but really we're quite into each other.

TREVOR It's a learning process, really.

The roles were set in your marriage. Your wife did the womanly things and you'd do the male things – looking after the car and the garden, the DIY?

TREVOR Except I never got round to doing it. I was always doing other things. Monday to Friday, I was in sales and then at the weekend I was an entertainer. I used to look forward to Saturday and Sunday.

What happens when two men come together? You've got two DIY experts and nobody to clean up after them.

IAN When Trevor was living with his wife, she used to get housekeeping money allocated each month and sort out everything financially. Trevor would just sign a cheque and that would be it. He wouldn't know or care about the finances because it was all sorted out. Now we live together, we have a joint account and we both put a certain amount of money in towards bills. When a financial decision needs to be made, it's done jointly. Trevor takes a hell of a lot more interest where his money goes – even food shopping.

How do you allocate the traditionally female roles?

IAN We usually do it together, as a couple.

TREVOR   Now if a plug needs putting on it's done, whereas before when it was my job to do it I would put it off and get nagged at until I finally did it.

IAN   We went through a stage where we had to get used to living together. Trevor never assumed he was the man and I was the woman. There wasn't much disagreement, more just getting used to each other.

TREVOR   Although we'd known each other for three years before we set up home, you don't really know somebody until you live with them. You find out their habits.

Tell me about this getting to know each other stage. What caused problems when you first lived together?

TREVOR   I've become a lot more tolerant now, but because of our age difference, music was a problem. Ian loves his music and he used to play it all the time. It used to be very, very loud. Untidiness used to be a problem – but we're learning to put things away as we go along. That's my breeding – being married it's done for you!

IAN   It sounds quite trivial, but one of the things that used to niggle me about you, and it still does, is your driving. He's all over the road. The car's a tip and I think, Just clean your car and stop driving over the cat's eyes. Little things, but they incensed me.

It's a bit of shock to discover these habits. Because in the early days you're everything to each other, then suddenly you discover your lover is not so perfect.

IAN   Since we first met our love has intensified. We were infatuated with each other in the early days. I don't think it's slackened off, but we do now understand each other's little irritations.

Is it more real? Before you were covering up your foibles, now you're getting the whole person.

TREVOR   Yes, because he never used to know my foibles. They were all at home with the wife and kids, and likewise Ian was in his flat.

IAN   When you're courting, every time you see each other you're perfect, the hair's right. Suddenly you live together and you wake up in the morning and you're beside a scarecrow. I think we took it in our stride, I half expected it.

TREVOR   We know each other's feelings now: if I'm a bit down or Ian's a bit down, we notice it whereas before we could hide the moods.

Were there any more serious problems?

IAN   Knowing straight away when each of us is lying, but not being able to say so. You know each other well enough to know when something isn't quite right but you're not confident enough to say anything.

TREVOR   One of our first arguments was when you went to Guildford. I regularly see the kids and on this particular night Ian failed to tell me he was seeing friends about fifty miles away. We needed to get to the bottom of that.

IAN   Before Trevor left to see the kids, he sensed I was on edge. There was something not quite right. I couldn't explain to Trevor why I was going.

TREVOR   Because of all the questions I would ask.

IAN   In the early days, like many relationships, it's quite insecure. We wanted to be with each other all the time. Trevor could go and see the kids, but I couldn't go and see my friends.

TREVOR   Why on earth would he want to go out?

IAN I found it difficult to say openly I wanted to see my friends. I just couldn't say it! It got to half past six, and in the end I thought I would just go and phone him later. That caused a bit of an argument, didn't it?

TREVOR It was just the insecurity. Why have you gone to Guildford? I immediately thought there was somebody else, I didn't think it could be just friends.

IAN Trevor sensed something and I knew he knew there was something. We couldn't communicate about it. That was in the first one or two months of setting up home.

Is this another difference between a gay and straight relationship? When you get married you expect it to last, while there is a different expectation for a gay relationship.

TREVOR Oh, yes, because boys will be boys! You marry a woman, that's it, you feel secure. Knowing each other's backgrounds and what a gay relationship is like, open to temptations, it brings a little bit of insecurity in. In a heterosexual relationship, if a boy sees a girl, there's lots of chatting up but it takes three weeks to get her where you want her . . . A guy meets a guy and he's there. There's none of this pussy-footing around and, of course, that brings insecurity into the relationship. You know that if you're with a guy you like, other people will want him too!

IAN Knowing that it could happen so easily has made us work harder at the relationship. It's become stronger. We know each other a lot better because there's no lying.

Are you monogamous?

IAN Not totally, no.

TREVOR I can't see how any gay relationship can be monogamous.

IAN We've got an arrangement. Yes, we are monogamous to an extent. We don't have any sexual relationships which could interfere with what Trevor and I have. If it happens like a bolt out of the blue, we meet somebody and something happens, that's allowed. As long as it's a one-off incident and doesn't threaten our relationship.

TREVOR We're open about it, we tell each other.

IAN It rarely happens, but when it happens it's not an issue.

TERVOR It's not like we've gone out to find something. It happens and we accept that.

How long had you been married before you had sex with another man?

TREVOR Probably about two or three years.

How did you feel about yourself?

TREVOR Afterwards there is the guilt, but during the act it felt good. I knew what the guy liked and the guy knew what I liked and I found that I preferred gay sex. It was more exciting.

How did it make you feel about yourself as a man? Did you feel it undermined your masculinity?

TREVOR You can be dominant in a gay sex relationship, or submissive depending on the circumstances. At one point you're dominant, in the next he is. I found it exciting, it was a challenge.

IAN When I had my girlfriend sex was OK. Physically, I enjoyed it – when I look back I wonder why [*giggle*]. When I gave into my attraction to men and had sex with a man, it was, Wow, this is brilliant! I felt guilty afterwards because I wasn't at ease with my gayness. I thought that to be a man I had to fuck women. It made me feel a little inadequate and I thought, What am I doing? For a couple of years I pretended I was straight but just had gay sex as a release. If I could convince myself, it was all right. Yet if I saw a man I had had sex with I would be terrified that they might say hello. Most probably they were in the same position. It was easier for me than it was for Trevor because nowadays the subject is talked about more, there's more information and more gay men about.

TREVOR In the early seventies, it just wasn't talked about.

IAN After a couple of years, I felt less guilty about not fancying woman. I felt more at ease with myself. I accepted my gayness. I'm a man but I fancy other men. For years I'd admired men's bodies but now I like their minds too. Once I'd got over the hurdle of accepting myself as gay, I was fine. I didn't feel any less a man − in fact I felt more of a man because I knew myself better and I understood more about men than some women do.

As Ian says, one of society's definitions of being a man is that you fuck women. Both of you went through a heterosexual phase [laughter]. What was it like, when you discovered you wanted to have sex with other men?

TREVOR When I was straight, I used to enjoy a man's body. I would admire rather than fancy his masculinity. That strength and everything about a man's body was magnificent. I didn't realize I was gay.

IAN I had a couple of girlfriends when I was sixteen, seventeen. I didn't feel gay then. I would see a man and think, he's very manly, I want to be like that. The lads would talk together in the pub or youth club. I enjoyed that conversation because I could relate to it instantly. I found girls a bit prissy – they would talk about girlie things, which was not what I wanted to talk about.

TREVOR When I was first married, I didn't fancy fucking a man. I conformed, it was a woman I fucked. I went through a bisexual stage and then you come out of that and go into a gay phase. I am gay and the bisexuality is now gone.

When you started living together what expectations did you have of each other?

IAN I didn't have any. It was my first proper relationship and the first time I'd moved in with anybody. But there was one surprise. Trevor's very affectionate and since we've moved in together it's intensified. I didn't realize he had it in him. He was never shy about showing affection but there's so much cuddling, caring and talking. Maybe I had some preconceptions because he was married that he wouldn't show his feelings as openly as he does.

TREVOR I didn't want to divorce a wife and have yet another wife. The expectations were someone who could share as much affection and caring as I had. I didn't get this from my wife. Although I had a loving relationship with the wife, it was not the same as what I have with Ian. I get a lot of love and respect from Ian, and I can respect him because I can empathize with him. When I was his age I had a lot of similar problems. We come from similar backgrounds and lived in similar conditions. My father died when I was very young and Ian didn't have his father around. I know what is going through his mind and that's what's made us closer.

IAN We both come from the same class. We were both brought up on a council estate. Mum divorced when I was quite young and my dad was never a strong influence in my upbringing – he was only there for holidays. Trevor understood me more than somebody who had had a normal family upbringing.

If you haven't got a father about, how do you learn what it is like to be a man?

TREVOR In the upbringing I had on a South London council estate you didn't learn much at school, but you learnt a lot about life. You needed to be one step ahead of the others, so the lack of a father's influence didn't matter. I knew how to get one over on the other guy before he got one over on me. I was a survivor.

IAN I do regret not having a father around. My mother did a very good job but there are some things a mother just can't provide. Being a woman she would never truly understand how a young boy would feel. She was a bit soft sometimes, the house would be a riot.

Society tries to push boys towards sexual stereotypes. What happens if you don't conform to those stereotypes?

TREVOR I had to conform. I was a working man and I went to a working-man's club, I couldn't go into that club and drink Martini, which I drink now. [*Puts on a working-class accent*] I 'ad t' drink light 'n' bitter [*usual speaking voice*] and talk like that with my mates from London. We used to play cards – we'd have a school right through the night and the next morning play golf straight from the game and that sort of macho thing. You'd be expected to know about cars. Now I dread going into that club and seeing all my old mates. I could hold my own but my way of life is so different. I now live life to the full. Before, because of my sexuality, I was uncertain in this crowd. I didn't belong there, I was putting on this act.

Are you bringing up your sons differently from your daughter?

TREVOR Oh, yes, girls are very pro-Mum and boys are very pro-Dad. My young boy is split between the two of us. He sees more of his mum than he does his dad. He's mollycoddled by his mother and domineered by his father.

Is it a father's role to lay down the law?

TREVOR His mother lets him do what he wants and gives in to him but I won't. When he comes to spend the weekend with us it's our house and there's the house rules – he finds conflict with that.

If the man of the house lays down the law, did you try and do that when you first got together with Ian?

TREVOR Yes. I suppose, when I come to think about it, I did. I found it very challenging. I have this domineering personality. I'm a leader and with my family I'd been setting down the rules. Ian has been the reins, he's pulled me in.

Trevor do gay men know more about themselves than heterosexual men do?

TREVOR Oh, yeah, crikey, a thousand times more. You know what you want, your needs, your strengths. A lot of married straight men don't know their own strengths or their weaknesses. You can tell a straight man a mile off – the way he holds himself.

IAN Straight men tend to plod along, in their life, in their marriage, and do the things that straight people do. Take the kids out to the swimming pool on Saturday and watch telly all week. The wife does the wifely things and the husband does the husbandly things. They don't seem to be in contact with their inner selves. They don't seem to talk about things like feelings.

TREVOR If you're gay, you're more aware of the world and issues. If you're straight you don't give a damn about the rest of the world – you're more into yourself.

IAN Trevor once said that he had a passion to do different things. That's why he was so into his weekend job as an entertainer – it was a release.

TREVOR I feel that I'm a better father now, in comparison with when I was at home, because I give the children my undivided attention. I'm learning their intersts, rather than being wrapped up in my entertainment career and other pastimes.

Having been officially a heterosexual man, but having gay sex on the side, what advice would you give to others in the same position who are dabbling on the side?

TREVOR Come out, you'll feel better for it. I know what you're going through – the turmoil in your mind, the guilt. You will feel more at ease with yourself. I used to have the same advice given to me but I couldn't comprehend what it would be like when I came out. I gave up a hell of a lot to come out but I found that I had to do it. For twelve years, I was living a lie and it was getting too much. I'm not saying it's not secure now, but I've given up my family, my property and a secure home.

IAN Trevor remembers what he was like when he first left his wife and children and he was in a right state. Some days he would think, Have I done the right thing? He felt so guilty. He'd given up stability and gone into something completely fresh. Sometimes it was quite hard for both of us, but that passes when you become stable in your relation-ship or perhaps when you realize there can be stability in a gay relationship. All the fear levels off.

It must have been difficult for you – somebody that you loved was always asking whether he had made the right decision.

IAN   Yes, it was. Trevor was at a very vulnerable stage. He used to ask it quite a lot, especially when we had small arguments. Although he'd had disagreements with his wife they would rarely argue. You asked earlier about role play, male and female, and when I think about it perhaps Trevor did have slightly stereotyped expectations. What Trevor used to say went, or he'd always get his own way. Whereas with me I'd say, 'No, I don't want that – what about me?' There was a bit of conflict there in the early days but it's sorted itself out now.

TREVOR   I was very alone, I had to make this relationship work, I couldn't go back. When my wife found out that I was gay we tried to live together for twelve weeks. I lived in that house with the wife and kids as a gay man, and there's no way that will work. At first, she decided I was bisexual. She couldn't accept that I was gay because I had lived with her so long. She arranged for me to see a counsellor – who needed counselling to counsel me, he'd had no experience of this. He couldn't understand what he was hearing. In the end, it was my wife who needed counselling.

IAN   She hoped that when he was cured the marriage would be OK again. It was definitely hurtful sometimes, when Trevor used to say, 'Have I done the right thing?' A tear would come to his eye when he phoned the kids up – maybe one of them was being naughty. At one stage the six-year-old was very clingy to Trevor whenever he saw him. I understood because I remember what it was like needing my father around. Luckily, I was not at all jealous so there was no conflict.

Ian, how did you cope with this?

IAN Luckily, I was a friend of the family. I met Trevor on his own and he was comfortable with me because I didn't act gay. He introduced me to the family and that way we got to see each other a lot more. We were mates in front of everybody else but having a relationship when we were on our own. I got to know the family and understood the children's needs. I don't think even if I'd never met them that I could deprive them of their dad. I haven't got kids but I'm no stranger to what love feels like. I would never ever try and break the bond between Trevor and his children. I just had to take a back seat, console him as much as I could.

How did you meet?

TREVOR I knew his mother because we used the same local and then Ian started drinking there. One day we got talking and quickly realized we both had the same sexuality. We arranged to meet in another pub and started talking about it a bit deeper and went from there. It really was a matey relationship to start off with.

IAN When we first met, I was eighteen and I had had one fling with a guy when I was on holiday in Austria. We'd written and phoned and he'd come over. It lasted about three months so I wasn't inexperienced. It wasn't a situation where we were matey matey and then suddenly realized each other was gay and then had sex. We both knew from the start and the whole friendship and relationship were built on that understanding.

TREVOR We got to know each other first. It was a slow development. It took me three months to realize that I was in love with this guy. I can still visualize it now. I was out one Saturday and I called you up and said, 'I have just got to talk to you.' I was getting very het up about it. I had had relationships in the past with guys but I knew I was falling in love and that it was a different type of love.

IAN   From when we met to when we moved in together was two and a half years. One of the reasons the relationship became strong and survived all the strains and hassle of Trevor being married was because we knew each other well. He could respect me. Although I'm a young guy and he fancied me, he didn't see me as just a sex object, he respected my brain as well. Through this he came to love me and I love him too.

TEVOR   We had empathy with each other and the relationship evolved. If it had been infatuation it wouldn't have lasted.

Ian, how did you feel about falling in love with a married man? It's not really a long-term prospect.

IAN   It's interesting, this point. When I first met Trevor, I wasn't accepting my gayness and neither was he. From the start Trevor said to me, 'I must let you know I would never ever leave my wife – that's totally out of the question.' My prompt reply to him was, 'Don't worry, I wouldn't want you. I'm straight too, you're just *my* bit on the side!' That was fine to start off with. We got to know each other and fell in love. Our attitudes changed not only towards each other but also ourselves. We felt more gay, more into each other. We moved in together because we felt at ease. It was what we wanted and needed. In that period of two and half years, I changed from being a so-called straight person with a girlfriend and lots of straight friends to being totally into Trevor. Our circle of friends and interests have changed. If we hadn't accepted our gayness and our love for each other, Trevor would still be with his wife now and would never have had the chance to explore his inner feelings. Before, Trevor had always been very wary of the guys he was having relationships with. They were never good enough or secure enough for him to leave his wife.

TREVOR It was sheer love, Ian was the catalyst for it to happen.

It sounds like you were catalysts for each other.

TREVOR Ian needed it to bring out his gay life and I needed it to take me away from my marriage.

IAN Because we were so-called straight people, we could relate to each other. We were straight but we were gay and helped each other along.

TREVOR Six months into the relationship, I wanted to live with Ian. Another three months later, we made love one night and the earth just moved. I had never experienced anything like that and I can still visualize it now. In the eighteen years of marriage I had never experienced so much energy between two people. I knew then that it was Ian that I wanted to be with for the rest of my life.

Is there such a thing as bisexual?

IAN I don't think there is. It's maybe a straight man's excuse not to face his sexuality. If there is a genuine bisexual person, it must be a gay man who can make it with straight women.

TREVOR There's no such thing, I've been there. It was my excuse – I'm bisexual [*laughter*]. I used to say to myself, 'I live a very fast life, I'm either up or I'm down. The gay side of my life stops me from going down.' To anybody I met that was my alibi.

IAN When I had my girlfriends I felt straight, but I felt a little bit gay as well. I called myself bisexual, but when I let my feelings take me over I knew I was gay. I felt gay sex and a gay relationship was more complete. I didn't have as much in common with a woman and although I could do sex and enjoy it to an extent, that was all. However, for me, what I have with Trevor is natural.

TREVOR I am sure about being gay. Since I had that experience with Ian, I couldn't think of having sex with a woman now – even though I was married for half my life.

IAN Do you think that when you had sex with your wife you were going through the motions?

TREVOR Yes, I wasn't enjoying it.

IAN You had sex with men because you wanted to, not because you had to. You wouldn't go out and pick up women now?

TREVOR Recently, I was in America and there was a woman who made it obvious she wanted to go to bed with me. I told Ian about it, because it didn't interest me at all. Five years ago I would have jumped in bed with her and satisfied her.

IAN We have talked about this, and five years ago Trevor would have thought, I can fuck another woman, that makes me a man. It made you feel straight and more comfortable with yourself.

TREVOR That woman didn't interest me, the flaps and the lumps. I'd much rather have a guy. I have come to terms with my sexuality – I am honest with myself. I've been a married straight man, dabbling with a guy, becoming bi-sexual, and then becoming gay. I've been there. If I'd been allowed to be gay at sixteen, it would have made such a difference. I wouldn't have got married. There wouldn't have been three fatherless children. I got married to con-form, but if I'd been allowed to explore my sexuality I don't think I would have. A lot of guys of my age group have got to forty and are leaving their marriages for a gay relationship. There are three couples we know of and all round about the same age.

How does your wife feel?

TREVOR Devastated. She asked me outright if Ian was gay, and I told her, 'If he's gay, what does that make me?' She just flipped and she hasn't really come down since. She has digs at me.

IAN She's not at ease with his gayness, which is why she makes derogatory remarks.

TREVOR She sends strange clippings through the post and anything from the children is always addressed to 'Daddy' to try and break me down. There's also the denial of Ian – she won't even have his name mentioned anywhere near her. It's as if he doesn't exist. I can understand that because he was a good friend of the family. It was a double kick in the face.

IAN She wants to know about our relationship but doesn't want to ask. Is it better? Am I the feminine one?

TREVOR It must be torture for her because she hasn't got anybody now. But if I'd left it another ten years it would have been even worse; she's still young enough to find another life.

Would you like to buy a house together?

TREVOR We're renting at the moment, but we've chosen the type of house we'd like to live in. We've both got the same taste. Most of the stuff in here is ours.

IAN Up to now we've rented fully furnished, but this is the first time we've started to add little bits, tables, lights, appliances. When we first moved in together we had nothing, just our clothes. We went out and bought a kettle and an iron.

Going back to when you were married, Trevor, who used to choose things for the house?

TREVOR   Mainly the woman. Now I hope I've got more style, an eye for colour and taste.

Do you argue over what the two of you buy for the flat?

IAN   Trevor's got this thing about Austrian blinds. They're quite nice but all over the house they're a bit too poofy for me. We've compromised! When we buy somewhere he can have them in the bathroom – behind frosted glass!

TREVOR   Ian's got this thing about having a rug on the wall, in the bathroom. Personally I can't see the point.

IAN   It's a nice rug, it will soak up the moisture.

TREVOR   Slight conflict, he will most probably end up getting his own way.

What sort of house would you like to buy together?

TREVOR   We would dearly love a terraced house which we can make our own.

IAN   Maybe a two-up, two-down or a bit bigger than that with a nice garden. We want to get a couple of cats and a dog.

TREVOR   Make it a family. My last house had a hundred-foot garden and a carport. We'll work towards that but it's not necessary.

How difficult would it be for you to get a mortgage?

IAN   We went to an advisory centre.

TREVOR   We'd didn't tell them we were gay, we told them we were friends and sharing for economic reasons.

IAN   But the girl said, 'Are you a relationship?' We looked at each other and had to be honest. She said, 'I thought so. It's better I know because that way I can find the right mortgage and insurance company for you.'

TREVOR   We had heard one or two bad things about people getting mortgages together and having doctors' records looked at. She was helpful and sympathetic.

IAN   I learnt so many things I didn't know before. Two men having a mortgage together creates all sorts of problems with mortgage companies. They push the premiums up if they think you're a gay couple. For instance, a straight married man who is fifty-five with a history of three heart-attacks applies for a mortgage and his insurance premium is lower than for a single gay man who's had a negative HIV test. That seems unfair.

TREVOR   If you're openly gay, it's compulsory to have an HIV test.

IAN   The lady at the mortgage-advice centre told us that some insurance companies lay down guidelines about careers. If you're a single male of a certain age and have a job like an airline steward, catering or hotel work, they assume you're gay. So we told her we were in communication and sales and she told us that wasn't a problem. It seemed a bit of a minefield, really.

TREVOR   You've got to tread very carefully. We went just to see what was available and came back with our tails between our legs. When I applied for my first mortgage I was a married first-time buyer – no questions asked. Now you've got to watch what you put down, what you say, what you do and the way you act. If the guy from the insurance company comes round you've got to be butch and macho, and put the football on the telly.

IAN   A friend of ours was told to take all his gay pictures off the wall, switch the telly on as soon as he answered the door, say that Arsenal had just scored! The lady at the mortgage-advice centre told us that one mortgage company automatically passes on what you say to all the others.

TREVOR   Although they have to safeguard their interests, they have it totally out of proportion.

Trevor, you've said that your relationship is more intense and that you're more aware than you were in your marriage. Is there a danger of becoming too intense, too aware?

TREVOR   To the point of suffocating? No, I don't think so.

IAN   I know Trevor would never get too overbearing and neither would I. I can't imagine you being too much for me because I know you so well, anyway, and what I know, which is a hell of a lot, I love to death.

When I met Ian and Trevor I felt like I was in a soap-powder commercial trying to persuade them to swap two boxes of their old straight lifestyle for one box of new improved HOMO! Although the recently converted tend to sing the praises of the new-found faith more than someone who is more assured of their sexuality, it is marvellous to see how their lives have improved by coming out. Their story shows how once you have been through this process you are much more likely to find a fulfilling partner. One of the wonderful elements of a good relationship is the amazing potential for growth that it offers. Individually, Trevor and Ian were both having problems coming to terms with being gay, but together they were able to come out. They could understand each other's fears, support each other and boost each other's confidence. This is another example of the 'falling in love' process that I described in Chapter Two: when searching for a partner, we subconsciously look for someone to help us deal with the unresolved issues that are holding us back as individuals.

Trevor and Ian also illustrate the importance of knowing each other properly before embarking on a relationship. It was this that helped them to cope with many of the issues involved in setting up home together, all of which were magnified by the crisis of Trevor leaving his wife. Looking from outside into their relationship, I was struck by how worried Trevor was in the early days of their relationship. I could see the incredible rapport and understanding they have, but both he and Ian were blinded by their and society's expectations of fickle gay relationships. Stability was particularly important for Trevor because of everything he had given up when he left his wife. It is fascinating how both men only recognized the stability and strength of their partnership once they had been settled for some time. Although this also happens with heterosexual couples, engagement and marriage reinforce their relationship, acknowledge their love publicly and mark stages on the road to commitment. For a gay couple the concrete reality of stability is not enough on its own. We also have to be 100 per cent aware and confident of it. We have no ceremony to mark stability and commitment; we have to recognize for ourselves when we have achieved them. The realization can often lag a long way behind reality.

STAGE 2 OF A GAY RELATIONSHIP
Nesting

Trevor and Ian are a good example of a couple who have moved into this second stage. When you are in limerence you don't care where you live – you probably only see the bedroom anyway! 'Nesting', as the word implies, is principally about setting up home together. The couple are still very involved with each other but now they become interested in their environment, too. Nesting is the beginning of a real commitment to each other.

Although there is still an intense feeling of togetherness the couple no longer shy away from dealing with difficult topics. Ian and Trevor are close enough now not only to feel secure but to recognize each other's shortcomings, which has not undermined their relationship, but, rather, has enhanced their compatibility. At this stage, the strongest elements of limerence will have worn off, which may leave us worrying about whether our partner still loves us or, even, if he is the right person. Sex is less frequent than the three-times-a-night euphoria when you first met. A folk legend that has always amused me suggests that if you put a penny in a pot every time you make love in the first year of marriage and then take a penny out every time you make love from then onwards you will always have bread on the table. An exaggeration, but it makes the point that it is normal for sexual desire to lessen to a more manageable level – after all, there are now lots of other things to share apart from your bodies. Fixing up a house together is a new way of saying, 'I love you.'

At this stage, familiarity can also breed annoyance. His little ways are no longer eccentric but have been transformed into nasty habits. Dealing with them can be awkward, first, because we are anxious about how he will take criticism, and second, it seems churlish to complain because so often they are only small irritations. However, if you say nothing, your resentment builds up while he may have no idea what is causing your darkening mood. My parents claim that their marriage worked because my father gave up dunking his biscuits in his tea and my mother stopped reading in bed! Even if you cannot trade off your nasty habits, talking about how you both feel will clear the air. At least you will know where to tread carefully in future. It is tempting either to ignore the habits or to snipe at them, but if you do, annoyance will spiral into a bitter row.

Ambivalence about the relationship and each other is a common feature now, a product of limerence wearing off. Setting up home together inevitably throws up disagreements as well as harmony. You know enough about your partner for the first flush of excitement to wear off but not enough to feel secure. The 'Blending' stage is one of intense sharing, but when you move into 'Nesting' the ambivalence may be difficult to admit to yourself and impossible to share with your partner. Each keeps their feelings to themselves and hopes the ambivalence will disappear. Each intuitively knows that something is wrong, and the silence can sometimes lead one partner to fear that the other has fallen out of love or has a new boyfriend. If you discuss the ambivalence you can begin to tackle the underlying issues. 'Blending' is all about how similar you both are, and the ambivalence is about the differences that need to be highlighted. Sort them out and you are on a firmer foundation.

Bitchiness about each other's tastes and values is a natural response at this stage. You may fear that the wonderful feelings and excitement about the new home cannot last. Although a couple is still bonding and beginning to accept each other for who they really are, money, for instance, may still be in separate accounts. They do not feel 100 per cent committed to each other. However, when they look back on this period they will recognize how much trust had been built up. Commitment to each other and the relationship is present but most gay couples do not fully recognize this until they have passed through this stage. Although each couple moves along the developmental model at their own pace, the nesting stage normally lasts between one and three years.

Expectations

To negotiate the issues of setting up home together sucessfully it is important to understand what you expect from your relationship. If you are thinking of living together, try to visualize the day-to-day reality – like it or not, you will have a mental picture of how life will be. Just as you had a tick list of what your ideal partner would look like, you have one not just of who does what but where you will live and how you'll arrange your life together. In the same way that we normally end up not with Mr Right but Mr Bit of All Right, you will need to compromise over your living arrangements. Although intellectually we know that the couple who walk off into the final frame of the movie do not live happily ever after without an argument, the fantasy touches something inside us and emotionally we believe.

In the past gay men have often created a pastiche of male/female relationships. In his 1976 book, *A Lasting Relationship*, Jeremy Seabrook interviews a gay couple, Len and William, who were then in their late fifties. Len confesses, 'I stay at home and do the washing and baking and say to the woman next door, "nice drying day". They talk to me as if I was a woman, and I do get a feeling of pride that my washing is perhaps whiter than hers.' While I was researching this book, couples reported that their 'in-laws' often treated them like the wife: 'She expects one of us to play the woman – and it certainly won't be her precious son!' There still seems to be some residual expectation among gays that one partner will take on the female role, but many of the couples I interviewed were keen to stress that they did not take on roles. In general, my research shows that modern gay couples share out the household tasks equally.

What do you expect from your home?

It is a good idea to discuss what your home means to each of you. For some people it is a haven from the outside world, for others it is a place to entertain friends. How important is your own personal space? Is privacy necessary? Do you want an office or den of your own? Is your home somewhere to express your artistic flair and personality or just a base to recover from work and other outside interests? My partner and I often disagree in this area: style is all important for him, while comfort is equally important to me. He does not care if the sofa is suitable for cuddling up together and watching television, he's more interested in the fabric and the design. It is important to voice your feelings: until you do this it is impossible to negotiate properly. Although these environmental issues are often considered less important than 'being in love', they are vital for creating a happy and stable relationship.

What do you each expect the other to do around the house?

The expectation in heterosexual relationships is that the man will carry out home, garden and car maintenance. The woman cooks, cleans and runs the house. Trevor's hetero-sexual experiences show that these stereotypical roles are alive and well. They have been inculcated into us as we grow up. Already, my four-year-old niece has a play kitchen and my nephew, who is five, has a crane and a garage. A gay man living on his own has to be both man and woman, performing all the tasks around the house. However, when we enter a relationship the roles we learnt as children may reappear and cause problems. It is vital that you do not make assumptions. You might agree to share the housework, but who is responsible for cleaning what? How often do you expect things to be cleaned? What do you mean by clean?

(1) Make a list of all the jobs in the house and talk them through, discussing whose responsibility each is.

(2) Explain to each other which tasks are priorities for you personally, the jobs which make you feel uncomfortable if they are not done and the ones that can be left until there's more time.

(3) Discuss what happens if a job is not done. How often are you allowed to ask for something to be done before it becomes nagging?

Tidiness, or the opposite, causes the most rows. We are tolerant of our own mess, but our partner's is quite another matter. If you have the money, invest in all the labour-saving devices: buy the dishwasher rather than fight over whose turn it is to do the washing-up. Hire a cleaner. As more couples fall out over tidiness and cleanliness than anything else, it is money well spent.

If you have problems talking through these kinds of issues, Chapter Twelve, on communications skills, will help. As a Relate marriage guidance counsellor, I spend a lot of time with heterosexual couples negotiating through these issues. This is partly because a revolution has and is taking place in women's expectations: while they are no longer prepared to wait on and play nursemaid to their husbands, their expectations of their men may still be deeply rooted in their upbringing. I remember the anger of one woman whose husband never seemed to get round to cleaning their children's shoes. He could not understand what the fuss was about. When we explored her feelings we discovered that her father had always cleaned her shoes and she felt that all good fathers did the same. When her husband was a child he had been taught to be self-reliant and clean his own shoes. They had different expectations because of their different upbringings, but the issue was so important because of what the shoes symbolized: their different attitudes to bringing up their children. She wanted to nurture them and he wanted to make them self-sufficient. It is important to explain your expectations to your partner by discussing them. Then you can begin to understand the hidden issues that make these matters more important than they seem at first sight.

Gender identity

The 'who does which household tasks' issue throws up the complex subject of gender roles. The process of coming out and coming to terms with your sexuality makes us all look at what it means to be a man. Some young gays feel deeply unhappy with society's stereotypes, while others, like Trevor and Ian, are more comfortable with them. Although we have confronted what it means not to have sex with a woman, we need to deal with other expectations about men before we can have a fulfilling relationship. Let us look beyond the macho heterosexual posturing, which few gay men would buy into, and concentrate on some of the underlying qualities that men are supposed to possess.

(1) *Men are competitive*. When their wives earn more

money, it nearly always creates discord. When I asked Trevor how he learnt to be a man, he explained that his tough council-estate upbringing had taught him to get one over on someone before they got one over on him. His definition of being a man revolved around winning.

(2) *Men do not show their feelings.* We are told that real men do not cry and that showing our feelings is a sign of weakness.

(3) *Men are rational problem-solvers.* We tend to think through a problem rather than looking at the feelings involved.

(4) *Men have careers.* We put a lot of energy into our jobs while our relationships often take second place. Our jobs are often a source of identity. If you ask a group of women to describe themselves they are more likely to tell you about their children and husband.

(5) *Men are the head of the household.* In market research, the man of the household is often used to classify the rest of the family, even if he is earning less than his wife. The man is the law-maker and the decision-maker. Trevor demonstrated this.

It is impossible for two competitive, rational, problem-solving heads of the household who don't talk or show their feelings to have a fulfilling, loving relationship: we need to get in touch with the other, traditionally feminine, side of our personalities before we can create a real partnership. The successful couples in this book are those who have allowed themselves to come out of the rigid gender bunkers. They share out the 'male' autonomous feelings which allow both partners to be individuals within the relationship, with the caring 'female' feelings that nurture it and provide closeness.

The gender stereotypes over who does the laundry and the gender identity issues can come up simultaneously for a gay couple and reinforce each other. For example, I remember how uncomfortable I felt when my partner began staying at my home with more and more of his possessions. I thought it was caused by someone intruding into my privacy and personal space but the roots were deeper than that. He rightly criticized my interior design and the kitchen layout, which I had inherited but done nothing about. I did not have much confidence in my taste, but when he started wanting to cut back the bushes in my garden I felt threatened. I did not mind him taking on the female homemaker role but I became uncomfortable when he also wanted to impinge on what I considered my male preserve – the garden. I also felt that I was no longer head of the household, that my authority had been questioned. (Nowadays, we're better at talking through our differences: I take more interest in the home and let him chop back the bushes.) We are more integrated both as a couple and as individuals. Although, as gay men, we think we have come to terms with our sexuality and what it means to be a man, becoming part of a couple can bring back childhood expectations and give us more work to do on our relationship.

Buying a house

It is always best to buy a house together rather than for one person to move into the other's home. If you have been on your own for some time, adjusting to living with another person can be difficult. We are territorial animals. If you stay in your own home, your partner may feel like an intruder disrupting your settled routine. No matter how hard you try, it will always feel like *your* home rather than your *and* his home. The person who owns the house has a lot of power, and if the relationship goes through a rocky patch he can always ask the other to move out. If the home is jointly owned, both partners have an equal say and equal security.

It is not unusual for gays to settle down later than their straight brothers and sisters. Homophobia can hold back our personal development and mean that we are settled into a home before we are ready to become settled into a relationship. If you have been used to considering only yourself, it is quite frightening to think about living with someone else. Confide your feelings to your partner because, however much we love someone, it is natural to have fears at this time. Often acknowledging how you feel is enough, or you might discover that you need to build some space into your relationship. Give each other permission to have occasional weekends away with friends or to pursue separate hobbies.

When you are planning to buy a house together, it is a good idea to consult not only a mortgage adviser but also a solicitor. You need to make certain that your interests are protected if one of you dies unexpectedly or if the relationship fails. If you are self-employed it is also a good idea to explain your new circumstances to your accountant, who can advise on ways of sharing profits from your business with your lover in the most tax-effective way, and can suggest other schemes to make the most of tax allowances and equalize tax rates. Always be honest with your advisers about the nature of your relationship: it allows them to understand your short- and long-term strategies.

Practical issues

(1) Try to buy important assets like your home jointly as joint tenants. This means that if one of you dies the other half of the property automatically goes to your partner. Unlike heterosexual couples the survivor will have to pay inheritance tax, but if the home is jointly owned this will reduce the final tax bill.

(2) The most popular way of buying a house in Britain is by using an Endowment policy. This is an insurance policy that pays out normally at the end of twenty-five years and provides enough money to pay off your mortgage and, hopefully, a cash bonus. The problem comes for the mortgage company if you die before you have finished paying and this is why they insist on your having life assurance. Insurance companies have the risk from HIV out of all proportion. They have increased the premiums by 250 per cent (at best) on policies for gay men and, despite the number of deaths from Aids coming nowhere near government predictions, have not downweighted the risk. You must take full advice before starting to buy a house using any kind of life-assurance policy. The worst scenario is that you could be placed on the Impaired Lives Register and be blacklisted from any insurance policy. There is the danger of being asked to take an HIV test and the trauma that involves. The best scenario is to pay an inflated premium. If you are not honest about your sexuality and the insurer discovers the truth, they will refuse to pay up if you die before the end of the term of the policy.

(3) There are ways of buying homes which circumnavigate the life assurance problems. These include repayment mortgages, PEP mortgages (Personal Equity Plan), pension mortgages to name just a few.

(4) Getting good financial advice, preferably from a company that specializes in gay finance, is the way through this minefield. In the UK, financial advisers fall into two camps: tied and independent. Tied advisers are either employers of a company or have an exclusive deal with one company. This means they can recommend only their company's products and although they can have a wide variety of plans they will have one set of guidelines on dealing with gay clients. They are also unlikely to tell you that one of their competitors has a better deal. Independent advisers are

just what the name suggests. They will know the attitudes of different companies to HIV and which companies are likely to ask you potentially embarrassing questions.

I cannot recommend too strongly that you take full financial advice and think the issues through carefully. Money is an explosive subject and one that many couples find hard to talk about.

5

MONEY: THE FINAL GAY TABOO

All couples have disagreements about money, whether to spend or save and where their priorities should lie. It represents much more than just purchasing power and in this chapter I will cover the issues and feelings it symbolizes, and how you can use this knowledge to explore and understand your relationship better.

Sean and Michael have weathered a lot through the five years they have been together: illness, loss of job (twice), failure of a small business and all the personal stress and financial problems these difficulties create. Sean is forty but has a youthful elf-like quality while Michael, although younger at thirty-five, has a more cynical, world-weary approach. Life has now taken a turn for the better. Sean has a senior position in a university finance department and they are about to leave their cramped flat and buy somewhere larger together. Michael plans to return to full-time education.

MICHAEL We met at the London Lesbian and Gay Centre where I was a volunteer working behind the bar. I was unemployed and Sean was a regular there. He kept on coming up and buying drinks.

94

SEAN   I fancied you [*laughter*].

MICHAEL   I had no concept of that at the time. Basically, one night at the tea-dance I just got pissed and decided to pick him up.

SEAN   Well, thank you!

Michael, what was the attraction?

MICHAEL   Mainly because he was older than I was and, I viewed at the time, more stable. I was missing a lot in relationships then. The younger people that I mixed with were immature.

SEAN   I just fancied him [*laughter*] to start with. Then I liked him as a person, because we talked quite often over the bar about all sorts of things. I hoped he liked me as well. I fancied Michael to start with but when I got to know him, I got to love him deeply.

How important do you think it is that you spent time getting to know each other before you had sex?

MICHAEL   I don't consider it that important.

SEAN   You've got different views on that from me. I think it's important. Remember when I went out with Henry – this was before I met Michael – I fancied him, picked him up and went back to his place for a few nights. That was just sex, nothing else in it. When I went back with Michael for the first time that was very different. I knew Michael and had grown to like him. I didn't just fancy him and therefore sex was much more – oh, it sounds so clichéd – it was an expression of love. But you think sex is sex and nothing at all to do with love.

Is that an issue between the two of you now?

MICHAEL We talk about it, and agree to disagree. It doesn't really rear its head.

SEAN Neither of us goes out with anybody else, sexually. We are faithful to each other. If for nothing else in this day and age – it's safer.

MICHAEL I was brought up in a small northern town. My father died when I was young. As I was the eldest I took it on myself to see that the family was OK. It wasn't until I was twenty-nine that I launched myself on the gay scene in London. I was fortunate that my sister was gay as well, so she knew all the haunts. I had a whale of a time, but then I realized this was stupid, that what I really wanted was a relationship.

What about you, Sean?

SEAN I was in teaching, a schoolmaster until I was thirty-six. I was found out in a relationship with a pupil, and I had no alternative but to resign. Even then I didn't face up to my sexuality. It was weeks later, having spent time with a psychologist, just talking and coming to terms with what had happened, what I was doing and where I was going. Then I started going to London several nights a week. I lived at home with Mother, and one evening she asked, 'Where have you been?'
    'Up to town.'
    'Same place as before?'
    'Yes.'
    'Same people again?'
    'Yes.'
    'Gay pub?'
    'Yes.'
    That was it, really.

MICHAEL She most probably thought it was Sodom and Gomorrah.

96

SEAN To start with, but after that everything was fine because things were just open. I think Mother's first shock was when I brought Michael home. We had been to a party, came back to my place and stayed over. We didn't say anything but just went straight upstairs and went to sleep. The next day the whole family had gathered.

How many people is that?

SEAN I have a brother and three sisters, their husbands, his girlfriend and all the children – with Mother, thirteen in all.

Thirteen people waiting for you at the bottom of the stairs!

SEAN They were all sitting in the lounge. We sneaked out of the front door and bolted.

MICHAEL There was no way that I was hanging around for your entire family to integrate me – Freudian slip! – interrogate me!

SEAN Then we settled on one sister first, and went round there as a couple. Now everybody is extremely accepting.

MICHAEL Your mother isn't! She's still hoping that you're going to turn. Being a Catholic, she would rather that Sean was married and breeding.

SEAN But she's quite realistic about it now. It doesn't mean that she's not fully supportive of the way we are. She loves Michael.

Do you feel comfortable with her?

MICHAEL No.

SEAN You don't?

MICHAEL She's very much a matriarch. I'm not saying she's not nice or anything. She does insist on having an opinion and being at the pinnacle of the family.

SEAN Yes, she is very much a matriarch – even the next-door neighbours call her Mother.

MICHAEL Sean's family is very different from mine. It's much larger and they always want to have an opinion on each other. I'm not used to that, I like people to keep out, stay away.

SEAN That has nothing to do with us being a gay couple. She is exactly the same with my brother and sisters. Remember when Sarah and Steve bought the barbecue set. She went for them in a big way.

MICHAEL So that's the type of family I've married into.

Sean, is there anything strange about Michael's family that you have married into?

SEAN Just that it is very, very different from mine. Mine is a close family, there's a lot of us. We grew up close and stayed close. But Michael's family are further away and more independent. We don't see them as much as we'd like to.

MICHAEL My mother adores Sean. We take her to gay pubs – we take everybody to gay pubs. My mother is very off-the-wall. On that first Christmas when we went up to stay with her, we'd just finished dinner and we were all sat round the table. She reached down into a bag and said, 'Anyone for a joint?'

SEAN It would have horrified my mother!

What impact has the acceptance and the involvement of both of your sets of families had on your relationship?

SEAN   It's enormous. We don't have the thing that lots of our friends have at Christmas time. One partner is going to see his family and the other stays at home or goes off to stay with friends. Any family gathering, we're both automatically invited.

Has it enriched your relationship?

SEAN   Yes, when we've been through bad times our families are there.

MICHAEL   No. My mother brought up all the family to be independent. So we've never needed other people's approval or disapproval. It's nice that the families are there to help, but I don't feel enriched by it.

SEAN   I do. I like the support and being able to ring up and talk about things quite easily and openly.

What's the difference between that and having friends?

SEAN   Friends are equally important, but you have your family whether you like it or not. They are a natural part of you. When Michael lost his job a year or so ago, my mother propped us up financially until we were back on our feet again, because it was quite a bitter blow. The whole family were supportive. Within weeks of it happening, one of my brothers-in-law had a birthday party at a restaurant. We couldn't afford it, so the family paid for us. We were not expected to buy Christmas presents. The family are not wealthy, yet they were there to provide support if we needed it.

How do you feel about this?

MICHAEL   OK, basically.

Where does supportive end and interfering begin?

SEAN   As soon as we wanted to buy a house.

MICHAEL   Certain members of Sean's family are interfering and others, like Claire, are supportive. She feels she can turn to us, without wanting us to do anything about it. That's how I like people to be when I'm facing them with a problem, not to help me but to be there to listen.

Have you put some backbone into Sean so that he now stands up more to his family?

MICHAEL   It's not that he lacks backbone, he sometimes seems an easy pushover. There are times when you need to be a little more assertive towards people – if you're not you're going to lose out and get trampled. I tend to be assertive only on particular issues, otherwise I let the world wash over me.

Tell me about the financial issues between you, because you've had money problems.

SEAN   When we started out together, Michael was unemployed. God knows how you survived. I know partially how you survived – I left you money.

MICHAEL   When?

SEAN   Whenever I set off from your place in the morning, I left you enough money for ciggies and something to eat during the day. I got Michael a job with my then company in one of their bookshops. That got us over the first hump for a while. The pay was crap but at least it was dough coming in. My pay was crap as well, but the two of us together had a manageable income and that was when we moved in here. Sandy was a lesbian who Michael was then sharing with – they got this place from the housing association. Then Michael got hepatitis and went into an isolation room at the Middlesex hospital.

MICHAEL   I was being paid sickness benefit.

SEAN I was going straight from work to the hospital and then I would come back here. I moved all my stuff in here the day he was taken into hospital. Then things became quite tight. You came out of hospital in the November and were unable to go back to work.

MICHAEL I went back in the middle of December.

SEAN But you'd not go in every day, and if you went in you didn't stay for the whole day. The company was laying people off, and it was decided that Michael was unable to complete his probationary period, and therefore was sacked.

MICHAEL They did pay me nicely considering I had only worked for them for six weeks and they paid me a grand.

Why didn't your salary cover everything?

SEAN I was paying a mortgage on my mother's house in Surrey, and living here, paying jointly the phone, rent, electricity and gas as well as travel and food. At one point I'd used the last of my credit-card money to pay the rent. I didn't know what we were going to do, because next month's money would be gone as soon as I got it. You *had* to go to work, well enough or not.

MICHAEL I saw an advert for London Transport. I shouldn't have gone back to work when I did, but by then I was feeling a lot better although not brilliant. I became a bus driver and we had some money for once.

SEAN Other problems came out of Michael working on shifts when I'm on a straight day, and the hangovers from hepatitis. It's debilitating. After he came out of hospital and we were going to go shopping, he didn't even make it to the tube station before he had to give up, sit down, rest and go home.

MICHAEL I took no time off the buses because of post-viral syndrome.

SEAN But you'd come home totally exhausted and you wouldn't wake up until you were going back to work. The post-viral syndrome posed incredible stresses on us: anytime I wanted to do anything Michael just wasn't able to do it. I got to feeling things like, Why don't I go out and leave him at home? We had blazing rows about him wanting me to be at home for him and me feeling a prisoner here. I'd got a promotion at work and we were comfortably off. I'd gone from the extreme of not knowing where the next penny was coming from to having money in my pocket and thinking, Why can't we go to the pub? I like going to pubs, he doesn't. 'Oh I don't want to. I'm tired, Sean, I've done a week's work. I need to relax.' Christ, I needed to go out!

MICHAEL It was a poor time for us both. Sean was struggling to understand my position and, because of the way I felt, there was no way that I could understand his. I had no energy to try to understand what Sean wanted. It caused an awful lot of friction. I don't think the finances were that pressurizing.

SEAN They were for me, because I was the one that was thinking how the fuck were we going to survive for the next week.

MICHAEL You're a born worrier. You enjoy worrying!

SEAN I do not enjoy worrying.

You have different attitudes to money?

MICHAEL We have different attitudes to life. He's like my mother, which is probably why they get on so well, because he worries. I once said to my mother, 'You're looking ever so worried, what's up?' She said, 'I'm worried because I've got nothing to be worried about!' Whereas I don't worry.

SEAN As long as you've got a few ciggies to go through the day, you couldn't give a damn.

MICHAEL It wasn't like that. As long as you can accept what the worst is, there's no reason to worry. The worst that could have happened was being reduced to living on pasta.

SEAN I was thinking that the worst that could happen is that I would have to go back to my mother and you'd have to go back to yours, because we couldn't afford to stay here. You wouldn't go on the dole, you wouldn't sign up for social security.

MICHAEL I couldn't even make it to social security, let alone anything else. I should have had more help from professionals. I don't consider the finances of the relationship much of a problem. We could have a million pounds and you'd still be having kittens about something.

SEAN I found it worrying. Michael became out of work again. He stuck the buses only for so long – he hated the job. Our money together was good but my money alone would not have covered our debts and kept us rolling. I saw the writing on the wall at work after we were taken over, I was desperately looking for another job to give myself some security so that if Michael did come off the buses we would still be reasonably secure. As it happened I landed an absolute gem of a job – I run the finance division of a university. I'd barely started there and his lordship decided he was taking a week off. He said, 'I'm not going back,' and I was thinking, What am I going to do? Because we still hadn't fully recovered. Also, we'd just been to France for our first anniversary and when we came back Sandy had stripped the place and vanished.

MICHAEL   Apart from our room she'd taken everything! We didn't have a kettle, lampshades, fridge – anything.

SEAN   I had to go and talk to my bank, but was careful not to say things like 'My lover and I!'

Do you feel, as far as finances are concerned, you are an invisible couple? If you'd been married you could explain the family's financial situation and have got a more sympathetic hearing?

SEAN   Or boyfriend/girlfriend, but not as a gay couple. It's a very conservative area, Walton-on-Thames, and the thought of a pair of poofs . . .

A pair of poofs are a bad risk?

SEAN   Yes – and I wouldn't have got what I wanted. I told the bank about my change of jobs and they were very understanding. I got the overdraft facility I wanted. It was a tremendous help.

Is it more difficult for a gay couple to borrow money?

SEAN   Yes. For getting money, I'm an individual and Michael doesn't exist.

MICHAEL   But there are advantages. Sean can take out a loan as a single person and so can I. If we were recognized as a couple we'd only be able to take out one loan.

SEAN   Anyway, Michael had left the buses and we'd gone to visit my mother and he'd seen a CD player in a shop window and wanted it. I said, 'If you get another job that pays more than the buses, you can have it but not until.' I'm busy at work, I get a telephone call, it's his lordship. 'I've bought that CD player.' *'We haven't got the money. How the hell can you afford to buy the CD player? I'm struggling to make ends meet.'* 'No,' he said. 'We struck a bargain and I've done the deal.' Suddenly he had a job that was paying more than me again.

MICHAEL We always tended to leapfrog over each other.

You also had a failed business. Tell me about that.

MICHAEL It wasn't so much failed as never really got started. I decided to use the skills that I had and go into replacement kitchen doors. But there was absolutely no demand for it in this area. Fortunately, we invested very little and only lost about a hundred pounds.

SEAN But I worked my arse off, bloody bank and the rest of it, because I used my position in business. I deal a lot with banks so I applied the same professional techniques.

How did you explain your relationship when you went to the banks?

SEAN I didn't. They presumed I was his accountant or his financial adviser or something like that. They weren't going to give him a bank account and provide the overdraft facility but I put forward a good business plan. They eventually said they would grant the overdraft facilities as long as I stood guarantor, which I did.

MICHAEL He would have a hell of a life if he hadn't! It wasn't a major disaster, I didn't feel like doing a Robert Maxwell and throwing myself off the nearest ferry.

Do you have joint bank accounts?

MICHAEL *God, no.* I wouldn't let him loose with my money. No, we don't, and I don't think we want one. It's easier to play games with these people, than if we had a single account with us both on it.

SEAN I can tell you my company's bank account from the millions down to the single pounds, how much is in it and what the liabilities are. Yet when we were both earning quite well I couldn't even tell you if my own account was in the red or the black. Until we were back in difficulties again and I had to become incredibly responsible with my own money. There's no way Michael would trust me with *his* money.

Why not?

MICHAEL Experience. He's hopeless with money, he says it himself. He spends it. I used to be exactly the same when I came into this relationship. Then I realized that one of us had to take some responsibility because both of us couldn't carry on at the same rate. We were running up debt at quite a rate, so I did.

SEAN I was banned from shopping. I used to fill up all the decanters first – that's essential. A nice little joint for Sunday, a nice little bourguignonne or chasseur for Saturday night, mince for during the week. If it came to less than seventy pounds I was most surprised. Then I would say, oh those are nice cushion covers, I'll have those. I loved Selfridges. I could spend all day in Selfridges if I had a big enough cheque book and credit card.

How do you pay bills if you don't have a joint account?

MICHAEL We each took responsibility for certain finances. Sean pays for the car loans, I pay the telephone bill, the electricity bill, gas bill.

SEAN When Michael had no money, mine had to cover the rent, the bills, food, the car loan, tax and insurance. We'd bought a Range Rover two weeks before he was made redundant which gave me a mammoth debt.

MICHAEL When he was paying for both of us, he was very responsible with the money. But as soon as I became

106

employed again, he just went to pot again. But money doesn't worry me, things will sort themselves out. We've got two arms and two legs.

Do our attitudes to money come from our upbringing?

MICHAEL   Yes. Mine was middle class.

SEAN   I had a working-class background, and because of the profession I went into I became middle class. I always had more money than I needed, because when I was living at home with my parents my money was my money. I handed over some house-keeping but I had pots of dough left over. I was totally irresponsible with it.

Taking the lessons you learnt in your childhood, complete this phrase: Money is . . .

MICHAEL   A means to an end . . . freedom.

SEAN   I have to have money to survive, so for me it's not a means to an end. It's survival to start with and then it's *great* having lots more of it.

Sean, complete the phrase – money equals . . .

SEAN   From my childhood days, money equalled great unhappiness when there wasn't enough of it to go round and family arguments and hard times.

Sean, when there isn't enough now, do you bring unhappiness here?

SEAN   [*softly*] Yes.

MICHAEL   Thank you for pointing that out.

SEAN   When there isn't enough we row.

MICHAEL   You row.

SEAN   OK, I row. We've always bickered and squabbled.

MICHAEL   I go through life quite placid, but if somebody attacks me then they'd better watch out! I respond over the top, more than I need to, which is my failing.

SEAN   Then you shout at me and I go and sulk.

When you didn't have any money, Michael, how did you feel about yourself?

SEAN   He'd get low and depressed. The slightest thing, and he'd take it personally. I'd come home and say, 'It's freezing today,' and he'd come back with, 'Don't you think I've done my best to keep the flat warm?' I was only talking about the weather!

What does lack of money do to your feeling of self-worth, Michael?

MICHAEL   It doesn't affect my self-worth, I've got no money now.

SEAN   [*emphatically*] It does. The difference in him when he got a job – overnight he became much more outward going and responsive. Easy about everything, we didn't argue all the time. Before, you had to ask me for pocket money for ciggies and things, which was demoralizing.

Money is power, isn't it?

SEAN   Yes.

MICHAEL   No. Money is freedom, not power. The two concepts are entirely different. Freedom is allowing yourself to do what you want, but power usually involves having authority over others. The only authority you have with freedom is over yourself.

SEAN   That time you were off work, my mother gave me one hell of a stripping off for not making sure that you had money in your pocket. She said I was exercising undue power over you if you had to ask for money.

There's quite a power struggle going on between you.

MICHAEL Probably, yes.

SEAN At the moment as I'm the one with the money, I'm the powerful one. [*Giggle.*]

MICHAEL I realize that I'm in a fortunate position. As a student anything I get as money is pocket money. Other people are having to live on what I'm using for pocket money. In those terms Sean does have some form of power over me.

SEAN But, seriously, I don't really have power over you.

MICHAEL I think you'd like to. I'm far too independent to allow somebody to have power over me. If somebody used it in a threatening way – like, if you don't do what I want you to do I will withdraw my support – they would be out of the door so fast, packed bags on the doorstep. Sean realizes that, because he knows what sort of person I am. Threatening me is not going to work. Anyway, he's got the money, I've got the Access cards.

SEAN He has as well. It stops me using them. Both of us have got to be there to decide to spend it.

It seems that the power is balanced.

MICHAEL It is, in certain ways. At one stage I cut his Access card up. I've never seen anybody cry over a cut-up Access card before. The spending was just getting silly and out of hand.

Do you think that gay people find it easier to talk about sex than they do about money?

SEAN   Yes, I think so. Heterosexuals don't talk about sex, that's what you do at home. They talk about money. Certainly, with younger gay men on the scene, it's who you picked up last night, where you went back to and how big their dick is! But they wouldn't talk about their finances, because you have to maintain the image that you've got enough to afford what you want to do now, or you're not there.

How do you feel about mingling finances?

SEAN   When we move house, we'll probably end up with a more realistic attitude towards the dough. We're going to be financially comfortable, even though he's only on student money, and we'll probably set up a joint housekeeping account and transfer money from my account. Whatever contribution Michael can make is fine.

MICHAEL   This is a new one on me! This is the first time I've heard of this.

SEAN   You lying toad!

MICHAEL   You're paying the bills!

SEAN   Yes. The property will be legally mine and Michael will be my tenant, as far as social security is concerned. I will charge him rent and we have no relationship whatsoever. If we were a heterosexual couple I would be expected to support him.

Why do you think your relationship has survived?

MICHAEL   I'm satisfied with what I've got. I'm a bit too old to look at the grass on the other side of the fence and think it's greener, because it's not. I think that's where a lot of relationships flounder. You've got to make a concerted effort for a relationship to work and I put the effort in.

110

There were numerous times when I was ready to throw him out, but I realize you've got to stop, think, and weather it.

SEAN I love him like crazy. There are times when I could cheerfully pack my bag and go, but there is a relationship – something we have to work at. There are times when Michael is all soppy and sentimental. Just before our anniversary this year, Michael was in work and suddenly there was light at the end of the tunnel. I have wanted a wedding ring for ages, and on our anniversary I half opened my briefcase and saw a card in it. He said, 'Don't open it now, wait till you get to work.' I got there, opened the briefcase and found a little box, beautifully wrapped up with a little bow. In front of my entire staff, I opened it and there was my little wedding ring! So he's a soppy sentimentalist as well.

MICHAEL Just one of the many facets of my character.

SEAN So we're good for each other.

The three great taboos of our age are sex, death and money. Gay men have always been used to talking about the first. Through having to come to terms with our sexuality we question, explore and talk about what we enjoy in bed. During this process we overturn the sexual taboo, which, of course, includes talking about it. We are now having to deal with death: Aids has made us confront that too. However, money is something with which we feel less comfortable: I know my best friends' sex habits but I do not know how much they earn! Money is the last subject we talk about, and therefore we have seldom analysed our attitudes to it. All the issues are buried in our subconscious.

The most important rule in dealing with money is to realize that money is *never* just money. It is intertwined with a range of other issues, like power, self-esteem, security and freedom – which I discussed in the interview with Sean and Michael.

Most gay couples have two salaries coming into the household and, because men still tend to earn more than women, this represents a good income. With no children to support, money is normally less of an issue than it is for heterosexual couples. Money is always easier to deal with when there is plenty of it. Michael and Sean are acutely aware of this, because they have had to cope with so many financial crises. Many couples claim to have no problems with money, but if this is true, why do they insist on keeping their finances separate, even after many years together?

It is important for gay couples to understand the powerful feelings that are attached to money. First, jobs in the 1990s are no longer secure and financial stability cannot be relied on. It is better to have worked through the money issues in advance rather than coping with them when one of you loses your job. Second, money can offer important insights into your relationship, helping you understand yourself and your partner better, and enriching the relationship.

In discussing Sean and Michael's finances, I have shown the link between money and upbringing: Sean came from a close working-class family with plenty of togetherness. He enjoys their support, both emotional and practical, and has no problems being subsidized by them. Others might shy away from a loan, concerned about the strings that might be attached. When Sean was a child, money shortages caused rows and arguments, which happens with Michael too: they are re-creating Sean's childhood. Sean talks about money in two ways: he is either the serious adult worrying about budgeting or the carefree child who can spend all his pocket money. He seems more comfortable with the child part of his personality. He needs togetherness and closeness from his and Michael's relationship: when Michael is away a rota of friends have to keep Sean company as he cannot bear being alone. Therefore, his is far keener on the financial equivalent of intimacy: a joint bank account.

Michael was brought up in a middle-class family, and supports the traditional middle-class values of independence and sound financial management. He comes from a small family, where everybody values their own space and individuality. For him, the power of money is that it gives him freedom, something he values above everything else. Therefore, he reacts strongly against any idea of a joint account because he is far more comfortable with independent money. His grant money is *his* money. It is vitally important to him that he does not have to ask anybody for money – he did not sign on after losing his job.

When a couple come together each brings along their own personal issues about money. In the early stages, it is possible to have a similar attitude: both Sean and Michael were spenders. However, once the couple become truly committed to each other *emotionally*, and therefore *financially*, there is a tendency to polarize: Michael decided that somebody had to take responsibility for money. One becomes the saver, the other the spender; one worries, the other is carefree. The position you take on this see-saw depends not only on your personality and background but also on the way the two of you interact. A good relationship will find a balance for the see-saw: Michael holds on to the credit card while Sean earns the money.

There are five basic see-saws on which most couples swing up and down.

(1) *Saver and Spender*. This is the most common: one partner says we must buy new curtains for the lounge, the other points out that they cannot afford it. Spenders are

constantly buying gifts for themselves and others and hate balancing their cheque books. The saver does not feel secure unless he has plenty of money in the building society.

(2) *'Responsible Adult' and 'Irresponsible Child'*. The responsible adult works hard; buying a house, long-term security and pensions are all important. The last thing that money is for is having fun! The irresponsible child must have the original fifties' jukebox – now! They certainly enjoy their money. However, in saner moments they discover that they have no savings to see them through the hard times and have binged their way into debt.

(3) *Innocent and Wise*. The innocent are almost afraid that money will corrupt them, and may even fear becoming too attached to it. They shy away from money or are ashamed of their possessions, which seem to tie them down and commit them. In contrast, the wise are always looking for new ways to make money – these were the people who endlessly spoilt dinner parties in the late eighties by boasting about how much their homes were worth, and today they are into multi-level marketing. They know everything about unit trusts and nothing about people. While the innocent are afraid of being corrupted by money, the wise see the markets as their saviour and other people as their downfall. If partners polarize on this see-saw the relationship is bound to be stormy. However, if they achieve a balance, in which the wise uses money efficiently and the innocent reminds him that there is more to life than work and possessions, it can work well.

(4) *Hoarder and Gambler*. The hoarders surround themselves with money – they almost try to insulate themselves with their financial success. A hoarder does not need money just to feel secure but to feel good about and value himself. The hoarder takes no risks with money or with his life. His opposite, the gambler, is addicted to adrenalin. When the hot investment tip comes up or the roulette wheel

is spun, he's in there. The gambler never thinks about what will happen if he loses and may become depressed and feel worthless when he fails.

(5) *Worrier and Unconcerned*. This couple drive each other up the wall. The worrier is always fretting that he will not have enough money to meet the bills, despite the reality that if he budgeted carefully there would be enough – the house is not going to be repossessed tomorrow! Every decision is revisited a thousand times. The unconcerned closes his eyes to the problems. If your partner is a worrier, then reality is probably somewhere between your two ends of the see-saw. You need to be more concerned and he less worried. However, if you are both in the more balanced middle position you probably know the size of the problem and feel comfortable that you are managing everything just fine.

Obviously it is possible to ride more than one see-saw at a time and most relationships use a combination. Problems arise when the more you push down in your own personal direction the further your partner flies up in his. If you are the saver and your partner the spender, the more you clamp down on his buying the more tempted he will feel to hunt for irresistible bargains. Try to negotiate an agreed budget and stick to it. This places the responsibility on both of you, but also allows both of you the pleasure of shopping. In other words, one partner has learnt to enjoy money and the other to manage it properly. If a financial see-saw has become an issue for you, try to find a middle, balanced position. You probably have something important to learn from the other person. After all, their position is only a reflection of your own.

If you are unclear about which issues are intertwined with money for you, try the exercise I used in the interview with

Michael and Sean. Complete the sentence 'Money is . . .'
Next, think back to your childhood and the lessons your
parents taught you. How would your father have finished
the sentence and what would your mother have said? What
connections can you make?

Not only do different people have different attitudes to
money, they also place different values on things. Here is a
second exercise to help you understand the similarities and
differences between you and your partner. Write the items
on the list on cards or pieces of paper. Next, spread them
out and then create a pile with your highest spending priority
at the top and the least important at the bottom. Each of
you should do the exercise independently, afterwards com-
paring your results and talking each other through your
choices. Everybody has their own ideas about the types of
expenditure included in each of the headings so it is important that you explain your thought processes and decisions
fully. There is no right or wrong order in which to place the
items; it is your opinions that count. The results may
surprise you, as well as making you more aware and more
understanding of each other's values.

good food	investments
entertaining	treats
holidays	friends
nights out	booze
clothes	items for the house
car	family
savings	major improvements to the
basic daily living	house
	hobbies

and a couple of blank cards for you to add things that are
important to you.

Next, we need to unhook money from the other issues

that are attached to it – self-esteem, freedom, control, power, dependency, etc. Self-esteem is the key. Once you feel good about yourself, you have the confidence to deal with the rest. These days, few of us make or produce anything: we are a cog in a bigger wheel. For the lucky few, the satisfaction of creating the perfect hairstyle or designing a house is equally as important, if not more so, than the money they earn by doing it. The majority cannot show their work to other people: they are 'something in insurance' or 'a salesman' and their salary becomes the most convenient yardstick of their worth. However, you do not become a better person if you are given a pay rise, just a richer one. Michael was depressed when he was not working; now that he has become a student his self-esteem has improved. Not only has he found something to do, but something worthwhile and interesting and this is how he feels about himself.

Many heterosexual men feel threatened if their wives earn more than they do, which is less of a problem for gay men because we question male roles generally, and do not feel the same need to be the principal provider. You should still talk through your feelings about this with your partner, and try to find an arrangement where the lower earner feels valued and that he is 'paying his way', and the higher wage earner that he is not being taken advantage of. When the situation changes, with a new job or promotion, be prepared to renegotiate.

There is no normal way of arranging your finances. It is up to you to decide whether you want a joint account, separate accounts or a joint fund for joint expenditures. The real issue is whether you are both happy with the decision you make.

By understanding our attitude to money, we learn about our childhood and how it can still influence us as adults. The more you choose *not* to talk about money, the more you need to unpack and understand the issues. Therefore, the more a couple intermingles their finances, the greater their opportunity to confront the underlying issues about money and their past behaviour. It is not an easy decision to make but if you take up the challenge you have the opportunity to become more intimate with each other and will be rewarded with a more fulfilling relationship.

6

BOUNDARIES: COPING WITH JEALOUSY

When a couple first meet they are so wrapped up in each other that they are not aware of anybody else. Calls go unreturned and friends feel the couple must have dropped off the edge of the world. Although when they move out of 'Blending' into 'Nesting' they begin to start interacting with other people, they are still continuing to bond. It is only when they reach the next stage in their relationship that they fully begin to deal with the world outside. It is vital that the relationship is well protected and has good boundaries – or other people can interfere and create immense problems. This is important for all relationships, however settled or new they are, but it is most likely to become an issue at this time.

The experience of becoming half of a gay couple is a bit like marrying Elizabeth Taylor: your new man is almost certain to come with a past, a string of significant previous relationships. Many of his best friends will have been past lovers, there may be unresolved business, or somebody 'officially' in the past may tamper with the new relationship.

Jealousy is a destructive emotion, and it nearly poisoned the relationship between Steve and Andy. Steve is forty-two and holds down a senior position in a large financial services company, while Andy is only twenty-two and a buyer for a department store. No money has been spared in fitting their home with all the latest suburban comforts.

STEVE We first met when Andrew was only thirteen or fourteen. He was living in the flat next door to a friend of mine, who used to have parties. Dave, my partner at the time, and I used to go and, occasionally, so did Andy. He used to sit in the kitchen, looking nervous and sweet and innocent. I used to go to the kitchen because I didn't like the parties particularly and probe him, asking 'Why are you here?' and 'Are you gay?'

ANDY I used to deny it!

Was it a gay party?

STEVE Completely. Occasionally his father would come too, and sit in the corner and get drunk.

ANDY This friend would invite all the neighbours in and so we all went. They were good parties. I used to play footsie with Steve [*laughs*]. Well, he touched my knee a few times!

STEVE Around that time I was getting fed up with Dave. We were drifting apart, I suppose. We would go together to a party but tend to spend the evening separately yet although I didn't really like his company, I wasn't looking for an alternative. It was interesting and exciting to sit in the kitchen and tease this boy.

Were you sexually attracted to him, Steve?

STEVE At the time no – he was so young! He would have split! Wouldn't you, darling?

ANDY No, I'd been doing it for a couple of years before.

When Steve asked if you were gay, was the reason you denied it because you didn't know the answer?

ANDY I knew I was gay. I used to get into gay pubs at that age. I was lying because I didn't want to come out. I was only fourteen or fifteen. I just wasn't ready. I was out to our mutual friend, because he was the one I was having sex with!

When did it change from innocent bantering in the kitchen to something different?

STEVE We bumped into each other once at a gay disco. Mike, this mutual friend, was going out with a boy called Jason, and I was still with Dave. It was about six months before the end of me and Dave. I remember spending half the evening with you, being flirted with outrageously and then getting a real bollocking on the way home. The next time I saw you, you were in a shop window. Mike and Jason had split up and me and Dave had split up and I was going out with Jason. You popped out – and Jason was spitting fire at you. You were saying, 'Have my phone number, Steve.' But I didn't. I guess it was three years later that I was on a one-week course in Brighton. I knew it was close to where Andy worked so I wandered into the shop.

ANDY He came over to the cash desk and I passed out! My legs went to jelly! Later I phoned up the hotel where he was staying, got the room number and went round and put a message under the door saying that we must meet that night.

STEVE But it was the next night we got together, which was, coincidentally, Valentine's night. Dave and a few others had arranged to meet me in a bar for a drink. Dave was still chasing after me at this point, but I suggested to Andy that I meet him there. So we did. There was much hissing and spitting. Dave was pissed off because I was with Andy, and Mike was even more pissed off.

ANDY Because all those years before, he had tried to protect me. I was his, his bit on the side, and nobody else could get near me. He didn't want me to go out with Steve.

He wanted you for himself.

STEVE He often used to call and expect you to be there, and available. You weren't monogamous – you were only nineteen and you were tramping around all over Brighton.

ANDY I was getting fed up with sleeping around. I used to go to this club, flirting away on the dance floor and hopefully the person would be staying at the hotel above that night, go up there – have whatever, come back down and dance around, go and find another one.

Were you concerned that you were getting involved with a nineteen-year-old? The age of consent was then twenty-one.

STEVE Not initially. Neither of us had any intention of becoming involved. That first evening, we went back to the hotel after we'd been to the pub and were giggling about how annoyed everybody else was. Andy said that he had never seen the inside of the rooms at that hotel and could he have a look round to compare it with another hotel where he used to work. We certainly had sex that night, about 96 million times.

ANDY I just thought it would be a one-nighter, or perhaps a two-nighter.

STEVE In fact you stayed for the whole week. From my point of view, there was nothing there except for an overt sexual interest, which I assumed would wane as quickly as it waxed. So it did not occur to me that we could have

122

problems with the police until it started to become more serious.

What did you think when you realized you could be in danger?

STEVE I had to check with Andy's parents that they weren't going to be difficult. We did that fairly early on. It was quite traumatic for Andy because he hadn't come out.

ANDY I had – at seventeen I told my mother I was gay. It was upsetting then and I found it difficult to tell her I had found a partner.

Why?

ANDY I think she still believed it was a phase and I would grow out of it – like every mother. Telling her he was almost the same age as her made it even worse.

STEVE In some ways it made it better. I talked to his stepfather about us operating illegally and I said, 'I don't need your approval, but I'm looking for your consent. While it's making Andrew happy, I need to know that you won't cause us problems.' They were both, if not happy with that, prepared to go along with it. I also had to discuss it at work, because I was security manager and guardian of the morals and the crown jewels. I didn't ask my boss if I was OK. He had known I was gay for years. I just went into his office and said, 'There is something you need to know: I'm starting a relationship with a new lover.' He said, 'I hope you will be happy.' I replied, 'But he's under the legal age of consent for gay men, and I'm telling you because I hope I will not get into any trouble, any blackmail problems.' He said, 'You certainly won't have any problems from me, and I'll make certain the rest of the management team are aware of the situation.'

It's difficult to come out at work as gay, and quite difficult to go and meet your new partner's parents, but to have to go under circumstances where in theory you could be locked up in prison – that must have made it doubly difficult.

STEVE   I didn't think about it much. I rationalized it to myself – the police aren't just going to arrest us because I'm having sex with an under-age male, they will only act if we cause offence to somebody or if somebody makes a complaint. Andrew's father or mother. We squared it with his mum and then you phoned your dad and said, 'This is what's happening. Don't make trouble for us.'

ANDY   I hate my father. There's no real connection with him.

Andy, how did you feel about having sex under the age of consent?

ANDY   I didn't care. It's my life. This is the life that I wanted to have. I was old enough to make up my own mind.

STEVE   I don't have any respect for that law. I can understand why they put it there, and I hope they change it again, not because it limited or restricted us – and we know lots of other young gay people having relationships. It probably inhibits the development of some people. It's just profoundly unfair. The thought that at sixteen a boy can legitimately make a decision to have sex providing it's the 'right' – heterosexual – one but if he makes what the law deems the wrong choice, he has to wait till eighteen before he can do anything about it. I just cannot see how in today's climate that can be justified.

You had been in your relationship with Dave for seven years.

ANDY   And I'm going to beat the seven years. I'm going to send him an anniversary card.

Why did that break down?

STEVE   I stopped loving him. He had a kink, which he suppressed in the early days but, as time passed, he opened up more and more and I became somewhat sidelined from the sexual side of things. Character traits were developing in him that I didn't like. He had an absolute obsession with Mike, the guy that Andy was seeing. If I'd said the moon was round and Mike had said it was flat, it would have become flat, without question. Initially I was jealous of that, and later on I became indifferent to it. I started to go swimming, joined a gym, did things in the evening on my own. We drifted apart, I drifted away and he will probably still say now that I treated him badly but I'd just had a gutful.

Were you still living together when you first started courting Andy?

STEVE   No, we had been apart for two years in which I was busy catching up with all the fun I'd missed. I don't think I slept for more than two hours a night in the whole time. I was really having a wonderful time. I was beginning to get bored and burnt-out, so I was winding it down a little bit.

What was the reaction of your ex-partners, Dave and Mike, when you met on Valentine's night?

STEVE   Mike took Andy to one side and was hissing at him. Dave was quite unpleasant to me – he said, 'What are you doing here with that boy? Haven't you had enough boys and floosies?' I didn't really take any notice.

ANDY   [*quietly*] I've had so much trouble from Dave. Threats, he's wanted to hit me, and just be totally nasty. It's been quite upsetting. Probably about two years. I almost left because I'd just had enough. He'd phone just before I was getting in and so Steve would be all wound up and agitated from talking to him. If he phoned when I was in, I'd answer and he'd get annoyed because he couldn't talk to Steve. But Steve didn't want to speak to him, so I used to answer the phone. He got so nasty.

STEVE   He was being nice to our faces and vicious, really vicious, about us to everybody else.

Do you think he was being so difficult because he was jealous?

ANDY   He was still in love with Steve.

STEVE   And he was telling everybody that we wouldn't last. Andy was sucking me dry of all my money, that was the only reason he was interested and he'd drop me as soon as he had spent everything.

ANDY   I got used to it after a while, and grew to ignore it, but it did build up and was very upsetting. I'd just come home from work and I'd be all stressed up from the travelling and then Dave would phone. Streaming tears, it would be awful.

STEVE   I thought I had an agreement with him. We would behave in a civilized fashion towards each other and still be friends. I was trying to keep my half of the bargain, but I wasn't seeing what was going on behind my back. He used to come round here and say how lovely it was but then I'd be out of the room and he would always try to link himself back by saying to Andy, 'When I lived here . . . when I was with Steve . . .'

ANDY   He'd say something like, 'Parties that we had together, this is how we would do things' and 'We wouldn't put that there.'

STEVE Undermining everything.

ANDY Everything has been redecorated and bought as new. I call it 'de-Daving' the house.

When you realized how bad the problem was, Steve, what did you do?

STEVE Andrew said to me, 'I'd like you to stop seeing Dave.' I told Dave that we didn't want to have anything more to do with him, and that was that. He tried a few times to keep in touch.

ANDY He'd phone up for the most stupid things, the flimsiest of excuses.

STEVE It's not an individual set of words, more a cumulative effect. It's a drip-feed approach – he's incredibly clever. We've had hardly any contact with him these last two years. I can't tell you the profound feeling of relief that I have about that, because just talking to him would give me a headache – it winds me up so much.

As a new gay couple did you feel supported by your friends?

STEVE I don't think we were hindered, other than by Dave. Mike got used to it after a while. What I found difficult, was that Dave had alienated most of the friends he and I had shared together, and the neighbours both sides – to the point that one didn't speak to me for eighteen months!

You were unaware of this?

STEVE Yes; except when I tried to make contact with these people I got a frosty response. I thought, Bollocks, I don't need this. All the friends I had had as a couple we lost.

Andy's friends seemed to be ephemeral, club friends, so when we got together we didn't know many people.

It's often a problem for gay couples that their single friends are no longer appropriate.

STEVE   You certainly lose contact very quickly. Andy used to try but they weren't interested any more, because he wasn't a disco queen ready to go out dancing all hours. Most, if not all, of our friends at that point were straight, a mixture of family, work associates and others.

Do you think that is because straight people are more supportive, because they socialize more as couples? Or is it because gays are slightly jealous?

STEVE   Some gay people don't like couples. They do get jealous. We both know quite a lot of women who enjoy the company of gay men and aren't threatened by our having a relationship. On our Christmas card list there are only about a dozen gay men, singles or couples, and the other hundred odd are heterosexual.

Is it also to do with where you live? This town is not somewhere that's famous for gay life.

ANDY   Quite a few gay people live in this town. They've tried to pick me up in the shop! Honestly, I've had some amazing proposals. Thanks, Mr Gold Credit Card!

You've been together for four years now. What do you think has made the relationship work?

ANDY   Money, sex and power! [*Laughter.*]

Be serious!

STEVE   I think he is partly serious. When I got my manager's parking tag on the car, he was much more excited about it than I was.

ANDY   I do love you very much, but I suppose the money has helped. I'm not a kept woman or anything like that. I pay my way!

STEVE   Either that or he sleeps in the shed!

How do you think the age difference has affected you?

ANDY   What age difference? He behaves like a ten-year-old most of the time.

How old does Andy behave?

STEVE   He fluctuates between about twelve and thirty. He can be very childish and so can I. There are times when he acts with a common sense and wisdom that you would expect in a fairly senior person. It's not an issue and I'm surprised that it isn't. After he moved in it took me about six months to get over the thought that one day he would find somebody his own age and say, 'Sorry, I'm off.'

ANDY   Next week?

STEVE   OK, can you get my secretary to schedule it? Now, it doesn't bother me because I know that the feelings I have for him, which have grown stronger over the four years, are reciprocated. It's not something you can fake.

ANDY   When Steve is seventy or eighty – and hopefully I will still be living with him then – I think his body clock will slow down. I'll still be wanting to go out doing things. I think he's probably going to have to let me have some freedom, but we'll cross that bridge when we come to it. I hope he can still get it up at that age!

STEVE   My dad's still doing it and he's well into his seventies.

Andy, you said that you didn't get on well with your father. Is Steve a father figure for you?

ANDY   No.

STEVE   I think so, sometimes.

ANDY   The pocket money's good!

STEVE   There's a cliché opportunity here. If people have a dysfunctional relationship with their father they go and look for it elsewhere. Whether or not that is Andy's motivation, either conscious or subconscious, I don't give a damn. It's working.

ANDY   Twenty-six is my limit. Anybody under twenty-six – I'm just not interested, because they've got no experience. They're total failures in bed, they just lie there and do nothing. I don't think you are a father figure, not for me.

What have you learnt from each other over the four years you've been together?

ANDY   I don't know. I wouldn't have been to Disney World, or travelled first class on the planes.

You make it sound like it's all been for the money!

ANDY   Are you listening, Dave? It has helped, although I managed before. I didn't need to spend lots of money. Life has changed so much – we're heading towards a different circle of friends, going up in the world.

STEVE   I've learnt patience. In the past, I've always been used to issuing orders and not brooking any discussion or opposition. Early on Andy started to resist me and said, 'If you want me to do something, you're going to have to ask me, and justify it.' It was a difficult thing to learn. Although it was something I'd do at work, I never used to do it at home. I'm still not a patient person, but I'm much more patient than I was. I think Andy has learnt to take a longer view on things – maybe everybody gets that in time, with him perhaps rather quicker than most. He doesn't just live for today or tomorrow.

ANDY   Yes, I suppose so, we've talked about the future.

STEVE   I think we've both learnt the value of a relationship, and what you can get out of it. You have to put a hell of a lot into it as well. It's like a constant investment of energy, not something you can take for granted. If you don't keep watching it, it will boil over or go bad or whatever. It's not a financial investment, it's an emotional one, an investment of time.

ANDY   We weren't looking for a relationship, but we're both happy with the way it turned out.

How do gay men learn about relationships?

STEVE   There is no institution like marriage for gay men. We have to make the rules up as we go along. There are no role models, certainly not where we live. It's not something you learn while you're growing up, your aunts and uncles typically aren't gay, your parents generally speaking aren't. All the things you're trained to do by society drop away. As a single gay man, you kick over the traces and go wild and crazy. If you meet somebody and decide you want to live with them you're a couple, and you've got to make it up as you go along.

Do you think that you are aping heterosexuals, or carving something out for yourself?

STEVE   I'm not consciously aping anybody. I love Andy deeply and want to live with him, and that's as far as it goes for me. We could be the only homosexual couple in the entire universe or the whole of our road could be full of them and it wouldn't make any difference to what I want to do right now.

Steve and Andy are a good example of how ridiculous the laws about the age of consent are in Great Britain. Without knowing them, the law would immediately cast Steve in the role of seducer and Andy as the innocent who had been led into a life of wickedness. The reality is that Andy and many other gay teenagers started having sex well before they reached twenty-one. Now the age of consent has been lowered to eighteen, but there are still many young gays who will continue to be criminalized. The law forces them to have illicit one-night stands, and makes it difficult for them to obtain good advice.

Gay and heterosexual people all have to pass through adolescence; this period is about rebellion. Everybody challenges their parents' viewpoint and values on a range of issues, not just sexual ones. It is through this questioning process that the teenager transforms themselves from a dependent child to an independent adult. It is impossible to be a well-rounded adult without working through this life stage – otherwise you are still too tied up with your parents. For heterosexuals a lot of status is associated with marrying and having children, society indulges – or puts up with – rebellion and encourages young heterosexuals to join the adult world. It is not as confirming and accepting of gay youngsters and, therefore, some gay men become stuck in the teenage life stage, devoted to their elderly mother and secret sex. Promiscuous sex is the opposite of everything straight society preaches: for gays promiscuity is all about rebellion, freedom, and, like being a teenager, it carries no responsibilities. An adult has commitments. Because it is illegal to have sex as a gay man until you are eighteen, the period of rebellion and sexual adolescence is extended, making it difficult for us to settle down into an adult relationship. The unequal age of consent says to young gay men, 'What you are doing is so disgusting you can be jailed for it,' which may be accepted by gay teenagers, to the extent that it poisons their self-image at the time when they are forging their identity.

If you are under the age of consent, you are normally safe from the police if you have one-night stands. It is when you fall in love that the problems start. Andy was forced not only to talk about his sexuality in a family where sex was never discussed, but to come out as part of a couple at the same time. (The issues around coming out as a couple are covered in the next chapter.) I had my first boyfriend when I was twenty, at university, and he was in his early thirties. It was only later that I discovered why he would never stay the night with me: he was frightened that somebody might report him to the authorities and that he would be prosecuted. It is no wonder that it often takes longer for a gay man to make long-term relationships than his straight brothers and sisters.

If you are in a relationship and one or both of you is under the age of consent, it is important that you talk through the problems together. Follow the example of Steve and Andy: confront the issues head on. It is unlikely that the police will prosecute unless they have a complaint from your parents so speak to your mother and father, explain how much you love your partner and how they risk permanently alienating you. Most parents will see sense.

Steve and Andy are also an example of how negative images can be taken on board. Dave spent so much time telling everybody that Andy is after Steve's money, that Andy now half believes it. He enjoys Steve's money – who wouldn't? – but he is also deeply attached to Steve and uses humour to cover his true feelings. There is no problem with this indirect form of communication because Steve is reading the hidden subtext. However, if you are more open misunderstandings are less likely to arise. The other lesson to be drawn from Steve and Andy's experience is the importance of making both people feel that where they live is their home, especially so if one partner is moving into the other's house. Be sensitive to their feelings and their need to impose something of themselves on the home. If you are the owner it is tempting to have the last say in everything but this may undermine the relationship and prevent it being a partnership.

I was impressed by how Steve dealt with the gay issue at work. His employers are conservative: they insist that everyone wears a suit to work, even frowning on a jacket and tie. Yet Steve's openness about his sexuality has not damaged his career: he has been constantly promoted. In some ways his gayness has been an asset – recently he has been given responsibility for his company's equal opportunities programme because the company felt this was something he particularly would relate to.

Why do we need boundaries?

Imagine a relationship as if it is a house. It needs strong walls or the heat escapes. If you leave the doors and windows open, someone may steal the family silver. Good boundaries protect a relationship from other people and outside influences. Balance, of course, is important: a house should not be surrounded by such high garden walls that those who live in it cannot see out and no one comes to visit. A relationship needs boundaries strong enough to protect it but not so strong that they imprison.

Gay people are far more likely to remain friends with ex-partners than are heterosexuals. (For instance, Andy doubts that his mother would attend her ex-husband/his father's funeral.) Yet gays move quickly from being lovers to friends. When a marriage breaks down, a divorce takes time to be made absolute. Gay couples have no established marker, such as engagement or marriage, at the beginning of their relationship; they normally celebrate the day they met as their anniversary. The date on which one partner moves out marks the end. However, in reality it takes time to come to terms with the end of a relationship. The effect is similar to that of bereavement, except that the person is still around, and you experience similar feelings. An important part of creating strong boundaries is a clear ending of one relationship before you move on. You need to work through a range of feelings: disbelief (especially if it was not your choice), anger, questioning (why did it happen?), bitterness and regret. The first year is particularly difficult with birthdays, Christmas and the first anniversary of the separation. After that, you can begin to accept and come to terms with the end of the relationship – before then you are just not ready. Until you have been through this process it is too early to be 'just friends'.

The different types of boundary

The first boundary that we need to mark out clearly and firmly is between the end of one relationship and the beginning of the next. Make certain that the issues from one partnership do not spill over into the new one.

Overleaf is a diagram that shows the type of boundaries that gay couples often erect.

There is a strong outer boundary, which takes into account society's ambivalence towards homosexuality. Some heterosexuals are supportive and help a gay couple validate

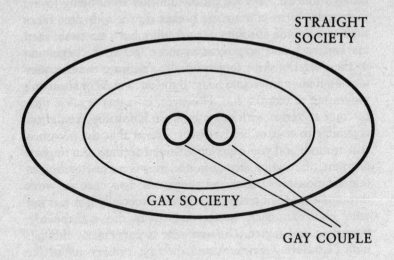

STRAIGHT
SOCIETY

GAY SOCIETY

GAY COUPLE

their relationship. When you become half of a couple your relationships change with friends you had when you were single. Andy found that his 'scene' friends drifted away, however hard he tried to keep in touch. When you settle down you're not as keen on a night on the town, and some of your friends will have little in common with your new partner. As a couple you will want a different kind of social life, and it is only natural that you will want it to include other couples. Although you should maintain individual friendships outside the relationship, the two of you need shared friends. Most established gay partnerships know more heterosexual than gay couples. Using Christmas card lists as an indication of social circles, partnerships I interviewed found a couple ratio of 2 straight to 1 gay. When my lover and I had just started together, I found that inviting round other couples helped us feel more like a couple and the majority of couples I knew were heterosexual. Therefore, try to make certain your outer boundary is not too strong: it is great to be able to tell sympathetic work colleagues what the two of you did over the weekend. Otherwise your life will become compartmentalized between home and work. After all, you look at photos of your heterosexual workmates' children and hear all their plans. Why shouldn't they listen to yours?

A weak boundary exists between a gay couple and the rest of gay society, but this can be a mistake. When a heterosexual couple splits up, the individuals often report that their social life falls apart. The people they knew as couples do not feel comfortable meeting up as a three. Some are worried that the 'spare' person will steal their partner and find the situation too threatening. By contrast, new gay couples find the opposite problem: some gay singles feel uncomfortable with the new partnership; they are either jealous or discover that they have different values. Gay singles are also more likely to try to seduce one partner than heterosexual singles, who normally consider the marriage vows sacred. A weak boundary may become a major problem where a previous relationship is unresolved. Steve and Andy had a weak boundary between them and Dave: he was invited to their home and they attended parties at his, which gave him the opportunity to attempt to poison their relationship. Once Steve and Andy decided they would have no further contact with him, it was not only a weight off their minds, it protected them: they had erected a strong defensive boundary. Gay society does not seem to recognize gay couples; they are often self-contained and invisible, which can lead to them having an unclear picture of themselves because they lack role models. If you are not certain how to function as a couple it is difficult to know where to set the boundaries or make them too weak, further compounding the problems.

It is not only couples who need boundaries and defences: individuals need them to preserve their own identities. Gay people often have strong personal boundaries. We define and erect these during our teenage years: parents complain about moody and withdrawn teenagers who do not communicate with them, but their teenagers are using the space to think about who they are and how they wish to live their lives. However, once they have begun to establish themselves as individuals, and therefore have set down the boundaries between themselves and the rest of the family, they will return to the family and become pleasant human beings again! Gay teenagers, though, have to build stronger and higher walls; after all, society denies their needs – and existence. Crucially, it is the growing sexual awakening of every teenager that gives them the energy and the need to break away from their family and think of finding a lover and setting up their own new family. Sometimes as emerging gay adults we have to build such high walls to protect ourselves from homophobia that it becomes difficult to climb out from behind them and be close to others. However, here comes the problem for some gay people: love requires us to think less about our own needs and become more aware of others' – letting down some of our personal defences and boundaries. In this way, we can begin to respect the needs of our new loved one as well as our own.

What is the secret of making good boundaries?

(1) *Be aware* . . . of how important they are. If you understand boundaries you are in a much better position to

implement them than the majority who haven't thought about them, but may have set them up instinctively.

(2) *Good communication and co-ordination within the partnership*. It is important that you talk to your partner and decide together where the boundaries are. For example, may your parents drop round and visit any time or should they phone first? There is a point at which being supportive and giving advice becomes meddling and interfering. It is up to the two of you to decide when this happens. Once you agree where the boundaries lie, it is easier to implement them.

(3) *Cut out the dead wood*. For many couples ex-partners are among their closest friends, but make certain that enough time has passed for the transformation from lover to friend to have taken place. It is good that gay people are forgiving: we are less likely than heterosexuals to be bogged down in old hatred. I have known cases where twenty years after a divorce a woman has left a party because her ex-husband has arrived. But if you feel that a friend or someone in your family is undermining your relationship, be prepared to expunge them from your lives. Protect yourselves!

(4) *Be flexible*. Boundaries need to change with different circumstances. For example, the sick are protected and not expected to make unnecessary decisions: a strong boundary is placed around them, so that they can concentrate their energy on getting well. In the same way there will be times when you need to pull up the drawbridge if your relationship is under stress; you need to relax the boundaries when family or close friends desperately require your help.

A gay couple should aim to find a balance where their boundaries are permeable enough to allow support in from

139

their community, but strong enough to protect them when needed.

STAGE 3 OF A GAY RELATIONSHIP
Self-affirming

I have called this stage 'Self-affirming' because it is now that the couple's individual needs reappear. The last two stages have placed the relationship centre stage: the two men have let down their personal barriers so that they could fuse and create their partnership. Where Nesting is about both of you going to the DIY store to pick up tools, in Self-affirming you realize that it does not take two of you to choose a hammer – and, anyway, one of you hates DIY stores. Until now the couple have stressed their similarities, either stopping hobbies they enjoyed individually or one partner joining in an activity more to be with his partner than because he found it fun. Now the gay couple have enough mutual confidence to explore their own pastimes: one might take up football again and the other join a gym.

Self-affirming is about allowing yourself to be an individual within the relationship and affirming that your own personal needs are important. The boundary walls that the couple placed round their partnership are lowered and the bricks used to mark out that the couple are two separate people. Before, there was one entity: the relationship. Now, there are three: each man *and* the relationship. Many heterosexual couples find this difficult to achieve. In counselling, I hear women particularly say, 'I want to do something for me', or 'I want to know who I am.' Self-affirming is re-establishing your identity. Wanting time apart and space of your own is no longer seen as a threat to the relationship. My partner often jokes about buying chewing-gum and liquorice because he knows these are the only two sweets I hate and this allows him to 'have something for myself'.

Some people complete this phase without thinking about it. Others find it disappointing that they cannot do everything together and be everything to each other. It is a vital stage, though, if the relationship is not to stagnate and if the couple are to sort out their differences. Self-affirming arrives around year four or five into the relationship. If you misinterpret your partner's and your own changing feelings as something sinister rather than a natural phenomenon, it can feel threatening. However, if you rise to the challenge you can begin to take risks, with the relationship, your partner and yourself. A couple might do this by changing from monogamy to allowing outside sexual partners. They will also risk bringing up other serious issues, like money or feelings about an ex-lover. They will risk admitting their own faults – 'I'm not that good with money, you take over the finances.' Before the self-affirming stage we tell our partners about their good qualities; now we can criticize and complain, too. We can even show emotions of which we might be ashamed, like anger. Sean and Michael can let their feelings fly because they have enough confidence in their relationship to know that it will not make the other pack his bags.

The most important lesson to be learnt at this stage is how to deal with *conflict*. It is so vital that if the couple fail to develop this skill they will inevitably separate. It can be a difficult lesson for gay men because our biggest conflict is over our sexuality. The typical coping strategy is avoidance – we say nothing and pass for straight. However, avoidance is not the answer to dealing with conflict inside a relationship. In the blending stage disagreements are too threatening and we swallow our individual tastes or feelings to restore

141

harmony. We use our different views about the house and household tasks in the nesting stage to rehearse differences which emerge in the self-affirming stage. By allowing ourselves to be different from our lover we know what we personally need and want out of life. It is only when both partners are clear about their own agendas that they can begin to find a working agreement on all the larger and more personal issues. The relationship is secure enough – and recognized by both partners as such – to cope with conflict.

Traditions are beginning to be established at this stage. The couple devise ways of celebrating Christmas or each other's birthday. Steve and Andy annually transform their home into a Christmas grotto with two Christmas trees, hundreds of lights, a three-foot moving musical Santa, a model village covered in snow, and every inch of the living room is covered with decorations from all over the world. Each year they invite all the neighbours in to admire their handiwork. Traditions announce the existence of a shared history and show that you expect to share a future. Customs like reading the papers in bed together on Sunday morning becoming increasingly important – especially if the couple are no longer monogamous. If in the past they used sexual exclusivity as a sign of commitment, the shared customs and traditions become the outward demonstration of their bond.

Other people increasingly become important to them (hence the need for good boundaries so that the relationship is not undermined). Friends, work colleagues and the local community begin to accept the two men as a couple. The partners themselves admit that they do not like all of their lover's friends and allow each other to socialize alone. We no longer fear that if our partner goes off to follow a hobby with a new friend that he is looking for a new relationship – it really is a round of golf he wants! Self-affirming can also be the time when we link up with our families again.

Although they might already know about our sexuality, parents often choose to ignore the news. They will also ignore their son's new relationship and conveniently forget to invite his lover to the next family gathering. It is now that we begin to demand to be treated as a couple by our families too.

7

FAMILIES, IN-LAWS AND OTHER STRANGE CREATURES

A gay man has first to come out as an individual before he can find a partner. Together they have to come out as a couple and it is a struggle to gain their families' full acceptance of the relationship. This is one of the major differences between heterosexual and gay couples. Parents will quiz their straight son about the women in his life, but even if they know their son is gay they would usually prefer not to know who he is sleeping with. It takes much longer for the gay couple to be viewed as such, and they need plenty of confidence both in themselves and in their relationship to campaign for the proper status. Yet it is important to win these battles: in the long term, families can provide affirmation for the couple as well as financial and emotional support.

Martin and Roy have been together for seven years and have been through their version of a 'wedding'. They felt it was important to make a public statement about how they feel about each other and to help explain to their parents, brothers and sisters just how important the relationship is to them. Martin is thirty-three and an HIV health co-ordinator; Roy is thirty-two, a business analyst. Although he is from Scotland he has spent a lot of time in America and his accent is an engaging mix of the two countries. They have bought a flat together in London.

How long had you been going out before you told your families about the relationship?

ROY I don't honestly remember saying anything.

MARTIN I don't have that kind of relationship with my family. I don't think they ever asked. My mother lives in Guildford and I don't speak to her very often and my father died when I was fourteen.

ROY His mother's a nice lass. I get on very well with her, but from the start she didn't like me. She's a gutsy lady, and I grew up in an orthodox Jewish household where the women were treated with the greatest respect. The combination of being terribly respectful to my 'mother-in-law' and she wanting somebody she could fight with wasn't a good combination. Once after she left I started a string of descriptions with 'that poisonous bitch' and didn't repeat myself once in four minutes. About a year ago I decided screw this and I don't take prisoners any more. She has to get used to the fact that I fight back.

MARTIN That's linked in with lots of things to do with you and your past rather than her.

ROY Women in my family are powerful but in a retiring way. In Jewish family life, you do not argue with women inside the household and they do not argue with you outside the household. It is a terribly stratified and restrictive society. It was very strange for a woman to take me on. I kept taking over all the cultural references which I was brought up with to somebody who they did not fit. I kept on making assumptions about her outlook which were totally inappropriate.

What would you fight about?

MARTIN They won't fight.

ROY We would have wonderful non-fights.

MARTIN He wouldn't say much to her at all, which she took to mean either that he's weak or that he doesn't like me or both. Probably both.

ROY As far as his mother was concerned, one of us had to be the woman and it couldn't possibly be Martin.

MARTIN That's part of it. My sister asked us who plays the wife! My mother knows intellectually we're together, but emotionally it's confusing. She tries to understand but she's got no references and no models to work with.

ROY To be fair to her, she does a hell of a lot better than your elder sister. She breezes through life trying to convince everyone through gritted teeth that everything is just fine. Claire, his younger sister, is wonderful.

What's your family like, Roy?

ROY My mother, being a standard Jewish mother, is on the phone about once a week so I discuss most things with her.

MARTIN They saw me on TV first. I was doing an interview for the Terrence Higgins Trust – I was press officer at the time. I was stretching a condom and saying, 'Use these things.' Apparently his mother's comment was, 'He's different.'

ROY My mother is a master of diplomacy when she wants to be and her only comment was 'He's not like your other boyfriends, is he?'

MARTIN   I went up three months later to be introduced to the family. It was New Year, and I was introduced as er . . . 'This is Roy's friend.' You weren't in the room.

ROY   If I had been, I would have cheerfully throttled her. The real problem is that there has never been anybody else in my family who is openly gay. That's not to say that there was nobody else in the family! My mother was one of seven and my father was one of eight. One of my uncles suddenly decided that his future lay in running a tea plantation in India – any idiot with eyes in their head could tell you he was about as straight as I am, but that wasn't discussed in the thirties or forties.

MARTIN   Then we bounce in and say here we are, deal with it or not. We weren't aggressive, I don't go out to say we're gay and you're going to have to deal with it. I just say this is who we are, we'll help you as much as you want. However, I am a human being with the same rights as any other and when you step on them, that's when I say, 'Stop.'

So how did you feel meeting all these close-knit Scottish-Jewish people?

MARTIN   Incredibly nervous. I thought, I'm not part of their system. We've been up quite a few times and every time, except the last, Roy reverted to being about fifteen. His father treated him that way – and in fact treated the rest of the family that way too. I wasn't having it and I told him on one or two occasions. He accepted it because there wasn't anything he could do.

What prompted this?

MARTIN   It was New Year's dinner. There was Roy and his two brothers and their wives, his mother and a couple of other family members. Just as we went into dinner, Adam, his father, told me that I would be the barman and he expected me to keep everybody's drinks filled up. I thought, OK, that's the boundary, I'll accept that for now. I didn't like the way I was told rather than asked, but it was nothing to get big about. Dinner went quite well, it was fun, relaxed, but at some point just after the main course he made a comment about what a bad job I was doing, how everybody's glasses were empty and how I should be filling them up.

ROY   It was made out to be a joke but really it was serious. That's how things are done.

MARTIN   I said, 'Excuse me, you may treat everybody else round here like they are your servants but you don't treat me that way.' Dead silence. 'Now, would anyone like another drink?' He was just confirming his position as head of the family – I give the orders, you jump. They were all very uncomfortable but I thought, Sod it!

Roy, why did you laugh hysterically just now?

ROY   There are 140 people who are still alive in what I describe as the family, in nine countries, speaking three different languages, and we find it most comfortable when we can keep at least one time zone between each other. It is a family in which nothing is said. I am the ogre of the family because I say nasty uncomfortable things. I am gay and I'm married. I just happen to be married to a bloke. I bounce through the family like a hot knife through butter. I'm the uncomfortable one to have around which is why I say he doesn't fit in with the family. Certainly he doesn't – thank God!

In what way is Martin different from your previous boyfriends?

ROY   The names have been changed to protect the guilty! When I lived in the States, I had this boyfriend Mike. My parents would never have been able to deal with him. Mike was a district attorney and six foot four and a half, 225 pounds and he took shit from nobody. The only boyfriend of mine my mother met was called Vince. How do you describe him?

MARTIN He should have been born in the fifties. My impression is that he doesn't like himself.

You were the first boyfriend to stand up to Roy's mother?

MARTIN I get on great with Roy's mother, we talk about lots of things – about Adam, about Roy, general difficulties. The thing that stands these two apart, Roy and his mother, is the skin problem, psoriasis. It has had a hell of an effect on both their personalities. I understand because I've always been tall and picked on; for protection you go on to the offensive.

ROY My mother had to learn to stand up for herself and not upset the family too much. Without the family background you don't exist in Jewish society. If you're ostracized from the family you might as well be dead.

You're in the same position, aren't you?

ROY No. I gave up bothering a long time ago. I have two brothers – my eldest and I are like a couple of five-year-olds together. We get on wonderfully. My middle brother, I saw him about a week ago. He said about five words the entire time and I found myself wondering why he even came to see me. My father had invited him along . . .

MARTIN To support him.

ROY Largely.

How did having psoriasis as a kid affect you?

ROY Up until about six years ago I had about 85 per cent coverage. It's not a pretty disease. It made me defensive, insular . . .

MARTIN   It didn't turn me off.

ROY   But that is not the point. You expect to be rejected.

MARTIN   That's what confused you about me.

ROY   It affected my self-esteem in lots of ways. Children can be vicious about anything that sets a child apart, and they were.

MARTIN   At school there was a kid who had what I now recognize as psoriasis or something similar and all my friends called him Cornflake because of the skin scales. Do you remember a time when you didn't have psoriasis?

ROY   [*sadly*] No.

That must have made it difficult for you to form a sexual relationship with somebody.

ROY   Oh, yes. It didn't stop me trying, though [*laughing*].

MARTIN   It hasn't affected us – it's everybody else's reaction. He picked me up at a training day I was running for the Terrence Higgins Trust and we went to bed the following week. I can't remember when I noticed it. I just thought, So what?

ROY   The worst thing about psoriasis is that anybody with it is more aware of it than anybody else is.

You were afraid that Martin would reject you.

Silence.

Why was that?

ROY   I think part of it has to be my mother's reaction to it. She had such negative views – like cover yourself up. She would assure you that it's nothing to be ashamed of but was proud that two of her brothers didn't know she had it until she was twelve. I rebelled against that because I'd rather be disliked for something I am than liked for something I'm not. I inherited my mother's independence. I'm also deaf and neither that nor psoriasis are first starters in the recommendation league. However, I just decided if you don't like it say so now and let's forget it rather than wasting our time, shall we? Now I have only 2 per cent coverage but I'm still very much of the opinion if you don't like it that ain't my problem. With my mother it was always verging on something to be ashamed of – and that, with me, is right up there with being ashamed of being gay. I've decided that my opinion of me is much more important than anybody else's.

You seem to have come a long way. Has Martin helped you with your relationships with your parents?

ROY No. What helped me was six years with a good psychotherapist. Martin and I decided after about a year together that I needed to sort my head out because I was fucked up. Anybody who grows up deaf, gay and Jewish doesn't have a great deal going for him in the confidence stakes! Martin gave me the financial support to do it, because we split the bills for the first year or so, and he gave me the background of security, emotional support, reminding me that I was doing the right thing for myself. Just somebody being there, someone that I could talk to.

Your relationship has been part of the process of readdressing all these issues from the past – which obviously includes family issues.

ROY Martin provided the support for me to be able to do it, rather than becoming involved in the process itself. One of the things that used to piss me off about my mother was that she would thank Martin for all the help he's been. I just found myself thinking, Gee, thanks, let's ignore the six years

151

I've worked my duff off in therapy to achieve some of the changes – which isn't to denigrate Martin's support.

Do you think it was more difficult for each of you to introduce your new partner into your families than it would have been for your heterosexual brothers and sisters?

MARTIN Infinitely. I had an easier time than Roy did because there are fewer in my family. I had been out – and out publicly. What I was saying was 'This is who I am and this is the work I do. If you don't like it then we'll talk about it, and if you still don't like it – goodbye.' We are only related by genes. Roy coming along was just another part of that. If I had stretched them by coming out, this was just another bit of it. It was following the pattern.

It was still more difficult.

MARTIN Because it's not expected, there are no formulas, no patterns, no structures. There are when somebody dies or gets married.

ROY It requires people to think and they don't like having to think.

MARTIN They like to be told what to do.

ROY Most have an expectation about what will happen: number three son will grow up, get married, settle down and have 2.6 children, 1.9 family cars and a sensible job until sixty-five when he will retire and start an allotment. That's nice and predictable and safe. It's also supported. You go into a shop and there's all these cards for birthdays, engagements, weddings and even divorce now. There's a structure and you're supported by it. When you bring home your boyfriend they can't go to a shop and find a card that says 'Congratulations, Son, on Your Boyfriend'.

Do you think that you have to come out as a gay individual and then come out all over again as a gay couple?

MARTIN   Yes and no. It's a stage further on. There's the difficulty that anybody has about bringing somebody home – gays have that extra difficulty because there's no structure. We joked about going home to see the in-laws to ease the tension. I was not sure what ground I was walking on. Would we be sleeping together or not? How would they react? 'Oh, you're the person, fine', the words being fine but the tone dismissive. As it turned out, this wasn't the case.

Does your family's involvement in your life add anything to your relationship?

MARTIN   If they weren't there would always be a gap, because I'd like them to be involved. I have a brother who Roy's never met. We've sent messages and talked about each other through other family members. He'll contact me when he wants to.

ROY   The Red Cross pass messages between them since they broke off diplomatic relations.

He doesn't approve?

MARTIN   He's inflexible. The first anybody knew about him getting married was when the wedding cake came through the post to everybody except me. He's made his own decision – I don't waste time or worry about it. I think as time goes on it's becoming less important.

Does interacting with your parents reaffirm that you're a couple?

MARTIN   For me, it reaffirms that we're real people.

ROY   The same for me. I was going to say it reaffirms, but no, it just makes it easier. As far as I'm concerned we'd still be a couple even if we never talked to them again.

What made you decide to have your partnership ceremony?

MARTIN We did it three years ago. I'll show you the photograph album. What we came up with I wouldn't call a wedding but when you see these photographs it's a wedding. We sent a letter out with an invitation explaining a little about what it was. We used the word 'partnership' rather than 'friendship' because that's a word we hate.

ROY I have several friends, I have dozens of acquaintances, I have one partner. I can't stand the word 'friend' to describe him. A euphemism straight out of the sixties that makes my flesh crawl visibly.

MARTIN 'Benjamin Britten and his friend of thirty years, Peter Pears', excuse me!

Partner can mean business partner?

ROY Believe me, I make it clear exactly what sort of partner I mean.

MARTIN That's why I tend to use the word husband. This again is the problem with taking people home. What are the structures in which you can get 80 per cent of what you mean across to somebody in one word? They don't exist – that is what the difficulty is. The British are so much into having structures.

ROY John Cleese in *A Fish Called Wanda* says, 'Being British is being permanently embarrassed.' It's true!

MARTIN This is embarrassment piled upon embarrassment. Even more so because we're breaking out of the mould of the expectations of what should happen. Partnership was the least problematic. There's lots of baggage that comes with 'wedding', but as soon as we sent the letter out the whole thing had a momentum of its own.

ROY I had one stipulation, I was not going to stand there with four unterfuhrers and a glass under my heel for anybody! Unterfuhrers are literally 'other fathers' in Yiddish. The people who make certain that the groom turns up at the wedding. A Jewish wedding finishes up with smashing a glass under your heel to prove that worldly goods are worth nothing.

Roy, you wanted to make certain that it wasn't like a Jewish wedding. What didn't you want, Martin?

MARTIN Neither of us wanted the old queens in kaftans through Golden Gate Park either! We didn't want some kind of camp crap.

ROY You didn't! I wanted to hold out for the leather wedding dress and the wilting daffs. [*He leans away to avoid being hit by Martin.*] Sorry, that's our little secret, isn't it!

MARTIN We wanted something public to say our relationship is important and we wanted our friends and family to be involved in it. We're not ashamed of ourselves and we're not going to hide away. This was a chance for them to come along and show us support. There were heterosexuals there as well as homosexuals.

ROY We had to allow some heterosexuals along, we felt we should. We decided to be liberal. I know they're benighted, poor, damned creatures – we have to be nice to them. They can't possibly be happy that way! [*Laughter*]

MARTIN The interesting thing is that Roy's middle brother drove the family down from Glasgow to the Forest of Dean where we had it. We thought something would happen so they wouldn't get there on time. My mother told me that she said to Roy's brother, 'Your trouble is that you want everything to be black and white, and nice and easy. Life isn't like that.' She told me that he just turned away at that

155

point. He can't cope because he has no tools. The thing in his favour is that we actually talk, my brother doesn't. If you took away my two sisters our families are very similar. My eldest brother and I chat and get on well, but my middle brother – Roy's never met or seen him.

What were people's reactions when the invitations dropped on their doormats?

MARTIN I heard through the rest of the family that my brother who we don't meet thought we had got in with the Moonies and that we had been brainwashed. They said to him, 'What? Grow up! Get a life!' Most people who came along loved the idea.

ROY Mild confusion. Once we had talked about what we wanted to do they were quite happy about it.

MARTIN They got a letter from Linda, a friend of ours, who organized it.

ROY It made a big difference, particularly to my father because he suddenly found that most of my friends were at least within spitting distance of normal. Although I wouldn't curse them by referring to them as normal, most of them are fairly presentable in polite company – which came as a shock.

MARTIN They expected to see lots of men in dresses, being terribly camp and lisping.

What actually happened?

MARTIN Everybody arrived and got mildly drunk. Then we went into King John's bedroom, where we had the formal thing. A friend read a piece of poetry.

ROY I'm an orthodox spiritualist. So for the most part it was an orthodox spiritualist ceremony, which is mostly about making an affirmation of responsibility for and to each other.

How did you pledge yourselves to each other?

MARTIN Mine was . . . 'I promise to love and comfort you, to listen and hear you, and to hold you and care for you. I ask you to accept my commitment to you and be with me now and always. As a token of this bond I give you this ring, for as a ring has no end so my love for you has no end.'

ROY I took out the bit about financial responsibility, [*laughter*] if you're in debt you're on your own! My vow was . . . 'I promise you my love and commitment, an ear for your joys, a shoulder for your tears and my arms for you always in all things. I ask you to stand by my side, my partner and lover always. As a token of this bond I give you this ring, for as a ring has no end so my love for you has no end.'

That's beautiful. Then you exchanged rings?

ROY Yes. Except I put the ring on the wrong finger.

MARTIN He was more hyper than I was.

ROY Unfortunately I put it on the third of the right hand by accident.

MARTIN I was almost in tears at this point. It was that emotional. We then turned round to all these friends and told them it was time for them to say whatever they wanted to say, which for a group of largely English people is difficult with people they don't necessarily know. They weren't silent – a few people said they didn't know quite what to make of the whole thing.

Did any of your family say anything?

ROY No.

MARTIN One of our friends said that she wanted to hand her heart out, to be included.

Did you get presents?

MARTIN The present was the wedding.

ROY What we recognized was that both of us had been living on our own for so long that there were few things that we needed so we said to people that if they felt a need to give, they should hire something for us like the plates or the cutlery or pay half the vegetable bill. Which is what people did.

MARTIN A friend who was in PR did all the photographs.

ROY My parents hired the crockery, your mother bought the champagne and paid for the cutlery. An old friend of mine made rolls, which isn't very exciting until you realize it was for 120 people. She arrived with a crate full of the damn things.

MARTIN One of the things I found difficult, if difficult is the right word, is that we walked into the kitchen during the afternoon. There were eight or nine people busily preparing food, four or five of whom we didn't even know! They had been drafted in by friends.

How did you feel about the ceremony?

MARTIN If you look at the photos taken afterwards you can see the release of tension. That's relief on both our faces. It was everything that I wanted. I can remember being in the room and everybody else being around us but I remember more the whole thing together. There wasn't pressure but there was emotion.

ROY   The biggest thing from my point of view was remembering that we had to feed 120 people in about half an hour. Praying like hell that nothing had burned.

MARTIN   This is called denial.

ROY   No, it's not.

MARTIN   It meant more to me.

ROY   As far as I was concerned I was heavily married anyway. It didn't make me feel any more or less married than I had previously.

MARTIN   It did for me a lot.

ROY   For me it felt a bit like I'm doing this because if I don't my family won't entirely understand. Up to that point it was a question of us living together – as far as they were concerned. They would have loved for me to walk down the aisle with a woman. No matter how different from a standard Jewish ceremony this was about the nearest they were going to get, so fair enough, they'll live with it.

MARTIN   One of the things that worried Roy was that it took me either a year to fall in love with him or to recognize that I had done. Whereas he fell much quicker. That's why the wedding was very important. That was the display and the seal, not for anybody else or for any legal reasons but for us, for me.

ROY   So I was on a dodgy number for the first three years. Fine! Great!

MARTIN   For the first six months. Yeah, you were. We had long talks about whether I saw Roy as a project. Here's somebody who needs help and [*intense voice*] I can do something for this person. [*Normal voice*] I had to think, Am I doing this because this man has psoriasis and he's hurting and I can take some of the pain away? [*Intense voice*] Am I doing good?

ROY [*Uncontrollable laughter*]

How come you find that so funny, Roy?

ROY [*More uncontrollable laughter*]

MARTIN We were both working at the Terrence Higgins Trust and he was asking about and got all these Martin Weaver stories.

ROY I'd met him at the training day and you know the saying don't sell yourself up the river without a paddle. I decided to do a little research and I got all these Martin Weaver stories. You could tell to the moment when people had tumbled why I was interested because suddenly they would dry up. Two days later I walked into the office and the manager commented, 'It's Mrs Martin Weaver.' I thought, You're dead! Next time I make coffee – two of arsenic and one of rat poison in it, sweetheart.

MARTIN You also told me that somebody said beware because I was a 'professional carer'. That was one of the things I had to think about in the first year. Was this an actively caring relationship rather than an emotional human commitment? Professional carer to me was an insult. I don't know what they meant.

For me, when somebody is a professional carer in a relationship it doesn't mean that the person is not genuine, but sometimes if you're always the one who's looking after somebody, you're the one who has the power and is in control all the time. Professional carers cannot let themselves go and be vulnerable. It's very different from a full relationship.

MARTIN I think all those bits were jumbled in there, and I thought, Do they have a point? When we were parted, and I wanted you to be around, that's when I realized that it never was a project. What I had stumbled across was something very special.

What advice would you give to somebody who was thinking that they, too, would like to get married or have a partnership ceremony?

ROY Don't do it. [*Laughter*] Hire caterers.

MARTIN They have to be clear about what they want and what they want to come from it. It develops a momentum all of its own. You need support from other people. Linda who was organizing said, 'Just turn up on the day — leave everything else to us.' It was an immense amount of trust that we gave to people. I kept saying, 'It has to be right. We cannot rerun it the following week.'

You say you have to be very clear about what you want, and why you're doing it. Why?

MARTIN It could turn into a disastrous attempt to model and copy a heterosexual marriage. If you don't know why you're doing it and exactly what you want, then you'll find yourself bending and twisting to other people's needs and you'll end up with an event that won't fulfil you . . .

ROY And will say more of what other people want for you than what you want for yourself. Other people have their expectations about what two gay men getting married will be like. That isn't necessarily what *you* want, or feel reflects you. So keep strongly in mind what *you* want out of the event.

Has this wedding changed your relationship in any way?

MARTIN Yes, oh, yes. It's made me much more secure. I

don't worry that if we have arguments he's going to walk out the door and the whole thing fall apart.

ROY   I would love to believe that it didn't change a damn thing but it has made me more comfortable. More settled without becoming complacent, because I think the one thing that I have learned is, for Christ's sake, to talk. In any relationship you're under pressure, I'm not the easiest person to live with and I don't find it easy to live with someone else. With a gay relationship you face pressure from the outside as well as the inside. You face, as we have, bottles thrown at you in the street. You name it, it happens. If you're gay you come in for some shit.

MARTIN   Especially as there's no cultural structure for it to fit in. In fact, the cultural structure is one for it to be taken apart, which comes even from within the gay world not just from straights.

ROY   I could deck some people who say, 'Oh, you're still together?' They seem amazed. They would never dream of saying that to a straight couple. When I talk about going back to the States to work, 'Oh, would Martin go with you?' No, we were thinking of getting divorced so I could find a new job. What the fuck do you think?

MARTIN   We were in a bar last night and Roy was hugging a friend of his and this guy turned to me and said, 'Doesn't that bother you?' People often say this when either one of us is off having sex with somebody else or just being intimate with somebody else. I feel, whether they mean it or not, that there is pressure for us to be clinging together all the time. Nobody else should come between us. A long time ago we decided we couldn't be everything to each other all the time.

ROY   There are friends of mine that drive Martin up the wall, and there are friends of his to whom I can be polite if I work at it. We didn't suddenly stop having a life apart from each other when we got married. There is this bizarre assumption that you must like all of your partner's friends. It's OK to have friends that are exclusively yours rather than yours in the plural.

What you've been doing is creating your own cultural structures.

ROY We have to because there are no cultural structures. No, that isn't true. Unfortunately there is a cultural structure: you get together, you fuck like rabbits for three months and then you never talk to each other again.

MARTIN Or you don't talk to anybody else again.

ROY You're never seen again, you drop all your friends that you ever knew when you were single. You have to build your own social structure because the ones that are there are either so negative or don't apply. In some ways it is an advantage that there aren't any social mores involved in a gay relationship because, quite frankly, you can suit yourself and people don't get too upset because you haven't done the right thing, because there is no right thing. The other side of that is that it leads to an immense amount of hard work. You have to make decisions about everything.

Martin, what have you learnt from Roy?

MARTIN I suppose it's as much about learning to love myself as love anybody else – to have a right to existence. To love somebody and know that it can work, and it does work. I don't know how to answer the question because I'm not the person I was when we first met but I'm much more secure and confident and understand more of what makes me tick and him tick and us tick. I've had five people come up to me in the last month and say, 'You're so lucky.' They don't see the work that goes on.

163

ROY My childhood was emotionally violent, to put it mildly. What I got out of this relationship was the security to do the work that needed to put my head back between my shoulders. What I get out of it now – somewhere between a lover, best friend, straight man to my comedy act, playmate, two ulcers and high blood pressure!

MARTIN We haven't mentioned the intimacy and the vulnerability. Outside in the big bad world, rightly or wrongly, we don't believe we can get that.

ROY Knowing that you're safe with one person at least.

MARTIN A lot of people out there are very frightened – frightened of themselves and everybody else. You can suck dick till the cows come home. That's quite fun, I enjoy it, I never denigrate it, but most people are scared of intimacy, of exposing their vulnerability, and I think that's the ultimate thing that we have from our relationship.

Following on from the last chapter and the importance of dealing with conflict, some counsellors feel that gay couples sometimes over-communicate the stressful and difficult areas of their relationship to one another. I have found no evidence to support this. There is a fine balance between ignoring problems – in which case they may grow and threaten the relationship – and being so aware of the issues that you blow up the problems out of all proportion. Martin and Roy have achieved an excellent balance: Roy uses humour appropriately; he makes his point but the seriousness is lightened by the joke. He still gets angry, but Martin has learnt to deal with it. In the past he tried to soothe Roy, which was like throwing petrol on a fire. Recently he has learnt to acknowledge Roy's anger – just to let him be angry and allow the anger to take its natural course. When they have both calmed down, they talk over the problem.

The difference between the self-esteem of Martin and Roy and that of Andy and Ian in Chapter Three is extraordinary. It has been hard-won, and Roy, in particular, has achieved a lot. The old cliché is, if you cannot love yourself it is difficult to love anybody else. It was only when Roy overcame the self-hatred caused by his psoriasis, his deafness and being gay that he was able to commit himself. Although most gays do not have as difficult obstacles to overcome, we can all learn from his perseverance and determination to fight for what he needed – respect and love.

Martin and Roy decided to have their partnership ceremony when they had been together for four years: the beginning of 'Self-affirming'. It is at this stage that their families began properly to recognize them as an item. Although it has not been easy for the families, it shows what can be achieved over time. The parents' problems are not because they do not care about their sons and love them, but more because they do not fully understand. We often imagine that our parents have no experience of gay people: as Roy's family shows, with the uncle who obligingly disappeared overseas, there is often one member whose lifestyle is 'deeply suspicious'. The problem is not so much ignorance but more a conspiracy of silence with everybody deliberately shutting their eyes. Parents often have only negative experiences to draw on. When I came out to mine, I discovered that one of their oldest friends was gay but had made his and his wife's lives miserable by repeatedly running off with different men but always returning home. No wonder they expect my relationships to be a 'vale of tears'. However, families are important and human beings have a deep-seated need to belong, which is why we feel the need to persevere rather than cut them off. And although Martin does not seem unduly worried about his middle brother's antipathy, there is still a photograph of him and his son on Martin and Roy's kitchen noticeboard!

Coming out as a couple

It was only when I came out as one half of a couple that I experienced real discrimination. My gayness had been something to which my parents could shut their eyes. The day after I came out I asked my mother what my father had felt; he had been quiet and had given few clues. She replied that it was something they would need to talk over together, but about a month later when I asked what had transpired I was told that they had been too busy to find time to talk to each other. In contrast, my gay partnership is a problem for them that could not be ignored.

When we introduce a new partner to our parents we want them to feel the same excitement as we do: we want to share the elation. My mother's comment to my sister after first meeting my partner spoke volumes: 'I could find nothing wrong with him!' Roy's mother's reaction to Martin was similar. Even if a mother loathed a future daughter-in-law she would manage to find an adjective like 'nice'. I didn't speak to my sister for six months after an invitation to her son's birthday celebrations was withdrawn when I had expected the invitation to include my partner. She felt that she wanted to meet him first on neutral ground. What is even more strange is that she was surprised that I was upset and angry with her. She could close her eyes to one queer but not two. By having a partner I am also obviously having sex. I am no longer safe and neutered. At the time I worked for a radio station, which was planning to broadcast a week's programmes from Florida. Everything was paid for by the tourist board and I was responsible backstage for producing the shows. At other participating radio stations the senior staff were allowed to take their wives or husbands to America for a holiday. When I asked to take my partner, it presented a huge problem: the station was also giving away tickets in a listener competition and the head of marketing was worried about the station's image. I had been openly gay at that company for over five years and there had been no problems – but suddenly, as half of a couple, I became a liability.

Coming out as a couple is part of the same process you went through when you came out as a gay man: you face the same ignorance and the same prejudices. This time, at least, you have the support of each other. However, when you feel angry it is important to direct it at the right people – the boss, the father or brother-in-law – rather than let it turn in on the relationship and blame your partner.

Having a good relationship is the ultimate revenge: it challenges society's preconceptions that we end up miserable and alone. It is also a radical statement. However open we are about our sexuality, our families or employers can choose to pass us off as straight (particularly if we are not camp). When we become one half of a gay couple they have to face reality and deal with their real feelings.

Do we need to go through partnership ceremonies?

Despite the high divorce rate, marriage is still popular. The reasons why couples marry fall into three areas: personal, social and legal. Gays cannot profit from the legal benefits of marriage: we still need to fight for the government to recognize our relationships and offer us the property, taxation and financial security that is the right of married heterosexuals.

On a personal level, marriage is about commitment – swearing before witnesses to love, support and build a life together. I counsel a lot of heterosexual couples who are living together, and the reason why they have yet to marry is always because they are not ready to make a commitment to each other. It can be caused by previous painful experiences, problems in the relationship or because, deep down, one or both feel that the person they are living with is OK for now but they are not sure about for ever. When gay couples are ready to make a commitment to each other, it is important to mark the event with a ceremony. Mankind needs rituals, which is why every civilization has found ways of celebrating birth, a couple's union, and death. Martin and Roy found their ceremony helped them feel more committed and secure, which are qualities all relationships need.

Living together is a personal arrangement, while marriage is a public, social institution. People might claim, 'I'm marrying you, not your family' but however much they might like to pretend otherwise, they are allying themselves with their spouse's relations. Families can provide financial support, and emotional solidity: it is one thing to fall out with a boyfriend your parents have never met, but quite another to break up a partnership with someone they know and like. Our relationships are sometimes viewed as less 'serious' and 'grown-up' as they do not normally involve child-rearing. A partnership ceremony helps us explain our relationship. It also makes society take us more seriously, reinforcing rather than undermining the gay couple.

Coping with the in-laws

It is vital that you sort out your feelings about your in-laws or you are likely to fall into the worst kinds of arguments – those that are not about yourselves but about other people – and therefore out of your control and far more difficult to solve. A major problem encountered by newly married heterosexuals is interference from in-laws: it is one of the top five issues that they bring to Relate. (The others are money, sex, children and sharing household tasks.) I counselled one couple whose in-laws came on the honeymoon! By contrast, gay couples' in-law problems are more often about neglect than interference.

(1) *Don't Assume.* When we come into contact with our partner's parents, brothers and sisters we automatically draw on the experiences of our own family. Martin and Roy expected there to be cultural differences: one was from a Christian, southern-English family, the other from a Scottish-Jewish background. Even being aware of these differences, Roy still used his own cultural references to deal with his mother-in-law. However, for most gays meeting their in-laws, the variations are not so explicit. Each family has rules, often unacknowledged: in Roy's, nothing important is said. If you find that you cannot communicate properly with your new mother- or father-in-law, ask yourself if you are treating them in the same way as your own parents or if you are expecting them to behave similarly. Try to think what the unwritten rules of the family are, and discuss your thoughts with your partner. It will not only help you understand your in-laws better, but will help your partner understand his parents, too.

It is interesting that there are as many similarities as differences between Martin's and Roy's families: both have strong mothers and problems with their middle brothers, which illustrates how we need some similarities so that the new families we are joining are not completely alien.

(2) *Try to see things from their viewpoint.* To deal effectively with your in-laws you have to try to understand how they will feel about you. Your parents will always cherish the hope that the last twenty years have just been a phase and one day you will surprise them and meet the right girl. Any girl – an overweight call-girl wearing a tight leopardskin mini-skirt and whose dyed blonde roots need touching up – is preferable to even the most charming gay lawyer or doctor. On top of this, there is the natural parental jealousy that they are no longer the most important person in your life. Your finding a partner reminds them that you have indeed grown up and are no longer a child. It makes them aware that they are getting older and, for parents of heterosexual children, they become acutely aware that they will become grandparents. They are moving up the mortality ladder and are next in line to be pushed off the top. Even if you had come home with the wife they always dreamed of, there would still have been resentment and, even, depression. It is not an attractive or comfortable sensation to be jealous of your children; which is why parents often take out their bad feelings on the new daughter- or son-in-law, branding them unsuitable, rather than dealing with their real feelings.

(3) *Acknowledge what is going on.* Although it might not change a situation, talking about what is happening between you can change the way you feel about it. In Chapter Three Andy discovered this – he felt that he was not spending enough time alone with Ian. Talking to a friend has not changed the amount of time they spend together but it has made Andy feel better. When you discuss what is happening between you and your in-laws some painful emotions will be expressed, and it is easy to become defensive, but once everything is out in the open, you can begin

to change what is changeable, and everybody will have got their feelings off their chest.

(4) *Set appropriate boundaries.* Some parents will always be more supportive than others. You need to protect your relationship from pain and decide what behaviour is tolerable and what is not. For example, if they run down your partner, tell them you will not listen and put down the phone. If they expect you to come home for Christmas alone, explain it is either both or neither of you. It is important that you appear united and present yourself as a couple to them. Once parents realize there is a line they are not allowed to cross, they will learn to accept you both and to treat you as a couple. Only the most bigoted religious zealots will risk losing their son.

An adult, committed relationship is the closest thing we have to the relationship we had as babies with our mothers. Lovers often use baby talk and childish nicknames, and all the holding and touching is the nearest we can find to our mother's womb. Psychologists believe that a good parenting experience sets us up to become balanced, happy adults and that bad experiences in babyhood may set up frustrations and unhappiness that can last for ever. However, it is never too late to work through the experiences. If you felt unloved and rejected as a child yet loved and wanted by your partner, much of this hurt can be worked through.

A gay partnership can also help you to improve your relationship with your parents. Your partner is detached enough to spot the out-of-date ways you behave with them. If he points out the patterns you can choose to change them. Martin stood up to Roy's father and since then Roy has not behaved like a child when he sees his parents. Your partner can provide you with the emotional support to challenge and improve your relationship with your parents.

171

Alternative families

We also create our own version of families who are just as important as our biological ones. Roy has 'adopted' a father, who is a judge in Ohio. He feels he has much more rapport with him than he does with Adam. His adopted father tells him when he is being a fool, and Roy listens to him in a way that he never bothers to listen to anybody else. The judge has a way of validating and challenging Roy, a perfect combination for good parenting. In his normal conversation, Roy always refers to this man as his father and to his real father as Adam. Sean, in Chapter Five, has been using some of his parenting instincts on their lodger, who, in return, calls him Mother. Michael fixes the car for him and the two of them have been round hundreds of flats with him advising and helping him on the right choice. After he moved out, Sean and Michael were invited round to his new flat, and found a tablecloth, sandwiches and cakes to re-create the traditional family Sunday tea.

It is difficult to find adequate words to describe these relationships which go way beyond friendship. I have a female friend whom I ask for advice and call 'Auntie' to show that it is a special friendship. I have a gay male friend whom I have known for so long that when we first knew each other we were both officially straight! We share so much history that we jokingly refer to each other as sisters. All gay relationships have the same language problems. How do we describe our 'significant others'? *Friend* is too discreet – the only thing it shouts is closet. *Long-term companion* was the euphemism used by Americans in the obituary columns. *Boyfriend* sounds too trivial. Although I like *lover*, there is always the confusion over gender when you are talking to people who do not know you, and it suggests that the relationship is purely physical. Martin and Roy use *husband*. Although *partner* can describe a business relationship, it describes a depth which goes beyond sex and friendship. It suggests a long-term commitment.

8

CHILDREN AND GAY PARENTING

Once heterosexual couples have settled down and feel committed to each other they normally think about having children. Gay couples also look for another dimension to their relationship, and some consider adoption, fostering or even having their own children.

Although straight society sometimes portrays gays as corruptors, the reality is that a significant number of homosexual men are involved in successfully raising children. These can be their own, they can be 'step'-children, or they can be nieces and nephews who visit regularly.

Gareth and Adam look incredibly alike, although Gareth is almost ten years older. Both have the same number-two hair crop and open welcoming smiles. What makes them unusual is that Adam's two children of twelve and eleven live with them, and Gareth is advertising for a woman to have his baby. Both have northern accents, but Adam's becomes stronger the more passionately he feels about something. They live together in a northern town large enough to support a gay scene but small enough to ensure that all your neighbours know your business. Gareth and Adam's relationship is a new one and they offer a good example of a first-stage couple – limerence is at its height. I have placed them in this section of the book because the issues of child-rearing are normally faced by more established couples. They also contrast with the later-stage couples and are a reminder of how we face different problems during the different phases of our relationships.

ADAM We've only known each other around five months, and we've lived together for just two. It was a whirlwind affair.

GARETH We met in a supermarket car park, and within a week of meeting Adam, I'd told a sixteen-year affair that it had finished. We've gone through a marriage ceremony, a blessing with the vicar, and have lived together since.

So what was the attraction, because it was obviously very strong?

GARETH I don't know how can you explain that, it's something we will never know.

ADAM It was just meant to happen.

GARETH I don't even know why I was there. I was going to the local supermarket and I thought, No, for a change I'll go to this supermarket where I never normally go. I parked my car and, lo and behold, I met Adam. A week later I had parted with my affair, although we did not live together. Since then we've all become firm friends. He's been on the telephone tonight, he's accepted it. He didn't at first, he took it very, very hard, but now he's a close family friend. He comes here for his tea.

ADAM He babysits from time to time.

GARETH The kids like him because he's quite a clown.

ADAM The kids know everything we do.

GARETH   We've got no secrets.

Adam, you've been married in the past.

ADAM   Yes, I was married for ten years. I knew my sexuality years and years ago but I wanted children, that came strong in my life. I could cope, muddle through with marriage, but I wanted my own children.

How old were you when you got married?

ADAM   I was twenty-one. I knew in my heart that I was gay but I wouldn't accept it, or admit it to myself. The most important thing in my life at that time was that I wanted my own children and I wasn't prepared to let anything stand in the way. I suppose if I lived my life again, I would most probably do the same because I feel so strongly about kids.

When you were twenty-one, did all your friends want children as strongly as you, or were you unusual?

ADAM   I suppose I was, in that I was a homely person. I wasn't the type that was out every night. I lived on my own, had my own flat for about three years before I got married.

When you met your wife, what sort of thoughts were going through your head?

ADAM   She was a right bubbly character and we seemed to have a laugh, a bit of fun. One thing led to another and one of my friends told her that I had a flat, because I hadn't told her. As soon as she found out she turned up with a suitcase. She'd left home and that was it. Within five months she were pregnant, but that weren't a mistake. It was all planned. We got married but told everybody the baby was a mistake because everybody was totally against the wedding, my family more so. I don't know if my parents knew that something wasn't quite right.

What was it like becoming a father? How you expected it?

ADAM   Better. I was there for both births, I helped deliver the little lad. It were brilliant, an experience you can't explain to anybody until you're there. Thirteen years down their lives they're still with me. My life has changed but they're still there, I've still got them.

What was your relationship with your wife like?

ADAM   A lot of people described us as friends rather than lovers. We worked really well as a team but as friends. People couldn't understand why we got married because we were so opposite. We had a lot of bad times, and I went through a lot. She had a violent streak in her – you've heard of battered wives, well, I were a battered husband.

How did she get on with the children?

ADAM   She were a good mother to 'em. I always jumped in to protect them – I was the soft one in the relationship. If she said something they'd do it, no questions asked. If I say, 'Do something,' they just look other way, don't bother.

Were you ever badly hurt?

ADAM   No, but when I went to the solicitor's, for divorce and that, I had bruises where she'd hit me. But I put up with it for the kids because I didn't want to lose them. I put up with a lot, but you can only take so much. The crunch came when I caught her in bed with somebody else. It was the final straw. I threw her out that night, clothes and everything.

When in your marriage did you begin to think that you might be gay?

ADAM   I suppose I did begin to admit to myself, towards the back end. The first five years were all right. It were later that it started dwindling down. The kids were getting that bit older. They were starting to find their own feet, they don't rely on you so much and I used to start wondering, thinking, well, this ain't really what I want. So I suppose it was in my mind a lot but it didn't come to the front.

Gareth, did you find it difficult coming to terms with being gay?

GARETH   I've always had a double life. I've had heterosexual relationships throughout, apart from the last few years. I think I've admitted these last few years that I am gay, or 99.5 per cent gay. I think I've kidded myself. In the early stages, I would have a girlfriend and a boyfriend. Usually each would know the other.

Would they know about the real nature of the other relationship?

GARETH   Yes. I had a seven-year relationship with one girl and at the same time I had an affair as well. I told her early on that I was gay. She said, 'Well, I know.' I don't think she was saying that to save her face. I had quite a happy relationship with her and almost got married. I've almost got married on two or three occasions. Before I met Adam, I thought, What is missing in my life? And I thought it was kids. This is why I put an advert in the paper. I think at forty-four I'm too old, but maybe I've got another year to do it – but this was something I decided six months previous to Adam. I was doing things before I met him. I think the only way now that I want children is through a lesbian, artifically. Because that's the only way he would allow me to have it, anyway. He wouldn't allow it naturally conceived.

ADAM   *Cold silence.*

GARETH I think gay men make very good fathers – Adam is a shining example. He's a doting father, and I have another gay friend with three children. He's an excellent father, too.

What makes them good fathers?

GARETH I think they have a maternal *and* a paternal instinct.

ADAM From my children being born, I was like the mother and she was like the father, 'cos I was the one that stopped in night after night with them. She was the one that went out to the pub and enjoyed herself. She hasn't really got a maternal instinct. I've been into court four times for custody and four times I've won. First time she never even turned up. The last time she went to court over my sexuality to try and get the kids back. That was the first time I had a social worker come to see me, and the social worker said, 'Why change them after two and half years down the track? There's no harm come to them.' Suddenly because my wife knows what I am, I'm a threat. After they'd interviewed me for the courts, the social worker went on to ask me if I'd like to foster, but that's something I can't do because I couldn't give them up. I could adopt but not foster because I get too emotionally involved.

So it was only after your ex-wife knew you were gay that she wanted custody.

ADAM I didn't have any other sexual relationships except with my wife. I'd never been with nobody else until we'd got divorced and then after that I was with various people. I went into another relationship with a woman to find out what I really wanted. That relationship lasted for a year but it didn't seem right. None of my family knew I was gay, and I couldn't cope with that, because I don't like lying. In the end I disappeared for three days, I got to the point that I knew what I wanted but I couldn't accept telling everybody. I thought, I can't live with myself unless I do. In the end I came back, told everybody, and everybody's been fine – they all said, 'So what?'

How long is it since you confessed you were gay to everybody?

ADAM About a year. It's been brilliant. My parents are nearly seventy and, at their age, it's hard for them to accept it, but they don't bother.

How did you feel when, after letting you have custody, suddenly your ex-wife tried to stop you because you're gay?

ADAM I were annoyed. I thought, She doesn't want them – she's let me have them for all this time, and just 'cos of that, she doesn't think I'm fit enough or I'm going to put them in a bad environment. I think a lot of it is just ignorance, because she didn't know anything about it.

'Annoyed' is a weak word for somebody trying to take your children away!

ADAM I suppose I'm just being kind. It really upset me. I love my kids. I fought for them with all I've got. I'm not an intelligent person but I've fought with what I've got to fight with. If you want something strongly enough you've got to fight for it.

What do you think people imagine that gay fathers are doing with their children that makes them unfit?

ADAM I think my wife thought I'd put them in an environment where they'd get molested or abused or whatever.

GARETH Other heterosexual people think we wear frocks. Your mother asked you that, didn't she?

180

ADAM Yes. She says there's only one question I want to ask you. She said, 'You don't dress up in women's clothes, do you?' I told her no. She said, 'I can accept everything but I can't accept that', which were fair comment. Before I came out, I used to go to all gay pubs and get babysitters for t' kids, but when people used to ask where I lived I never told them. Nobody knew where I come from because I would never put my kids at risk. You meet somebody in a pub, and you know next to nothing about them, so you can't really tell what they're like. There was no way I would *ever* put my kids at risk.

GARETH That's why, in some way, me and Adam just gelled, because within quarter of an hour of knowing him, I knew he had children, their ages. I knew where he lived, everything. He just seemed to want to tell me everything. He'd never told anyone before.

ADAM I'd had relationships and the kids had never been in contact with them.

How did you feel when you found out that this man that you were terribly interested in came with two children as well?

GARETH It didn't influence my decision at all. I said to him, right from the word go, I accepted him as a package. I wanted Adam and if the package was three, I accepted the package. I would never ever say to him I want you and I don't want your children. I believe that if I love him, as I do love him, I'm capable of loving his children, because they're part of him. I can't say now after five and a half months that I love the children because I'd be lying, but I've grown very fond of them.

When did you tell your children that you were gay?

ADAM About seven months ago.

GARETH   We wanted them to come to the blessing, but unfortunately his ex-wife forbade it.

ADAM   They've seen photographs so they know all about it. When I told them, the youngest one, Michael, he said, 'So what?' That was it.

What did you tell them?

ADAM   It was the hardest thing I've ever had to do. I just sat down and more or less asked them if they knew what gay men meant. They said, 'Yeah, it means two men what like each other', and then I told them, 'Well, I'm in that category'. My daughter, the eldest one, Sarah, she just cried. She sat and she cried buckets. I just sat and cried with her. Then we just talked and that's when I told them about Gareth. Michael weren't too bad.

What do you think your daughter's tears were about?

ADAM   A lot of it is, she's frightened she's going to lose me – that's the top and bottom of it. When their mum went, she went the same night, clothes and everything, after I'd caught her in bed with the other man. The kids never saw that. The next morning I had to sit them down and tell that their mum had gone, that I'd told her to go, and what had happened, without going into too much detail. That was on the Friday. Friday night they slept with me – they hardly slept because they just cried. Saturday she rung 'em, so they weren't too bad and she says to 'em, 'I'll ring on Sunday at seven o'clock.' She never rung. They sat there until nine o'clock, waiting for her to ring. I've never seen two kids so upset – it was as if she ripped their hearts out. I'll never see them upset like that again. We were up all night and she was in the pub. I got in touch with her next day and she said, 'Oh, I forgot.' I said, 'You'll never do it to them again.' Since then they've clung and they won't let go.

So are they frightened that because you are gay they might lose you?

ADAM Sarah thinks I'm going to turn my back on them, and I've got to try and reassure her. I suppose her mum's done it to her so she thinks if I do it she's got nobody. It's awkward trying to see it from a child's point of view.

Do you think you would have got a similar reaction if you'd told her you were going to move in with a woman?

ADAM Probably, because when I was in the relationship with that woman I was seeing she was a bit like that, although we didn't live together or anything. She was very clingy, she didn't like her.

How did you feel, Gareth, when you were going to meet these children for the first time?

GARETH Dreadful. It was like going for an interview, having teeth drawn. I can't describe the emotions I felt, I was so terrified that they knew I was their dad's new partner. We met for the day, went to a local carnival, had a pub lunch and came back here and played some games. It went remarkably well. The first time I met Michael he beamed. I'll never forget that child's smile, he just looked at me and smiled and all the barriers were gone. I felt, Why was I so worried? But I'll never forget it. I even fell in the pub, didn't I? It was quite comical, a nice ice-breaker. I was still very nervous, and coming back from ordering I tripped and beer went everywhere. The kids were falling about laughing. That was it. I wouldn't say it's been one laugh ever since – it hasn't – but we've had a lot of laughter here.

ADAM Michael is the type of kid whoever he meets, he gets on with them.

GARETH We have a lot in common, we both love sport. Adam doesn't like it – he doesn't know the first thing. You don't know a rugby ball from a football. Michael and I chat away merrily and watch the sport together.

How did you feel when introducing your children to your gay partner?

ADAM Nervous, because I didn't know what the kids' reaction would be. I was uptight for the kids and I was uptight for Gareth – it was like I was in the middle. I didn't know how they were going to get on, they could have hated one another.

GARETH He's the one that has to pull everybody together, he's the head of the family. We all look up to him and he's the one that has to do everything. The hardest thing I found was when we had to live together because I was dreading the moment when the kids came into the bedroom and saw their dad in bed with another man. Yet it was so easy, wasn't it? They didn't bat an eyelid.

ADAM Yes, we were dreading that moment but when it happened it was so quick we didn't think about it, as much as they didn't think about it, 'cos they always know they've got to knock on the door before they come in. They just knocked, and we said, 'What do you want?' and they just opened the door, stood there talking ten to dozen about what they wanted. They never stopped for breath or nowt. They just carried on as if it were normal.

Children ask embarrassing questions. Have they ever asked you anything embarrassing?

ADAM No, it's surprised me.

GARETH The only thing that was quite embarrassing, I felt, was the picture that Sarah drew of all us, and she drew me pregnant [*laughter*]. She said, 'That's you.'

So she thinks you're her mother?

GARETH That's what I thought. She can't have two dads so she's looking to me as a mother figure.

What about schoolfriends? People say it would be terrible to be brought up by a gay father because you get a hard time in the schoolyard. Are there problems at school?

ADAM Michael copes with it and gets round it. Sarah doesn't. She's having a bit of trouble at the moment. I went down to school – you see, I've got to the stage where I can walk down that street and hold my head up high. I've nowt to be ashamed of. I went in that school and found out what was going on. The teacher was brilliant. We sat down for an hour talking. She knew the situation and it didn't bother her. She were honest with me. Sarah's finding it hard. She finds it difficult to make friends where Michael makes friends right easy. He's right quick if somebody says something – he can answer them back. She finds it hard, wondering what to say. I don't know how to help them, because I've always brought them up to be honest. I can't change that.

She's had a new school, a new home, a new 'surrogate mother'. There's a lot to cope with.

ADAM And she's just started her periods as well, that's another change to her body. She's having all this to cope with all in a big lump.

How do two men help a young girl through her periods?

GARETH It was a funny thing, the first time he left me in sole charge of the two children and went out for the day was when she had to start her first period, and she had to come to tell me. It was quite a warm moment. It was so sad Adam had to miss an important thing in his daughter's life. She knew what she had to do and she had everything. I just put my arms round her. She cried on me and I cried on her

185

because it was such a tender moment. She hadn't known me long, but she trusted me sufficiently to come and tell me.

ADAM   At the age of ten when she had her injections and saw the nurse, the nurse explained everything she should do. I sat in and she explained it all to me too. Me and Sarah had sat down and talked about it, like her mother should have done, but her mother hasn't been interested. We've talked about sex, because I don't mind discussing things like that with them. My parents never did it for me. I had to find out myself.

GARETH   Have you ever discussed gay sex with her?

ADAM   No, I've never been asked. That would be difficult, but I've always brought them up to come to me with their problems. They can discuss things with their mum but they find it harder because if she doesn't like what they're saying, she'll start shouting because she's right bombastic.

When people discuss gay people bringing up children, they say that children need a male and female role model. What would you say to that?

GARETH   I think Adam is the female role model.

ADAM   I've been on my own with them for just over three years, and I've had to be mother and father. I've worked full time, I've cooked, cleaned, washed, everything what two people should do. It just comes so natural to me. When I've got kids I just get on with it.

Playing devil's advocate again, your son could be growing up gay because he's got the wrong role models.

ADAM   Yes, that's what his mum says. She says, 'If he does, I shall blame you.' I told her, 'You're to blame, not me.' There were an article that my sister-in-law showed me, which said it comes from your mother. I said, 'For God's sake, don't tell me mum because she will be upset.'

Why do you think we're gay?

ADAM   I don't think it's from your upbringing, I think you're born it, it's in you. I always knew there was something different about me.

GARETH   I think it's just a chance meeting, you experiment, you like what you did. I don't think it's your upbringing. Not every child dabbles but I think that most children at some stage have a little dabble, quite like it and they carry on doing it. That was my experience, anyway.

Have you ever argued about the children?

ADAM   No.

GARETH   No.

Not one single argument? I don't believe you!

GARETH   I will not interfere regarding the bringing up of the children, although I don't agree with an awful lot of the things he does. One of the things I've frequently told him is that they watch far too much television. And the news is never on in this house. If I want to watch the news I have to go upstairs.

How's it changed your life, having children in the house?

GARETH   It's been difficult because I've never lived with anyone. I feel to some extent they've invaded my space, but maybe I go out for half an hour. At the beginning I thought, God, what have I done? I don't think I sat down and thought it through.

What was the biggest shock for you?

GARETH   Having to wear a dressing gown to go to the loo, and having to lock doors. I used to be able to walk round the house naked, but I can't do that any more. Suddenly the house isn't mine, it's ours and I have to consider other people. Not that we agree on everything.

ADAM   We disagree on a lot of things.

GARETH   I like antique furniture.

ADAM   I don't.

GARETH   My antiques have had to go into the dining room.

ADAM   We find it hard in the kitchen, because we both like to cook.

Adam, how do you feel about Gareth wanting to have a child of his own?

ADAM   I think it's a good idea. If it does come off, the child can come and stay weekends or weeks or whatever.

GARETH   There are very few women who would give the child up, but I would like her to give it up for me to bring it up – but that's an impossibility, I would think, beyond my wildest dreams. I would so love to bring the child up myself. I got a very promising letter the other day. I replied immediately to it and suggested she ring me. I was expecting the call tonight.

How are you going to have this child, if you're not going to have intercourse?

GARETH   I would like that, but Adam said no. When we first met, I'd had a very active sexual life. Adam hadn't quite the same as me. We obviously had protected sex, and I said that one of the things I want to do is to have our relationship built on firm ground and I said I was going to have an HIV test. He didn't say he was going to have one, initially at first. Within a week of meeting him I went and had an HIV test. The results were negative, and then you went and were also negative. But we kept on having protected sex because I wanted the three-month re-test. Now we've gone through that, he says, 'I don't want you to have sex with anyone again.'

Is it a fear of Aids or jealousy?

ADAM   I think it's the fear of Aids. I mean, you don't really know.

Would you be jealous of him going to bed with somebody else?

ADAM   Yes, yeah. Deep down, yeah, I wouldn't like it.

GARETH   I would like to think that any child born should be naturally conceived. I know we've discussed it and it can't be.

ADAM   I don't mind him doing it because I've already done it myself! I also have two children that I did artificially for a friend. Her husband couldn't have children and they were sick for children. I got on real well with her and I was so unhappy for her. So we went to see the doctor and sorted it all out, this was when I was married and we all agreed. I donated the sperm.

GARETH   What I'm wanting to do he's already done. It seems so strange that it should happen at this stage in my life, that I met Adam. But he knows it was going on before I met him. Unfortunately I haven't met the woman to have my baby yet.

How do you intend to do it?

189

GARETH Just do it yourself, that's the way I envision it. To put it as crude as anything you have a wank in a cup and take that in. You're in one room and they're in the other. Their partner or whoever injects it into the vagina and that's it.

ADAM When I did it for my friend, we did it that way too. The first one I did, it worked straight away. For the second child I managed to get the sperm to her, but something happened, somebody called round or something so she couldn't inject it. So she put it in the freezer, then she forgot all about it. It was so funny a few months after she went in freezer and found this bottle. She says, 'Do you think it'll be any good?' I says, 'No, I don't think so, no!' When her kids were born her face said it all, she was so pleased. She thought she would never have children. But she did, all thanks to me.

Are you worried, Gareth, that you might help a child be conceived and the mother could walk away for ever with it?

GARETH Strongly worried about that. I want contact. This is why the letter I received was so promising. She lives about thirty miles from here. My main worry is that I'm too old – by the time I'm sixty the child will be sixteen. I will not see the child grow up, if I'm taken at seventy the child will be just blossoming. The chances are I may see it marry, possibly grandchildren, but Adam will, having had his children young. He could even be a great-grandfather. Should I now say that I won't have children? Let it go.

Does the fact that you want children and Adam already has them make your bond stronger?

GARETH No. I think it's putting more pressure on us than anything.

ADAM The thing is with the kids, the time you get on your own you appreciate a lot more than other gay relationships would, because they can have more or less all the time to themselves. But when you've got children, you can't be holding each other on the sofa and things like that. You're restricted, but you don't take one another for granted as much.

GARETH I say, when that bedroom door is closed this is my time. We can't embrace in the kitchen – unless the kids aren't there. Then I'll go in and put my arms round him or whatever. We just live as brothers while the children are around. That I find hard, that we can't have any physical contact.

What do you think gay people who haven't got children do with their maternal and paternal feelings? You breed cats. Are they surrogate children?

GARETH Yes. When one of my cats was a kitten, I dragged her twice from the jaws of death. I've become so close to her. He's nursed his children through sickness and I've nursed the cats, in a different way.

Adam, what advice would you give to men who have children but are coming to terms with being gay?

ADAM They haven't got two heads, or owt like that. In this day and age, it's getting discussed more and more. They've even started discussing it in schools now. Children are coming to terms with it younger and younger and they don't seem to bother with it. Everybody's got their own lives to lead and I don't think gay fathers should hide behind corners. I have a friend who was married and he'd two girls. He told the girls everything, he told his wife, and he's never looked back. He says it's the best thing you could do. I suppose in some ways it's easier for me to come out – I

191

have the kids to hide behind. People will probably be thinking if two kids at that age can accept and still want to live with their dad, why can't we? Touch wood I haven't lost a friend through this, but my ex-wife has lost a lot of friends.

On one hand you say you should be open with your children, yet on the other you won't touch Gareth while they're there. Why's that?

ADAM   I don't think you should rub it in. They've got to get used to the situation. It takes time. Probably when they're older and they've lived with it so long they'll be so used to it, and they won't give it a second thought if they see us on the sofa together. I try to be honest with them, because their mum says one thing and does the total opposite. She'd promised to buy Michael one of those Raleigh bikes for Christmas, and she's now had to say she can't afford it. She'll promise to take them out and then ring up and say, 'Oh, I can't go.' She's done it time and time again, and it's not fair.

Did you ever think of giving up the children when you met Gareth?

ADAM   Before I moved in I told my ex-wife I was moving in and taking the kids with me, and said, 'If you don't like the situation *you* can have the kids if you want. I will sign custody over to you!' I didn't want to. I don't know how I would have coped with it if she'd said yes, but I offered it to her and she said no. She hasn't really met Gareth yet. I think she's ashamed that two men are having to bring up her kids.

GARETH   I didn't want him to do it, because I think he would have resented me. After the first argument he would have said, 'For you I lost my kids.' If he ever lost custody of his children it would have nothing to do with me. If it did I couldn't live with myself. I will not be the one to say I don't want your children. I will never say that.

How does the blessing you had before you lived together enrich your relationship?

GARETH   I believe we have a commitment and we will make things work. There's a rocky road ahead of us, we knew from the beginning, but we both went in with our eyes open. The fact that we've made this commitment to each other now makes us work at it a lot harder. We're not doing too bad.

ADAM   Not considering the obstacles in the way.

I have a lot of admiration for Gareth and Adam. They could be held up as a shining example to anybody who is worried about gay men bringing up children. I also found Adam an inspiration: sometimes, as gay men, we blend into the background not wanting to make a fuss in case we are discriminated against. Yet he stood up and fought for what he wanted and believed in, and he did it in a difficult arena. The attitudes of society to gay men and children is the litmus test for how tolerant that society is. People often use the emotive issue of children to hide their homophobic feelings; because the needs of children are rightly considered of crucial importance, it is more difficult to challenge ill-informed opinions. The children's mother's fear that Adam will be exposing them to evil, corrupting forces is a good example of this. The reality that heterosexual fathers and step-fathers sometimes abuse children is forgotten. However, I hope the example of Adam and Gareth shows that a person's sexuality is not a guide to how good a parent they will make. Adam's success is all the more astounding when you consider that he had only recently come out. It takes confidence about your sexuality to feel proud in the way he does. This normally comes with time and from winning minor skirmishes. It would have been easier to lead the double life Gareth was talking about. Adam also demonstrates how important it is to 'come out'. When he was not open about his sexuality and was lying about his identity he was also forced to lie to his potential partners – not a good basis for a relationship. If he had not come out he would still be conducting meaningless affairs, rather than enjoying his enriching relationship with Gareth.

My meeting with Gareth and Adam was a warm experience because they are obviously in love. They are at the beginning of their relationship, in the 'Blending' stage, which I outlined in the first chapter. When limerence is at its height the couple are bonding and concentrating on everything that is similar about them. I had to press hard to find areas where they disagreed. The arguments about the furniture, who does the cooking and the children's TV habits had no heat because they had been doused by the calming waters of limerence. Limerence allows Gareth to cope with two boisterous children when he has been used to only his own company, and gives Adam the strength to uproot his family and trust them with somebody else. When you look at the obstacles that this couple and other gay couples face, it is just as well limerence is strong!

Gay parenting

It is important to try to see the situation through the children's eyes, which is hard to achieve if you are under stress from the break-up of a marriage or coming to terms with your sexuality. The problem is compounded by our tendency not to act rationally in moments of crisis. In many ways adults, too, can regress back to childhood, becoming introverted, moody and less capable of the skills of thinking logically through something. Therefore it is better, if possible, to wait until you have survived the initial crisis and fully understood the situation, with all its implications, before you try to talk to your children. People often rush into discussing their sexuality with their children. However, you need to be sure you are over the initial trauma so that you have all your adult rational skills to hand. If you are able to talk to your son or daughter in this way not only will you explain it better, you will also show them how adults deal with complex problems and help them to draw on their own emerging abilities.

The good news is that the small amount of research into gay parenting (Professor Rutter, Maudsley Institute) shows few differences between children brought up by gay and lesbian parents and their heterosexually reared schoolmates. However, this investigation was conducted over only a few years and drew conclusions for the short and medium term. During my research for this book I drew extensively on the knowledge of a child clinical psychologist on the developmental stages of childhood. At first, he recalled few cases where the parent's sexuality was a problem for the child. However, with further thought he remembered examples where it was one of a range of issues, but by no means the predominate one, which fits in with the example of Sarah and Michael. Michael is more confident and able to reply quickly to playground taunts; he is therefore coping better than his sister, who finds it more difficult to make relationships. Children who discover that their father is gay will react in character. How they cope will depend on how they deal with problems generally. A parent's sexuality is not, on its own, such a huge problem that it will overwhelm them.

These days, increasing numbers of children are living in families quite happily which do not conform to the traditional view of what constitutes a family.

As a parent, you are in the best position to know what to tell your son or daughter – after all, you know them best. However, I have some guidelines to help focus your mind.

What do we tell the children?

APPROACHING TEENAGE YEARS

A bright ten- or eleven-year-old, and most twelve- and thirteen-year-olds have began to learn the adult skill of thinking conceptually through an idea. They can think toward the future and can begin to define their place in the world. They can deal with problems not only from within but also draw on schoolfriends, teachers and other significant adults outside the family. Therefore, they can begin to cope with abstract ideas like their father's sexuality.

SIX AND OVER

Being gay is a concept that is likely to go completely over their heads. The six- to ten-year-olds need to experience something before they can understand it. At this age they are good at identifying and following rules; they test them but cannot make them up for themselves. At school playtime children spend five minutes playing and the rest of their time arguing about the rules. Their reaction to your news would be something along the lines of 'You're an adult [you set the rules], you know what you're doing, get on with it.'

Unless you need to introduce a new partner, there is no need to explain your sexuality. If you do, keep it anchored in the particular and avoid the abstract. An example would be, 'I love Martin, and we are going to live together. I still love you, Mummy still loves you, we will always love you.' And, for example, 'You will come and spend every other weekend with me and Martin.'

This age group often finds strange ways of grappling with the issue, asking wacky questions: 'Why do you take it in turns to do the cooking?' 'Why have you got a double bed when you're not married?'

At this age it is not a once-and-for-ever explanation, but one that will need to be readdressed as they become older and can comprehend more.

PRE-SCHOOL CHILDREN

At this age all of a child's experiences are mediated through adults. Therefore, the disruption caused by parents splitting up is overwhelming. If you are separating from your wife because you are gay, there is no difference in the experience for your son or daughter than that of any child going through a divorce.

Children are now at their most egocentric: they see themselves as the centre of their universe and, therefore, are more likely to blame themselves. They need lots of reassurance that they are not responsible for your problems and that they are still loved. Pre-school children have creative ways of solving their problems: they make up stories to comfort themselves. Parents often think their children have started to lie when they hear them talking about their wonderful weekend with Daddy, when he was hundreds of miles away. Understand that this is wish-fulfilment rather than naughtiness, and take it as a sign that your child needs more help and reassurance in coping with your divorce.

DANGER SIGNS TO LOOK OUT FOR

If you find that your son or daughter is responding in a primitive way, perhaps rolling up in a foetus-like ball, or regressing and behaving younger than they normally would, it means that they can no longer cope, and need more help and reassurance.

First of all, try to discuss the issue with your ex-wife or partner. It is important to try to achieve a consensus between you and for them to be around when you finally talk to your child. Children tend to see everything through the eyes of the partner who is being left. Therefore the more your ex-wife feels abandoned, the more likely the children are to feel the same. For many women losing their husband to a man is worse than losing him to a woman. They feel bitter and begin to question their own 'womanliness'. It is important to try to keep this part of the break-up away from the children: the issues that are between the two of you should not involve the children.

When you are talking to your son and daughter:

(1) Try to communicate with the individual child. This is difficult if you have never spoken about emotional issues before, but try to build on the ability you already have to talk with him or her.

(2) Give information about being gay: that it is possible for two men to love each other and want to be together. Explain that this is how you feel. Be as honest and accurate as possible, although you should not overwhelm them with details.

(3) Reassure them. Explain that this will not change the way you feel about them, and that you will continue to love them just the way you always have.

(4) Give them a chance to tell you how they feel, and answer any questions they might ask. They will probably

198

find it difficult to respond at this stage, but *please* stay with the subject.

(5) Help them explore the implications and how it affects them. This exercise is like peeling an onion: start with the practical matters (this will depend from individual to individual, but topics that should be covered include where you will be living and, if you are in a committed gay relationship, information about your new partner), then move on to how society feels about gay men. This will allow your children to start to think about how other people will react to your gayness and how these reactions will affect them. Next talk about school, perhaps discussing which of their friends they should tell. It is important to warn them that in their situation some children share too much with their peer group. They will find a varied response, from the supportive and empathic through to abuse and gay-bashing. Help them think through who they tell, how and when. Finally, move into how it makes them feel themselves. Pre-teenagers are wrestling with their own awakening sexuality, and your news will make them ask questions about themselves. A long and involved debate on the origins of sexuality would not be appropriate, but it is important to reassure them that gayness is not socially taught or induced, and that your news will not change how they feel about the opposite sex.

(6) You should give them a chance to reopen the subject when they have had time to think. Give them permission to come back and ask further questions. For them to come to terms with your sexuality will take time, rather as it took you time to come to terms with being gay.

(7) Set aside time to reaffirm your father/son and father/daughter bond, backing up your words with actions that you still love them. This could involve anything from collecting them from school through to weekends away with you on your own.

CAN WE BE AFFECTIONATE IN FRONT
OF THE CHILDREN?

Each family finds an appropriate level of intimacy with which every member feels comfortable. Some are cuddly, and some do not touch in front of the children. Take your cues from what was acceptable in the family in which the children were brought up. When teenage children tell psychologists about their parents' new relationships, they often find it difficult to understand why their father is in love because they never see him touching his new wife – the Ice-Station Zebra syndrome – or, conversely, complain that they are embarrassed because the couple are all over each other – the Petting Teenagers syndrome. The problem arises because the new couple are not following the rules of intimacy with which the child has been brought up. Try to relax with your new partner in front of the children. They should be able to understand the difference between affection and sexuality.

STEP-PARENTING

If you have children from a previous marriage or have formed a relationship with someone who has, you have now entered the world of step-families. What follows are only guidelines because individual circumstances make hard and fast rules impossible.

Leave the discipline to their natural father. It is extremely tempting to have your say because we all have different standards for children's behaviour, usually formed by our own upbringing. They seem natural to us because most of us have been brought up by one set of parents, and we have no first-hand knowledge of any other way. Remember, your partner will have had different experiences, and how he is bringing up his children will be a compromise between these and those of his ex-wife. Disciplining children is difficult – they find it hard enough to take it from their natural parents!

When you are dealing with the children, show a united front. Although it is all right to disagree with how your partner is bringing them up, or perhaps they are treating you in a way that makes you angry, wait until the children have gone home or you are alone together. It is vital that you try to settle your differences when they are not there. Children have a clever knack of playing one person off against another, and if they discover that they can do this with you they will try to manipulate you over and over again. Form a coalition that is so strong the children cannot divide you.

Put each other first: the most difficult of my guidelines, but very important. Many parents put the needs of their children first rather than those of their partners, but this may undermine your relationship. Putting your partner first is often a difficult idea to grasp as our society almost worships the child. From being two lovers, parents can turn into Mummy and Daddy exclusively. Also, the power structure of the family can become unbalanced in favour of the children, who are not yet emotionally mature enough to cope with so much responsibility. They end up feeling insecure and anxious. Family therapists stress that the natural order is for parents to be the heads of the household. The families that function well consult their children but the parents make the important decisions.

It is extremely difficult for a step-father to put his new partner first because he feels so guilty about what he has already put his children through. He may try to make up for it by spending too much money on them and generally overcompensating, which may be even more marked because he is gay and feels extra responsibility for breaking up the family.

You should aim to find a balance that feels comfortable for you, your new partner *and* the children. There will be crises, and times when one needs more of your attention than the other, so build in flexibility to allow you to adapt as circumstances change.

MOST GAYS DO NOT HAVE CHILDREN

One of the major reasons why gay men are over-represented in creative and artistic fields is perhaps because most do not become parents. Creating a child, bringing a new life into the world is, I am told, a fulfilling and satisfying experience. As a gay man I have accepted that I will not be a father, but I am channelling my creative instincts into other fields – for instance, writing this book. Like children, our creations have an identity away from us. The father nurtures the child, while the author carefully rewrites the book; the father prepares the child for independent adulthood and the author prepares for publication and the opinions of the outside world. Both the child and the book give their begetters a small stake in immortality.

By generally not bringing up children, gay men have more time to be creative; the nurturing goes on our partners often leaving enough for us to share with society at large. It is no coincidence that so many male counsellors, Samaritans, social workers and clergymen are gay.

Postscript: Since the interview took place, Gareth found a lesbian willing to have his child. He is now the proud father of a baby boy.

9

SEX

Sex is incredibly important to gay people. It is the primary definition of what makes us different from straights. Although far more than sex is involved in the gay lifestyle, when it becomes a problem in a relationship it can overwhelm everything else. One of the most important decisions a couple has to make is whether they want to be monogamous, and both partners are forbidden outside sexual experiences, or whether they wish to have an open relationship.

Scott and Shawn have been a couple for sixteen years. Scott used to be a cake decorator but is now back at college studying to be a social worker, while Shawn is a computer consultant. They live together in Central London and have a completely open relationship. It nearly ended when Shawn fell in love with a work colleague.

Scott and Shawn's partnership also serves as a useful summary of the first three stages, Blending, Nesting and Self-affirming, of gay coupledom.

How did you meet?

SCOTT   I went out looking for a relationship. He was tall, dark and slim. I quickly clocked him and he clocked me but

I thought, Don't look interested. He'd come up and stood behind me and I thought, Where's he gone?

SHAWN   I was just standing looking at him.

SCOTT   He thought I was on the game first of all! Then he came and stood beside me at the bar and ordered a drink.

SHAWN   And I said, 'I suppose you want a drink as well.' That was it.

SCOTT   I'd come out on the gay scene when I was twenty-one. After a year I realized it was very lonely. Never had any trouble meeting anyone but I was waking up in bed the next morning beside another completely different person. That's why I decided to go out looking for a relationship. However, it was just one-night stands, more one-night stands. I thought Shawn was going to be yet another.

What made it not a one-night stand?

SCOTT   It was very strange, because I couldn't take him back to my place because I was living with my uncle and he couldn't take me back to his place. We just agreed to meet again for a beer or something.

SHAWN   I just thought he was interesting. I wasn't quite sure what sort of interesting, but he was interesting.

So the first time you met you just talked to each other?

SCOTT   Yes, I came up to you and asked, 'Have you got a hairy chest?' So he said, 'Yes.' I said, 'Have you got hairy legs?' He said, 'Yes.' I said, 'That's it.' I don't think we even had a wank or anything.

SHAWN   We didn't have sex for nine weeks.

SCOTT   That was against the usual rules because normally you'd have a bit of nookie on the first night. There must have been something there for us to meet up again.

So you were meeting each other over nine weeks, without having sex!

SCOTT   We were having wanks. We were finding places.

SHAWN   No, we weren't doing anything.

SCOTT   Don't you remember that place under Waterloo?

SHAWN   No, that was much later. It was nine weeks before I got my hands on anything! I remember these things.

Do you think that the getting-to-know-you stage was an important factor in you being here sixteen years later?

SHAWN   It probably retained the interest for the first year, because I knew more about him by the time things had really got rolling. If we had started with sex I don't think I would have had such an in-depth knowledge of him. Knowing him for six or nine weeks before things took off sexually did make a difference in the first year.

SCOTT   I see what Shawn is saying and it's true – up to a point. But sometimes there is a hidden dimension. You didn't come and see me again in the hope of getting me into bed?

SHAWN   No. I found him incredibly interesting and very attractive. He had hair and I had a waistline!

SCOTT   It sounds a strange thing to say, but I like Shawn as a person now more than when I first met him. Friendship is very important. When we first met it was purely physical. This was my man. We had some really big arguments and fights in the first few years because it was almost like a power struggle.

SHAWN   For the first nine months we were all cosy and for the next two years it was horrendous rows. It was half-way through the rowing that we began to live together. I'm not certain if that perpetuated or terminated them!

What were the rows about?

SHAWN Anything. Remember when I threw that frozen chicken at you in Sainsbury's? We frightened the life out of that poor old dear.

SCOTT During one fight Shawn actually ended up on my shoulders. We both said, 'What on earth are we doing?' We argued about the usual things – I'd want him to do something and Shawn would say, 'The more you want one thing the more I'm going to do the other.'

SHAWN He was like the typical wife. Get married and the first thing they want to do is change you.

SCOTT We don't have roles.

SHAWN We both bent to each other's way of doing things. He still drives me potty and I still drive him potty. We just accept it.

SCOTT I've always found Shawn insensitive. He used to phone and say he'd be home in half an hour and four hours later he'd come in drunk. It's like the classic domestic argument, 'Why couldn't you ring?'

SHAWN Why should I ring?

SCOTT Just to let me know. But that comes over as nagging. I felt like the wife at home but that was my choosing.

SHAWN I think that a lot of the roles we have chosen to take have been down to our work. Scott was always on an early shift and I was doing shifts too – nights and evenings and all over the place. When we didn't have a washing machine, it was me out doing the washing because I could do it at strange times. Scott did the shopping and the cooking.

SCOTT One time I was shouting, 'I cooked you this.' He replied, 'I don't ask you to cook' – that brought it home to me. I don't have to do this!

SHAWN We didn't have any traditional roles, there wasn't a dominant and a submissive person. It just rolled on and we sorted it out as we went along. It was down to who had the opportunity, the inclination and the skill. That's why the housework never gets done because we both hate it. Another reason we row is because we're both hot-tempered.

SCOTT When we first met I was the equivalent of a bimbo – a himbo.

SHAWN No, you're doing yourself down. That makes me cross.

SCOTT No, every time we went to a party, it was 'This is Shawn, and, oh, this is Scott.' I always thought that all I had going for me was the looks. I would be in his shadow. What changed things for me was when I went off to America in 1984. I decided on the spur of the moment to go and work there for six months. When I came back I wasn't aware of just how much I'd changed but a lot of people told me. It was really good because when you're in a relationship you forget yourself. It doesn't matter if it's gay or straight. You become one of a couple. Suddenly I was in America and people liked me. I didn't have to be with Shawn. I became a stronger person, much more self-opinionated.

SHAWN Our friend Ian said you became a much stroppier git! Whatever it was, it did you an enormous amount of good. I'm glad you did it.

Did you see each other over the six months Scott was in America?

SCOTT No, but we wanked over the phone a lot, didn't we? [*Laughter*]

SHAWN We kept in regular contact!

SCOTT I had a couple of good lovers over there. One of them comes over every year.

SHAWN Great.

SCOTT We've always had the classic – what you find on the gay scene – open relationship. We don't do anything behind each other's backs. If I want to bring somebody here, I tell Shawn. This started very early in the relationship – we were involved in threesomes.

SHAWN We were faithful for the first two or three years.

SCOTT The jealousy aspect has gone if you're being honest with each other.

SHAWN The suspicion goes but I'm not sure that the jealousy does. He's getting it and I'm not. Is that jealousy?

SCOTT No, it's envy. But I didn't know what I'd find when I came back from America. I'd said to Shawn, 'I'm going', he said 'Good', in terms of 'good for you'. I never said, 'Will you wait for me?' When I came back, I realized that I was a person in my own right.

SHAWN I always knew you were your own person, you just didn't know it yourself.

Why did you start having sex outside the relationship?

SCOTT The first time was with this friend, Ian. Shawn got very upset about it – that's when we realized that we're both voyeurs. The first time he watched someone fuck me it was like – I don't like this. He reacted in the way he felt he should react. Then we talked about it afterwards.

SHAWN   Ian is my best friend, by the way. Before and after! I was extremely irritated. I said, 'Do you mind getting your dick out of my boyfriend?' He got all upset.

SCOTT   You smacked him round the head!

SHAWN   I did cuff him gently, this is true.

You were angry, weren't you?

SHAWN   I was irate. It was strange, I was externally angry but inside that was not how I was feeling.

What were you feeling internally?

SHAWN   Resentful. I don't know why, but resentful comes to mind.

SCOTT   I would disagree with that, because we had quickly established that we both liked threesomes. It wasn't a case of you thinking, Scott enjoys it so I better go along with it.

SHAWN   Prior to that all my relationships had been monogamous. Except when they weren't – at least, they were supposed to be!

At first you were monogamous. What changed things?

SHAWN   I think it was simply that it was a 'new toy'. To start off with we were more interested in each other because we didn't know about each other. It was only when we started to get to a certain level of knowledge and felt comfortable that we started to notice other people. Prior to that they could walk past naked and you wouldn't see them. First flush of lust.

Is it a bit like mountain climbing? You go and find other people because they're there.

SCOTT   No, no.

So what makes you turn from being monogamous to having sex with other people?

SCOTT   Up to this time with Ian, we'd both been faithful. I can still see it! Ian had also been Shawn's lover. The sex bit wore out but they became good friends. At a party, people were drinking, you unzipped his trousers and started sucking him. For no reason . . .

SHAWN   As you do.

SCOTT   I can still see it now as clear as day. It turned me on. I thought obviously Shawn must want me to join in.

SHAWN   That's when I got upset.

SCOTT   Up to then we'd never really gone out looking for things. After we'd sat down and talked about it and knew each other's feelings, I said, 'I would like to try it again.'

SHAWN   It became another possible dimension.

Was it anything to do with what was happening in your sex life?

SCOTT   No. It was too early in the relationship. It was not boredom, more like another avenue. It wasn't a case of 'Oh, we've run out of ideas, let's try something else.' It enhanced our relationship. Interestingly, the two grew together and it's been like that ever since. It works for us.

Are there any rules?

SHAWN   Safe and honest.

SCOTT   We've never said that, but it goes without saying.

SHAWN   No discussed ground rules, just respect for the other person.

SCOTT To give you an idea of the way we work, one time I was coming home and I dropped into Kings Cross toilets, met this guy, brought him back. Shawn was at work so I phoned him up and said, 'By the way I've got a guy back here.' He said, 'I'll be ten minutes.' He just walked in, we did the business, had a pizza and sent the guy home in a taxi. It's not like, 'How long have you been here, have you done anything?'

Is it always threesomes, or are you allowed to have sex on your own as well?

SCOTT I'm a slut! I tend to do it more by myself, and the situation arises more for me because I travel on public transport. Shawn goes to and from work in a car, but if you're on public transport it's so easy to trick.

SHAWN The only people I meet are at work.

SCOTT We used to go to the Subway club's darkroom. We both enjoyed doing that – but together. I would enjoy watching Shawn fuck and he would enjoy watching me get fucked. It did enhance our relationship. Did it bring us closer together?

SHAWN No, I don't really think it's done anything but eradicated jealousy and insecurity – there's no hidden agenda all the time.

Do you still have sex together?

SHAWN Oh, yes.

SCOTT But I've gone off it for the last two and a half months.

SHAWN Scott has just started doing a social-work course at college, which is a lot of work and a lot of pressure. He's been concentrating on that.

SCOTT   My dad's in hospital too. My mind hasn't gone off sex. I've gone off sex with Shawn. If someone came up to me in the street and said, 'Do you want a quickie?' I'd have a quickie, right – I don't have to give any emotion to that. I can just have sex and walk away.

SHAWN   It's emotional commitment which is the problem.

Shawn, how are you feeling about this?

SHAWN   Fine. I know what he's going through. It's heavy stuff – in fact I've got a new contract at work. It's not a problem.

SCOTT   I said to Shawn, the other day, that I'm quite aware that I'm cutting him out of this period of my life. It's important to communicate although it doesn't make him feel any better. If I said, 'Fuck me now,' he would. He's always, always on tap. I go for periods when I don't like it. I think it's my premenstrual tension!

So sex and love are different things?

SHAWN   Oh, yes. Sometimes we have sex and sometimes we make love. We usually have sex.

SCOTT   You make love and I have sex. We have said that before.

SHAWN   I'm dreadful, I keep falling in love with everybody I have sex with! He says, 'Oh, God, not another one you're going to fall in love with.' Horrible.

SCOTT   When we have sex Shawn is very into the love-making. I'm into the sex. Cold sex and that's it. I've spoken about this so many times with counsellors and people say, 'It's your upbringing.' I know where I'm coming from, it doesn't make it right, but that's the way I am.

In what way is it your upbringing?

SCOTT I'm very open with my sister and she has the same problem. In our family we're not very affectionate. Both me and my sister recognize this in our mum. She never showed love or hugs – especially towards my father.

So, Scott, you find it difficult to show love?

SCOTT I think I do.

SHAWN It has to be very safe before you do.

SCOTT A lot of it is also a habit.

SHAWN It doesn't cause me a problem because I can see he loves me, he doesn't need to show it. But I can imagine it would drive other people barmy.

Do the barriers ever come down? Are there times when both of you make love together – rather than you, Scott, having sex and you, Shawn, making love?

SCOTT Occasionally.

SHAWN Funnily enough we do, but when we make love we don't have sex. I might sit for an hour nibbling his ear but that's as far as it goes. Once we get into a lovey-dovey mood, we can't be bothered with sex somehow. We tend either to make love or have sex. It's very rarely that we do both.

Has having these other people involved in your relationship ever caused a problem?

SCOTT Yes, but not because of the sex. A lot of people say that if you're not monogamous you're increasing the chances of finding someone else. I would disagree with that because sex doesn't make you want to go off with someone else. Sex is irrelevant. You could be in a monogamous relationship and go to work and build up a friendship with someone who happens to be gay. You've not had sex with that person but you start to feel a lot for them. This is what happened with you and Danny – he had gone off on a conference and met this guy.

SHAWN This was five or six years ago. It started off as a bit of fun and got dramatically serious, rather quickly. I was going to leave Scott and go with this other person. For a whole heap of reasons that didn't happen.

Why not?

SHAWN I don't know. It got to the stage when I was equally in love with two people and I had to make a decision which way to go. Initially I made the decision one way and then changed my mind within twenty-four hours. I decided to stay.

Scott, how were you feeling during this period?

SCOTT Without being melodramatic, you could call it traumatized. I had always thought that nothing could rock our relationship – we'd got a good, honest relationship. Suddenly this guy came into my life, and it was *my* life – up to this point I thought it was just sex between these two. Shawn told me about Danny and how he had just broken up from his lover and I said, 'Isn't that sad? Do you want to invite him up to London?' Shawn said, 'Would you mind?' And he walked in and he was stunning! He looked like Eddie Kidd and a really nice guy too. I thought he was just a flirtation and it would die out. But when Shawn said he was leaving me, I found myself doing all the things that I had always criticized other people for doing, like ringing up the other person and screaming down the phone. I couldn't believe that I was doing all these things! I was going into work and still keeping a stiff upper lip but one day I just crumbled. I was in tears and sobbing so they sent me home.

How did you feel seeing Scott going through all this?

SHAWN   Really fucked up. I was wondering if that was why I didn't go. But it's not. I just made the value judgement and decided that of the two, at the end of the day, I was staying with Scott. It was awful for me to see someone I loved, and I loved him just as much as I did before and as much as I do now, going through so much pain. To see yourself doing that to someone is horrendous.

What happened next?

SHAWN   A lot of repairing to the relationship and a lot of repairing to do with Danny. I took him to Paris and explained the situation.

How did you feel when your lover went off with your rival to Paris?

SCOTT   I had accepted that he was leaving me and I wanted to retrieve the friendship. I wanted to keep that going if nothing else. When you realize that someone you love loves someone else and that that somebody can make them happy, you let them go. That's when I recognized how much I loved Shawn. If Danny could make him happy, more than I could, then I had to let him go. Once I had accepted that I relaxed a lot within our relationship. Shawn was still living here and my attitude towards him changed. Before he was going to Paris, I was scrubbing his back in the bath, not knowing that he was going to end it with Danny. On the Sunday when he came back and sat down, I asked, 'How was it? Was it good?' There's no use crying because it would make it harder for him, I was all bubbly because I had accepted that he was leaving me. All he said was 'I don't think I'll be seeing Danny any more.' I remember that so clearly – he was sitting here. Inside, I was secretly happy. I don't know to this day really why he came back, and Shawn has never spoken about it.

Were you aware of this change in Scott?

SHAWN   Yes, I was. Highly visible.

Do you think that influenced your choice?

SHAWN   It influenced it in that when I was looking at both of them, instead of having one of them ranting and raving at me and calling me all sorts of horrible names, I had two people being nice to me. Had Scott still been ranting and raving, I would have been more inclined to go with Danny.

Is it almost that because he set you free you decided to stay?

SHAWN   Yes, that's true or at least a very large component of it.

So what repairing had to be done?

SCOTT   The relationship I had thought was safe and secure was no longer safe. What I learnt, in a positive respect, was that nothing is for ever. We can sit here all nice and cosy now, tomorrow it could be gone. For me the repairing was about reassessing how I felt about Shawn. Did I trust him?

SHAWN   The security went out of the window. There wasn't, in practical terms, anything that needed repairing, but we needed some realigning of attitudes and changing of some base assumptions. It sounds quite minor but in fact took about six months.

SCOTT   It's not about trusting again, because what happened wasn't intentional. He didn't set out to find someone else to love. It happened. It wasn't dishonest.

Were you seeing other people sexually over those six months?

SHAWN   We gave up everything over those six months.

You came back and started bonding again?

SHAWN   Yeah, it was almost like going back to square one. Except we didn't row this time.

SCOTT   I think it was positive. It taught me about my strengths – I didn't *need* Shawn, in a nice sort of way. If it happened again, I would react in the same way, even though I know I can cope. It taught me a lot about the relationship.

SHAWN   I learnt to distance myself effectively from my emotions, which proved useful because my brother committed suicide two years later – which totally fucked the family up and which, in many ways, it still is today. I was able to switch off emotionally and carry on working.

Playing devil's advocate, instead of going through all this pain, wouldn't it have been better to have stayed monogamous? After all, there had been nothing wrong with your sex life.

SCOTT   Oh, no. I enjoy having sex with other people – it's part of me. It's still part and parcel of the relationship.

SHAWN   We had a great sex life for two years. I don't think we'd still be having the same one today. It's also something about forbidden fruit – it's perfectly all right to have a munch if you fancy it – somehow you don't get the frustrations and the anxieties. Just that it's there gets rid of the temptation, and it makes life so much easier. You don't get guilt feelings and you don't have to do things secretly. Our one unfortunate incident is one of the dangers but we've managed to live through it.

Could it happen again?

SHAWN   Of course it could.

217

SCOTT   It's got nothing to do with the sexual relationship. I met a guy about four months ago and he was supposedly straight. I started to feel a lot for him before we'd had sex and Shawn recognized it. He said, 'Do you love him?' I said, 'I don't know.' Luckily he moved away. Yes, it could happen again, but it has nothing to do with an open relationship, I really believe that. We could be living in each other's pockets – and Shawn could just meet someone who changes his whole world around.

SHAWN   I can fall in love in three minutes.

SCOTT   When Shawn and I first met, we had that hidden something. The same thing can happen with someone else, and it's got nothing to do with sex or looks – it's something you can't put your finger on.

Turning now to work, you both have careers that are important to you.

SHAWN   My work is the most important thing I do, probably because it takes up so much time. I'm committed to it.

SCOTT   My working life is changing. I've been in the creative, artistic side – pastry and cake-decorating. About a year ago, I started to reassess what I really wanted from life. I don't know if it's got anything to do with age. In the voluntary sector, I was involved with the deaf, Samaritans, Aids, and I wanted more of that. I just said to Shawn, 'I'm thinking of doing social work.' It seemed like a good idea at the time and he just said, 'Go for it.'

Scott becoming a social worker means change for the relationship. Shawn, do you find that threatening?

SHAWN   It was a managed change. We sat down and agreed what would need to be organized and did it. I'm sure things will come out of the woodwork but it's early days.

SCOTT It has been a culture shock, going from cake-decorating to sitting in a classroom. We're all mature students so we've all given up jobs to go back to college and the majority come from a social-work background. I felt out of my depth when I started. There was a lot of background reading to do. I felt a loss of identity. You've got people who've done degrees and all I've got is a City and Guilds and CSE in woodwork. It's starting to gel now. I know I can hold my own among my peers.

Could there be problems in the future, with both of you having careers that could take you in different directions?

SHAWN I haven't said anything about it, but I've identified this as something that will dramatically change us. Before this, by and large, Scott has not brought work home with him – the problems have stayed there. I say 'by and large' because he's the sort of person who becomes very involved with whatever environment he is in. I think he's going to be a lot more emotionally mangled by the time he comes home. I'll wing that when it happens.

SCOTT When I was working in the voluntary sector I didn't have a problem. My own counsellor said, 'You're very good at separating yourself, you've learnt your defence mechanisms, you've learnt what's going to work for you.' At the moment I'm coping with superficial stuff like the politics of college. I've dealt with hard cases in the past and I know I'll deal with them in the future.

Do you feel Shawn supports you and is interested in your course?

SCOTT Shawn's interested, there's no doubt in that, but I'm pulling into myself at the moment. The support is there but it doesn't make me feel any better. There's a lot of other things I'm finding out about myself. It's bringing up lots of memories from school. Do they like me? Am I in this gang or that gang? It's very childlike but it happens in groups.

You both stress how important your friendship is.

SHAWN We wouldn't have a relationship without it.

You have other people who are good friends whom you have sex with as well. What's the difference?

SHAWN Friendship, sex and love, we've got all three, but we don't have love, except by accident, with other people. We can have friendship with other people, or sex, and sometimes both, but currently the only person that I've got friendship, sex and love with is Scott. They are three separate and unrelated components.

SCOTT I just know that I love Shawn, everything is encompassed by this thing called love. If somebody asked me what I mean by love, I couldn't answer. The sex bit is something I feel quite guilty about. Guilty, yes, because I'm not giving Shawn sex at the moment, but I can't have sex just to make him happy. I've got to want it, and even though I know Shawn understands I still think to myself, yes . . . but . . .

Are your friends doing the same as you?

SHAWN No. Most of them are dishonest. They have their little bits on the side. Normally what happens is one of them is slightly closer to one of us than the other, I find out what one of them is doing and Scott finds out what the other is doing. They're not telling each other and it's deceitful.

SCOTT In general, one does it and the other doesn't know or they're both doing it. It's a case that 'We're in love and as long as we don't talk about it we don't have to face any difficult situations.' Because we're both Samaritans we tend to talk more to each other about our own feelings. If we go through a patch where we know there's an underlying agenda, we'll talk. A lot of people say they talk but they don't really.

Do you manage the emotional complexity with other sexual partners because you talk through the issues that come up?

SHAWN Although externally it's complex, internally it's very simple. There's no jealousy, no secrets, no guilt. You need to be honest and open and prepared to discuss everything and accept that you might get angry or jealous.

SCOTT Do you remember Gordon? After this Danny episode I could see history repeating itself. He started to come down from Manchester and visit. I said to Shawn, then and there, 'I'm not feeling happy with the situation.'

SHAWN And I agreed and told Gordon not to come down any more.

Would monogamy have been a strain that would have damaged your relationship?

SCOTT The friendship and the openness go hand in hand for us. It's not just a case of having an open relationship. Because we're friends we give each other space.

SHAWN Part of that space is sexual freedom. You probably get the impression that we're out bonking every night, but it happens every now and again.

SCOTT Do you remember that time when we tried to be monogamous? You told me not to have sex. It was when I was seeing Tom up the road and you started to get a little paranoid about it. I had had a fling with this guy and he had started to fall in love. I wasn't in love, I was just having sex.

SHAWN He was going to get hurt.

SCOTT While we were trying to be monogamous, which lasted about a month, I found that I didn't like the constraints. It was important that I said to Shawn, 'I can understand why you're getting uptight. In future I won't have sex with Tom any more, but I can't promise you that I won't mess about with others on the side.' On that basis we carried on. Often when people say they've got an open relationship, if you ask them if they know that their boyfriend is having sex with someone, and they don't know – that's when the jealousy starts creeping in.

SHAWN Most people's idea of an open relationship means *they* can have sex outside and the other one can't.

SCOTT You've got to know yourself well enough and be pretty confident to sit down and say, 'Right, when I ask you how you're feeling, I really do want to know how you're feeling.'

SHAWN You actually are interested in the answer!

Scott and Shawn again illustrate the importance of getting to know somebody properly at the beginning of a relationship, because although sex is what normally brings us together, it is other qualities that sustain. Although they feel that their friendship is the principle ingredient in the success of their relationship, they also feel that sexual openness is important. To test this, I asked them to look through the following qualities that could have contributed and rate them, giving 1 to the most important and 10 to the least. If you try it on your own relationship, don't spend too long agonizing over the results. Initial reactions are important as the exercise is designed to reach your subconscious feelings.

Compassion	Respect
Friendship	Humour
Shared interests	Communication
Love	Sexual freedom
Independence	Similar values

Shawn and Scott were surprised at the results, which I have listed from most importance to least.

Scott	*Shawn*
Friendship	Friendship
Communication	Love
Similar values	Compassion
Respect	Respect
Love	Sexual freedom
Shared interests	Humour
Humour	Similar values
Compassion	Communication
Independence	Shared interests
Sexual freedom	Independence

They both rate friendship as the most important quality for their relationship but sexual freedom and independence are ranked low. It is interesting that love ranks indifferently for Scott and in second place for Shawn, which, in a way, underlines their different personalities. Although it is popularly supposed that 'All You Need Is Love', on its own love is never enough to sustain a relationship. If you have completed this exercise with your partner, it is useful to discuss together the reasons for your choices and your understanding of what each category involves: different words have different meanings for different people. Although a close match of attributes helps a partnership, it is also useful to know the areas in which you differ and to be aware of what is important to your partner.

Shawn and Scott also illustrate how couples do not pass simply through the relationship stages. You can slip back down the rungs of the ladder. At times of crisis we need to revert to an early stage: after the affair with Danny, Scott and Shawn report that they closed in on each other, into the relationship, and had no outside sexual contacts – in other words, they returned to 'Blending'. When the relationship had been reapired and the crisis worked through, they were able to climb back to their normal rung. Scott and Shawn have now passed through the 'Self-affirming' stage and feel confident of their own identities within the relationship. They are now moving into the next stage.

STAGE 4 OF A GAY RELATIONSHIP
Collaborating

This starts from about six years into the relationship, when the couple feel that their partnership is secure. They use this security and the sense of themselves within the partnership that they gained from 'Self-affirming' to launch successful projects outside the partnership. It can be a college course, a career change, or new hobbies and interests. Similarly, when children reach three or four the confident ones start to explore the world because they know if they are threatened they can run back to the security of their mother's arms. The stage is called 'Collaborating' because of the high degree of support given to the partner who is embarking on the new project; some of the excitement it generates is brought back into the relationship and both partners rejoice in the triumphs. It may also provide new ideas for the other partner and he, too, can develop the interest. In the 'Collaborating' stage, couples may start working together using their complementary skills on a new business venture or, perhaps, renovating a house. Communication is easy and comfortable; it may be so finely tuned that couples finish sentences for each other. All the negotiating and explaining needed in the earlier stages are now bearing fruit. With this sense of security, the partners are less concerned about maintaining the relationship and energy can be diverted outwards. For all couples it is a period of productivity, providing material and professional success. It is also a time when they can establish separate parallel sexual affairs away from the main couple relationship. By this stage, too, the couple are now more accepted as an item by their respective families, work colleagues and gay friends. Problems may arise, however, if one partner feels left behind while his lover is establishing a new and separate identity. (Interestingly, I have found that in the couples I have interviewed who are going through or have been through this stage, the partner who has made the most changes has been catching up on the other's perceived educational or social standing.) Boredom and taking each other for granted may set in and the outside sexual activity may also provoke crises. There is a fine line between separate identities and activities that enrich the relationship and those that leave the couple growing apart.

As a Relate marriage guidance counsellor I see many heterosexual couples who find this stage a time of crisis. Typically, the wife returns to education or starts a career, as opposed to a job to supplement the family income. The independence of the woman, who traditionally has been responsible for the home and nurturing, is threatening to her husband. Many heterosexual couples never reach this stage. Those who achieve collaboration on projects outside their relationship normally succeed after the children have either started school or left home. It is an area in which gay relationships come into their own: typically there are no children so the nurturing goes into the relationship and the partners have the confidence and support, both emotional and financial, to discover new career avenues and develop their personalities. The relationship is secure enough for each partner not to feel threatened by new experiences and people. Their independence stops the couple from living in each other's pockets – distance in a relationship helps to keep the attraction and interest alive and minimizes potential stagnation.

Two-career relationships is a problem that heterosexual couples are increasingly facing – but it is something that gays have always had to deal with. If an exciting job comes up at the other end of the country for one partner, what does the other one do? Give up their own rewarding job? Commute? Or should the offer be turned down and the status quo preserved? If this issue crops up in your relationship, you will discover one of the great joys of the 'Collaborating' stage: you can depend on your partner and together you can find a solution.

Faithful: to be or not to be?

The majority of gay couples are not monogamous.

Three couples in this book currently have a sexually exclusive relationship (Chapters 5, 8 and 10). Five couples have a completely open relationship which includes long-term outside sexual partners (Chapters 2, 3, 7, 11 and this one) while two couples, in the early stages of their partnership, have only occasional sex outside the relationshiop (Chapters 4, 6). Some relationships become more open as couples are together longer.

Our society believes in monogamy: a public figure can

be forced to resign if found to have a mistress. Although everybody buys into the idea of exclusivity we are not always able to deliver it, hence the high levels of adultery. The couples in this book who do not have a sexually exclusive relationship all stress that they are *emotionally* faithful. Men are generally good at compartmentalizing their lives – work in one box and home in another, for example. Women are less likely to do this. Men can also put their emotions into separate boxes: Scott and Shawn make love or have sex. For most women these two elements go together. By dividing sex from love, some men can screw around yet remain emotionally faithful, which might explain the famous double standard in which it is all right for a man to have sex on the side but not for a woman. In heterosexual couples an affair often ends a marriage. In contrast, it is not as threatening for gay couples. Heterosexuals who read this book may well find the idea of open relationships alien and frightening. Why do gay and straight couples view this issue so differently?

First, and as I explained, men separate love and sex while women do not. Most women feel that if you have sex with someone you must be emotionally committed to them, and a wife will feel rejected if her husband sleeps with another woman. Men are aware, if only at a subconscious level, that for a woman to have sex she is likely to be in love, and that if a wife has sex outside the marriage she is emotionally rejecting her husband. By the time gay men settle down they have had many sexual partners and are aware that sex can be a purely physical release with no emotional content.

Until recently, most women have been economically dependent on men. They are in danger of losing not only a partner but also a provider. Also, they have taken the status of their husband – they are often introduced as 'Peter's wife' or known as 'the doctor's wife' – so when a husband leaves, his wife is in danger of losing her status and part of her identity.

Years of cultural conditioning have made us consider monogamy the norm. In the process of identifying himself as gay a man has to challenge so many of society's expectations – what difference does one more make?

Man has traditionally been the sexual hunter. It is up to him to ask a woman out and woo her. When you have two hunters, two people looking, you have double the chance of a match. Even if you plan to be faithful, it is difficult when some handsome man starts flirting with you and propositioning you!

Sex is one of the few ways that is culturally acceptable for men to express their feelings and become vulnerable. Beyond fighting, sex is the only acceptable way for a man to become close to another human being. This is why men find it almost impossible to last for any length of time without sex, while women are more likely to complain when they are not getting kisses and cuddles and have less of a problem coping without sex. Sex is versatile: it can be a form of bonding, but also in fucking some stranger you can gain an illusion of closeness and intimacy until you zip up your pants and walk away because you have not allowed yourself to become emotionally vulnerable. Sex gives men the opportunity to experience feelings without challenging another part of the male gender identity: self-containment and strength.

Sex has often become a hobby for gay men, which, in the gay world, is socially acceptable. It is difficult to let go of sexual variety and settle with one person.

On the whole, gay men are not accepted by society, which can result in our not accepting ourselves. Sex can become a way of compensating for those feelings: if other men find us sexually attractive, we feel attractive and worthwhile. In an attempt to affirm ourselves we may believe that the more sex we have the better we will feel.

The phases of a couple's sexual activity

COUPLES NORMALLY START OUT BEING SEXUALLY EXCLUSIVE

During the 'Blending' stage, when limerence is at its strongest, there is a period of intense sexual exploration. According to McWhirter and Mattison's study, in the first years of the relationship 85 per cent of their couples reported having sex more than four times a week. The couples are so intensely into each other that they have no need or awareness of others. It is important to remain sexually faithful at the beginning so that the 'Blending stage' is properly achieved.

IMPORTANCE OF BEING SEXUALLY FAITHFUL IN THE EARLY STAGES

Limerence can create such powerful lovemaking, that it overwhelms any potential sexual incompatibility.

When a couple has moved out of the 'Blending' stage, sexual problems may emerge. You need to learn practical skills: how do you say no without hurting his feelings?; how do you deal with the fact that you need more sex than he does?; how do you maximize pleasure for each other?; what was he doing only because he knew you liked it? When the sex goes off the limerence boil it is easy to seek solace from uncomplicated sex outside the relationship rather than dealing with the domestic sexual issues. You can't solve the problems of your relationship in the arms of another man!

If you work at the sexual niggles as they arise, and keep learning about each other and how to give pleasure to each other, you can build a good, lasting sexual and loving relationship.

The other reason I believe in fidelity at the beginning of a relationship is that trust takes time to establish in a gay partnership, and it is dangerous to embark on secondary sexual relationships until this has been earned and built. Scott and Shawn had a monogamous period early in their relationship; when they had their difficulties with Danny they had something on which to fall back.

MOVEMENT FROM QUANTITY TO QUALITY

Although the frequency of sexual activity declines with the length of a relationship, couples often report an increased level of satisfaction. First, the partners know each other and how to please each other, and the trust they have built up allows them to become vulnerable. In many ways, vulnerability is what love is all about. You cannot love something that is invulnerable; we love puppies because they need our care but nobody loves an impenetrable armoured tank. When you really know and trust someone you can bring the puppy part of your personality into the bedroom and leave the tank outside. This is what Shawn and Scott were talking about when they made the distinction between making love and having sex. When you make love you spend a long time in someone's arms, caressing and touching and afterwards luxuriating in post-orgasmic warmth. Sometimes you almost feel that you can touch your lover's soul. In contrast, sex is a more physical act – it's more about having an orgasm than communicating. One is not necessarily better than another – a quickie can be fun and fulfilling too – but 'quality' lovemaking is only possible when a couple understand, trust and can be vulnerable with each other.

PERIODS OF SEXUAL INACTIVITY

It is natural to have phases in your life when you do not feel like sex. Scott feels no desire for lovemaking; he needs all his emotional energy to cope with his new career and his father's illness. Although Shawn understands and is not pressurizing him, Scott feels guilty. Nowadays, we are expected to be forever sexual and some people feel a failure if they enter a fallow period. Sometimes it amazes me how robust we expect our sexual appetite to be. I once counselled a heterosexual man who was worried about his impotence. I was not surprised that he had no desire when I uncovered all the problems in his life: his son was dying of Aids and wanted to come home, but my client was Aids-phobic and scared of catching the illness; his son-in-law was dying from inoperable cancer and my client was trying to support his daughter; and he had just started a new relationship and was not certain if it had a future.

HOW DO GAY COUPLES DEAL WITH THE SEXUAL EXCLUSIVITY ISSUE?

It is not as simple as deciding whether the relationship should be exclusive or open. Most couples can be placed along a scale: at one end lies monogamy and at the other the completely open relationship in which each partner conducts a secondary affair. This is why I have categorized my couples in three broad areas: closed, partially open, and open relationships. Couples find a position on the scale with which they feel comfortable, normally by trial and error, rather than through discussing the rules together. All of the couples I have interviewed were open and honest between themselves about all their sexual practices. Others have sex outside the primary relationship but do not discuss it:

perhaps one partner is not aware it is happening or, more commonly, both are aware but fear that by acknowledging the affairs they will damage the relationship. These couples did not come forward to be interviewed.

Even when sex outside the relationship is a 'secret' there are rules. Most couples cannot articulate them, but they will include one or some of the following.

(1) *When it can be done*. Some couples allow each other to have sex with other people when one is away on business. Some partners are allowed to cruise a club when their lover is also there, while others feel it is bad manners.

(2) *What can be done*. Some couples allow each other to play the field with anyone they choose but ban more intimate acts like intercourse.

(3) *Where it can be done*. Some couples have sex in saunas, cottages or cruising areas but not at home. By contrast, others might allow each other to bring contacts home only when the other is there, or out, or they are not permitted to use the marital bed for sex.

(4) *How often it can be done*. In some relationships it is permissible to have sex with other people but repeat business is banned!

(5) *Including the partner*. Some couples enjoy threesomes and group sex but ban each other from seeing outside contacts individually.

(6) *Friends*. Some couples put friends off limits.

(7) *It must not interfere with the relationship*. Outside sexual partners are tolerated as long as they do not hinder the regular running of the primary relationship.

(8) *Emotional involvement*. Everything is allowed as long as each stops when there is a danger of them falling in love.

Obviously these areas are not mutually exclusive and each couple will find a combination to suit them. The beauty of gay relationships is that there are no rules; it is up to the two of you to choose what is right for you. However, the more truthful you are with each other about what is happening between you, the more likely you are to spot problems and resolve them before they tear the relationship apart. If you are in a relationship and either of you is having extracurricular sex, then talk through the rules I have outlined so that they are no longer 'secret' but made explicit and understood by both of you.

Advantages of a closed relationship

The sample in my book is only a small one and therefore will not stand up to rigorous scrutiny but, in general, the more closed the relationship the more sexual activity between the couple. Some of the completely open partnerships were only having sex once every other month and in one case had almost stopped altogether. Martin and Roy, in Chapter 7, can go for months without having sex together. They enjoy the intimacy and the vulnerability they have together much more. Lovemaking is like everything else: the more you put into it the more you get out. Couples in closed relationships are more likely to invest energy in the sexual aspect of their partnership. There is a danger in an open relationship of having sex with everybody but your lover! In the long term, this may affect the relationship: lovemaking is a form of communication, another way of bonding, and, in a world that scorns gay relationships, we need every support we can find.

Sex is a useful barometer in a relationship. If the couple

are drifting apart or not paying enough attention to each other, their sex life is normally the first area to suffer. It can act as an early-warning system that something is wrong. If you are having sex outside it is easy to miss the signs.

Open relationships can be complicated by the secondary sexual partners falling in love and creating a triangle. Most of the 'open' couples have had to weather such crises. The risk reduces in the 'partly open' cases because it is difficult to fall in love with someone whose name you do not know or who you only meet once. However, a closed relationship is no guarantee that one of you will not fall for someone else – life does not come with guarantees.

Advantages of an open relationship

Monogomy is difficult and it is sometimes better to admit your weaknesses and learn to live with them, rather than cheat on the side. Deception is never a good foundation for a relationship. The couples in 'open' relationships report that they make some good long-term friends in this manner, and have a chance to try out new sexual experiences or indulge tastes that their partner does not share.

By separating having sex and making love, open couples can enjoy the best of all worlds: the excitement of the sexual chase, the gay scene, and the safety of a committed relationship.

Erica Jong, the author of *Fear of Flying*, claims that 'Monogamy is impossible among interesting people.'

Conclusion

In conversations with couples in both open and closed relationships, I was struck by how both sets are striving for the same ends. Both types of partnerships use the same words to describe their feelings. For example, 'The relationship is stronger, healthier, with more mutual trust and understanding'. These are benefits which one couple see from their closed relationship. It could just as easily have come from my interview with Scott and Shawn. The goals are always, trust, intimacy, safety and security, and couples in both open and closed partnerships feel their choice helps them achieve all of these.

The issue is one of personal taste. The problems arise when each partner wants something different. If you are in this situation it is important to listen to your partner's viewpoint rather than trying to convince him to agree with you. It is only when you truly understand each other's feelings and fears that you can begin to compromise. Always *explore*, so you can *understand* and then finally move to *action*, when you make a decision. This process takes time, so do not expect to sort it out within one chat; it will probably take several. The topic needs to be revisited as circumstances, experiences and time change your feelings. Some couples start with an expectation of monogamy and then renegotiate, while others decide to close a previously open relationship.

If you have chosen some degree of an open relationship it is vital that you are honest with each other. Like Scott and Shawn, when you ask your partner, 'How do you feel?' be prepared to *listen* rather than only hearing what you want to hear. If you and your partner are having sexual problems *talk about them*. As gay men, we think we are comfortable talking about sex. However, we are better at dishing the dirt about sex and gossiping with friends than being open and honest about our feelings with our partner. Lovemaking is about communication, so overcome your embarrassment and open up. It will make you more vulnerable but it will also bring you closer together.

10

AIDS

What is the impact on a couple when one partner is diagnosed as HIV positive? Barry and Brian are forty-five and forty-three respectively and have been together for nineteen years. Brian learnt in 1987 that he had the virus; since then he has been in remarkably good health. Barry took the news worst: his health deteriorated with drink, drugs and depression. Brian and Barry started in a three-way relationship but now only have sex together. They are a good example of how productive couples can be in the 'Collaborating' stage. They are both in publishing and live in a house crammed full of art-deco artefacts and furniture.

Barry, you were in another relationship when you first met Brian.

BARRY It had started with a colleague in South Africa, a fellow journalist. We set up home together in Johannesburg, I was fairly active in the anti-apartheid movement. I ran myself into problems with the regime at the time, and had to leave the country quickly. Richard, my partner, joined me later in London. I got him a job so we were living *and* working together. In 1975 I met Brian. The relationship had been getting a bit strained for a variety of reasons: Richard had never been an easy person to live with and I often felt that he had a chauvinistic attitude. I always thought that he ought to have been straight, and he would have used a wife like most straight men do. Very often I found myself playing Richard's wife – I got really, really fed up with it.

Can you give me an example?

BARRY   Richard couldn't cook, he couldn't wash up, he couldn't do any of those domestic tasks. He was not a home-maker. He just assumed I would be there to mop up after him. I enjoy cooking but I don't want to feel that something is thrown at me because nobody else wants to do it.

BRIAN   Politics came into it too.

BARRY   I was very involved with the Labour party who helped me stay in this country. Richard found this upsetting because he was dedicated to the Tories.

How did you come into the picture, Brian?

BRIAN   I came out very late. I had my first sexual experience when I was twenty-one. Nothing to it, really, just experimental, and then I backed off until I was twenty-three. I decided all at once that I would investigate the gay scene. My way of approaching it was to answer an advert for a room in a house for someone gay or straight. I didn't tell anybody there if I was gay or straight, basically because I didn't know. There were two gay guys there who befriended me. They were curious about me and invited me out one night. They took me to the Salisbury pub and I saw a guy there that I fancied very much. He just kept walking back and forth in front of me. Eventually he stopped and said to me, 'Do you know what the time is, please?' I just collapsed laughing because there was a great big clock on the wall behind me! Although I was naïve, I had read a lot of books and I knew this was the corniest line. We hit it off. It was

Barry, and he told me all about Richard, that he was in a relationship and it would just be a one-night stand, but I went back with him, anyway.

When did you meet Richard?

BRIAN I phoned Barry up the next week and invited them both for a drink. We ended up having a three-way relationship for about three years.

What was it about that kind of relationship that appealed to you?

BRIAN I think the three-way thing meant that I wasn't committed to anybody. I was just going in offering something additional to their relationship. When things between them started to get bad, I had to make a decision about who I was going to go with.

Why didn't you want to be committed?

BRIAN It was too early. It was my first affair.

What was it like for you, Barry, finding that this one-night stand had developed into something more?

BARRY Confusing. I was younger then and quite experimental, and although it was the first serious thing that had happened for Brian, I had the benefit of having matured early. My first gay experience was when I was twelve and I initiated it. From then on I had a full sex life and it was always gay. Emotionally I thought I was having infinitely better sex with Brian than I'd ever had with Richard. I had thought I was in love with Richard but I didn't know what love was until Brian came along. The thing with Richard held together as long as it did because I felt quite sorry for him, which is never a good reason to keep a relationship going. I felt there was a lot of potential to hurt him. In the

239

end, he was ultimately quite hurt when we upped and left him on his own.

Did you all sleep in one bed together or did you alternate?

BARRY   Ostensibly Richard and I were sleeping together in the big double bed and Brian was sleeping in the second bedroom. But I was getting up in the middle of the night and going to sleep with Brian.

BRIAN   To start with all three of us slept together.

BARRY   It couldn't last for long and it didn't. I've never ever, since then, been the slightest bit interested in a three-way relationship. There was nothing ultimately that was good for any of us as a result of it – but nothing permanently damaging. Richard was hurt because our original relationship had broken up. He's still a good friend, by the way.

Was it a long breaking-up process or were you genuinely a three-way relationship over those years?

BARRY   Richard and I worked together, we all ate together, we went to the pub together. We were three guys who were always together, but as far as I was concerned the sexual satisfaction was all coming from Brian.

BRIAN   As far as Richard was concerned as well! I ended up, not to put it too crudely, servicing both of them – they weren't getting on with each other at all. When it got towards the end I said I was going to leave and Barry said if I left he would leave anyway, so it wouldn't solve anything and Richard would still be on his own. I had to decide then which one I was going to go with.

What pressure does it put on you having two people in the same house desperate for your affections and not wanting to alienate either of them?

BRIAN Fairly heavy. I used to get quite depressed sometimes, but I'd always suffered from depression. There were
constant rows. They were always fighting with each other.
They would fly off the handle at each other about what the
prime minister said on television. At one stage Richard went
to hit you, didn't he? That was the point that I decided
enough was enough.

BARRY We never argued over Brian. The arguments were
almost entirely political.

BRIAN My relationship stayed stronger with Richard after
the two of them broke up, but eventually Barry and Richard
thawed out with each other and they remained friends. You
were quite jealous of Richard at one stage.

BARRY I think I was and I don't think I'd ever been jealous
in my life.

BRIAN I didn't feel I could drop him straight away because
he had been hurt by the whole thing. I wanted to let him
down gently.

What was it like going from three to two?

BARRY It became very settled. The number of rows we've
had you could count on the fingers of one hand. I grew up
in a household where mother and father fought like cat and
dog so I found the rows with Richard unsettling. Rows
really frighten me.

BRIAN There was much less tension and I knew where I
was. Even before we left it became a fact that we were
sleeping together and Richard wasn't with either of us. We
are very close to Richard now, we consider him to be part
of our family. He comes to see us when he's in trouble.

*Once you were just a twosome, did you get involved with
outside sexual partners?*

BARRY I think we agreed that we would not cramp each other's territory. If something came along, all right, we wouldn't make too much of a thing about it.

BRIAN It was an open relationship.

BARRY But there was no conscious screwing around.

BRIAN Barry used to go away quite a lot for work and if he met somebody and had a little thing while he was away he would come back and tell me. You've always told the people you've met about us.

BARRY Yeah. I've never misrepresented the situation to anybody.

Would you ever three-way sex again?

BRIAN No!

BARRY No!

BRIAN The experience with Richard put us off that. It's just too complicated. We both feel we need to concentrate on the person we're with and we can only concentrate on one at a time.

People suggest that in gay relationships the sex will have dropped off after nineteen years.

BRIAN I think it does with everybody. I don't think that's specifically gay.

BARRY But we have sex about once a week.

Which is what heterosexual couples who have been together for almost twenty years normally report. Do you still have sex outside the relationship?

BARRY Not any more. The opportunities don't arise. My client base is all in London so I don't go out of town. I would describe our relationship as monogamous since the time we set up home on our own, with the occasional bit of casual sex on the side.

How often would you have had casual sex on the side?

BRIAN Very rarely.

BARRY I reckon I have had sex with only four other people since we became a twosome.

BRIAN About the same for me. It's just too much effort to go looking outside.

BARRY At the moment, we're emerging from a period where we were under a lot of financial and emotional stress. I have managed to steer us through that and we are coming out the other side relatively unscathed. I don't want to jeopardize anything by involving a third party in any way.

Brian, you have been diagnosed as HIV positive. How did that happen?

BRIAN We went through a rough patch some years ago, where things were going badly for us. I met an American and had a three-night stand with him. Two years later I got shingles and it affected me very badly. My company insisted that I go to their specialist in Harley Street. Barry took me there because my eye got affected. This guy examined me and sent me off down the road for a blood test. When we came back he said, 'The good news is that you fought off the shingles very successfully, your eyes are fine. The bad news is that you're HIV positive.' We didn't even know they'd done the test.

How did you feel about that?

BRIAN He fell to pieces. I don't know how I felt. The main thing was that we weren't quite sure how to get home. He was in a state of shock and I was still shaky, still swollen and ill. We were looking for a taxi and all the time I was feeling that this was ridiculous – the world really ought to come to a stop. We shouldn't be doing things like looking for taxis. But we gradually came to terms with it. He found it much more difficult to cope with than I did.

BARRY   It affected me in every possible way – in my work and the way that I approached life. I just got incredibly pessimistic. I kept having visions of waking up with him dead beside me. I became absolutely incapable of planning ahead. I didn't see the point. I was just going through the motions and getting more and more bogged down and depressed. I did so many things that were totally out of character for me. During the early part of the eighties, I had this thing about dressing well. I just let that go. I took three expensive suits to the cleaners, put them in the boot of the car and then forgot they were there. When I found them they'd got mildew. I went through a period where nothing mattered. Just waiting for him to become ill and die on me. It was very traumatic.

Were you looking for signs that he was ill?

BARRY   No, and I still don't, but I was expecting things to happen.

BRIAN   We did something wrong as well. After a while we decided that we ought to tell somebody in our group of friends because if anything happened somebody ought to know and tell all our other friends. Previously, we had decided we weren't going to tell everybody. The person we picked on was our friend John. I told him but he wasn't interested – his reaction was odd. It was as if I had told him we were going on holiday. We discovered shortly afterwards that he was dying of cancer. So we had only recently discovered that I was HIV, and were thinking I would die, and then we had to help nurse John when he got ill, had to watch him die and ultimately had to organize his funeral.

That must have put an incredible strain on you.

BRIAN   It was difficult because we were having to deal with all these other friends. John became the sole topic of conversation and everybody was upset. We didn't feel able to tell anybody that we had problems too.

What was stopping you from confiding in your friends?

BRIAN   We had been dubious about telling John, or anybody, and his reaction put the damper on telling anyone else. It was also partly because we didn't want them to change towards us, to start treating me like an invalid. Also, we thought, everybody's got their own problems and we didn't want to lay something else on them.

BARRY   As it turned out it was a bad decision because the result was a gradual social isolation. I was scared that people would say something and everybody was talking about HIV and Aids, and not realizing that we were affected by it. That made me uncomfortable. I was paranoid about it.

BRIAN   It was like coming out as gay all over again. When you decide to tell people you are HIV positive it's very like deciding to tell them you're gay. Beforehand, you worry how they're going to react – you try to predict how they might react and think about which friends you are going to tell. There is one major difference: when I came out at work it did cross my mind that I could be forced out of a job, if the reaction was bad, but I knew I could go and find another job. If I came out at work now and told people I was HIV positive and they reacted badly and forced me out, I would probably never get another job. If I got a negative reaction, and I don't think I would, I would have to search for another job saying why I was forced out. That's a big difference.

BARRY It came at a time when we were involved with a disastrous property deal with a third party and I had to take legal proceedings. It was dragging on, wearing me down, and costing the earth. I got to the point where I didn't care how it ended. I had had a company car and I gave it up for a motorbike. I think I was feeling, 'It's fun, it's liberating and I don't care if I live or die'. I'm still on the bike but my attitude now is one of tremendous respect for it because bikes can be very dangerous.

Barry, how did it affect your health?

BARRY I was drinking a hell of a lot more than I should have been. I discovered that I was diabetic. There had been a time when I was incredibly fit, going to a gym three times a week, and I just stopped exercising. I started to smoke again and I hadn't smoked since I was twenty-one! I'd used dope infrequently, and I started to use it fairly often. I felt lousy.

Did you have an HIV test?

BARRY The same day that Brian was diagnosed I was given the test. It was negative, which, oddly enough, didn't please me at all because my feeling was we may as well go out together. There was also relief that it wasn't me who had given Brian the virus. And I felt there was something desperately unfair about this because if anybody had had more partners it was me rather than him.

How did it affect the sex life between the two of you?

BRIAN It didn't really.

BARRY We just stopped having penetrative sex. Which was never a big thing, anyway, as far as we were concerned. Now and again I miss it and I have introduced condoms.

Did HIV place a barrier between you?

BRIAN Oh, no. I remember that after I was diagnosed we were sent to a doctor who tried to counsel us a bit. One of the things that he'd noticed was that gay couples supported each other whereas, in his experience, heterosexual couples had broken up. If they weren't married the woman or man who wasn't infected had shot off straight away. The gay couples stayed together. Certainly there was never a stage when I thought Barry was going to walk out and leave me.

Brian, it seems that you came to terms with it much quicker than Barry did. Why was that?

BRIAN I don't know. I'm an atheist and I always used to be scared of death. Yet, almost as soon as they diagnosed me, I stopped being frightened. I just carried on as if nothing had happened. It wasn't denial. I have heard HIV people and other people such as cancer victims who say, 'When this happened I stopped doing silly things and went round the world – and did all these things I wanted to do.' I was quite resentful about that because when they diagnose you they don't stick a million pounds in the bank. You've still got to work for a living, you've still got to pay the rent, and it did annoy me when I used to think that I would die and I wouldn't have time to do anything, to have a nice retirement and relax. Other than that I got on with it.

But you didn't, Barry. One would have expected it to be the other way round.

BARRY Apparently not. The symptoms I had are typical of the partner who is all right – I subsequently learnt that. I was incredibly angry because we had been robbed of our future together.

Did you feel guilty that you were going to survive?

BARRY   Yes, and enormously angry. It was just coming out in all directions. Never at him or the cat, but third parties would find me absolutely impossible.

Brian, were you able to support Barry?

BRIAN   Yes, but not enough in the end. After John had died and the dust had settled we decided to tell other people.

BARRY   I told one of our friends and you were very angry about it.

BRIAN   Because you told him without consulting me. He'd done it because he'd got depressed and needed to talk to somebody.

BARRY   I'd written to this friend – I hadn't phoned him or anything. This was a turning point because I'd reached desperation. He was the only person I could think of.

What reaction did you get?

BRIAN   What we would have expected. He was very sympathetic and concerned. He phoned up straight away and we had long discussions. He's a very close friend. We discussed it and Barry went for counselling. I agreed that he should go.

How did the counselling change things?

BARRY   It helped that I could talk to somebody about the feelings. I was showing all the symptoms of having been bereaved – related to the perceived loss of the future. My counsellor was transferred away and I was rather left in mid-air because I felt that I hadn't quite completed what I needed to do. A year ago I subsequently decided to see a hypnotherapist and he did for me in about five or six sessions more than all the counselling did. He managed to extract a great deal of the anger I was feeling and injected a more positive aspect into my life. I think I've been a bit better in the last year.

You've become involved with Aids organizations. How has it helped you?

BRIAN Barry heard about this men's support group starting up. I didn't want to go because I've never been into all this group-therapy stuff. I resisted going but eventually I went along. The first time we were there, there was a good discussion and a good feeling. We ended up being two of the most involved people in the group. Through that we met Jody Wells, an aggressive personality who can rub people up the wrong way. Barry liked him straight away and I didn't! He was getting people's backs up at this group because he wanted to tackle difficult subjects, like telling people they shouldn't bloody well be taking AZT. People who are taking AZT don't want to be told this.

BARRY Not telling, but wanting to discuss the pros and cons.

BRIAN He wasn't saying you ought to come off AZT but that, in his view, it was a bad thing because of the side effects. The sort of things he was saying then he was the only person saying. I had felt for some time that somebody somewhere should be gathering statistics and there should be a database to see how people who are taking drugs like AZT compare to people who aren't. Was there any concrete evidence that one was doing better than the other? Jody got his group off the ground, Continuum, and he's using it to put forward his theories and to publish things that don't get published elsewhere. We've been helping him. I feel that they haven't established a link between HIV and Aids, and when Jody and other people say this they're dismissed as cranks. Yet the more you read, the less evidence there seems to link HIV with Aids. Maybe they are chasing the wrong damn thing. My whole attitude to being HIV positive has changed. So many people have supposedly died of Aids who were never HIV positive, and so many people who are HIV positive show no signs of dying and their T-cell counts are fine.

BARRY There are too many anomalies and too many unanswered questions. We believe that the medical profession have jumped in too soon. It's not entirely their fault because if you consider the pressure that was put on them, particularly in the States, to do something about this thing called Aids. There was a bespoke drug on the market that had been around since the sixties which had been developed for cancer but was found to be too toxic – AZT. We believe that people on AZT show symptoms which are automatically being classified as Aids symptoms but others who have not gone on to this drug are not showing these symptoms – weight loss and the rest of it. In our experience with Continuum, we've seen people who are being diagnosed as HIV positive who are immediately having a T-cell count which is found to be low. They are being put on medication and within six months are dead.

BRIAN I said right at the beginning that I won't take any of these drugs. Pure instinct. It was only later that I started reading things that reinforced the decision.

BARRY Both of us are sceptics and never have taken the party line on anything whatsoever, politics or religion or anything else. Now we're beginning to find that so much of what was said about Aids five years ago, three years ago, even a year ago can be taken with a pillar or salt, because there are too many contradictions with the HIV equals Aids equals Death hypothesis. Instead of being treated for whatever *ad hoc* diseases are arising they are using a highly toxic drug to treat Aids.

Brian, do you still feel that you have a serious illness?

BRIAN I don't feel now that I've got a serious illness. I have to accept that my T-cell count is very low in comparison with other people.

What does that mean?

BARRY Nobody knows.

BRIAN It could mean I'm going to get ill. If they are right.

Could it just be that we're all different? Some people lose their hair and others don't, some people have high T-cell counts and others don't?

BARRY There's a thought in the medical profession that says, 'OK, you've got a low T-cell count, let's start administering drugs earlier rather than later.'

BRIAN I think the medical profession is barking up the wrong tree.

Brian, are you more prone to flu and things like that than other people?

BRIAN I get flu about once a year, I've always had flu about once a year. If it goes round I get it, I always have.

Beyond shingles have you had any other illnesses?

BRIAN Nothing else, that was the last.

BARRY I have been much more unhealthy in this period, but all my problems have been stress-related.

BRIAN Even shingles is stress-related and could have been brought on, for all they know, because at the time my company had just been bought and people were being made redundant. I was having to help these people. I was part of the administration side helping to hand over to the new bosses and I was suffering an awful lot of stress. When I first got shingles they said it was because I was under so much pressure. There was chickenpox in the building as well, so it may have not had anything to do with HIV at all, but they have noticed a link between HIV and shingles which is why they sent me off to be tested.

How do you feel about your health now?

BRIAN I am aware that, compared to other people, my T-cell count is low and that could be a problem. I could be susceptible to diseases, but I don't accept that they have proved a link between HIV and the low T-cell count. At one point my T-cell count dropped to 300 and that is the measure at which they start thinking about putting you on AZT.

What would a 'normal' figure be?

BRIAN Between 600 and 1200. They had been putting people on AZT if it dropped to 400 and they lowered it, and then 200 became the measure. I went down at one stage to 200 but the next time I went up to 400 which is the highest. I was at a low point and then shot up to high point. My average is about 300.

So you think you've got a good twenty years ahead of you?

BRIAN I don't think I can tell. I don't think it's worth worrying about any more than falling under a bus.

How has this whole saga changed your relationship?

BARRY   It has drawn us closer together. We've always been close but we're closer now than we've ever been.

BRIAN   I think that's right. I hadn't expected Barry to behave in any different way. I would have been absolutely shocked if he'd walked out the door, but over the years you think about what a big thing this all is. Although he was badly affected by it he fought and stayed by me. He tried to hide from me how badly he was affected because he didn't want to upset me. So even if it didn't bring us closer together it at least made us realize that we had something good.

What would be your advice on coping with HIV?

BARRY   We've started to run into real problems with insurance policies. When we had our financial difficulties we cashed in all my policies and kept Brian's because of the knowledge that he would never get another insurance policy – not the way that things looked then. He was going to act as a guarantor for a friend and even as a guarantor they sent him an insurance form which had some incredibly offensive questions. He promptly sent it back, saying that he flatly refused to have anything to do with the company. So we found another way round, but the problem comes up quite often.

BRIAN   I would not advise taking the test. There are all sorts of reasons why you should have safe sex anyway – all sorts of diseases around. Eating healthily and having a healthy lifestyle is common sense, anyhow. The test doesn't tell you anything helpful.

BARRY   You can't do much more with your life knowing that you're HIV positive.

But it seems it would have been better for you if you had told your friends and not carried the burden alone?

BRIAN   That's very important, but you have to be careful who you confide in. It's not just like coming out as being gay. You can lose friends – but I suppose if they're not going to stand by you they don't matter.

Trying to shield each other from your individual pain made it worse.

BRIAN   Yes. If you've got a long-term partner he's entitled to share the pain as well as everything else. It is a bad thing to withhold.

BARRY   Where we went badly wrong was in keeping friends at bay. We stopped going to see people, and we had been very social animals. We liked to do a lot of entertaining in our home but that just dropped off. I was becoming uncomfortable around the whole subject of Aids. I had turned myself into a liar, we were holding up a shield to a certain part of our life. Before, we had been completely open with all our friends. The shield got bigger and the retreat more dramatic. Finally there was nobody left. We were isolated until I realized we must break out because it was becoming damaging. I would stomp out of the room because there was something about Aids on the television.

BRIAN   Whereas I wanted to watch everything. I was curious, I wanted to know what was going on. Then, I'm the sort of person that would – if my leg had broken and my bone was sticking out I would be examining it.

So you've still got to be yourself, even if you have got HIV. You've got to react to it in the same way that you deal with all the other problems in your life. You have to use the same coping mechanisms you always use.

BRIAN   Absolutely.

BARRY   We went to a workshop run by this Australian. He talked about 'pointing the bone'. In aboriginal culture if somebody had the bone pointed at them it was a curse. It literally said that you were going to die. It was used sparingly but effectively because anybody who had the bone pointed at them upped and died. It was as simple as that, and this guy thought that HIV was the modern bone in civilization. Somebody digs around in your vein, comes up with HIV and, although they won't say it, the whole culture around it points to the fact that you will die. There's no cure.

BRIAN The thing that was said to us almost immediately was 'This does not mean you are going to die.' Doctors say that, all the people we've spoken to are told that, and then they immediately act as if they believe you're going to die. You hear them on the radio saying, 'All these people with HIV and they will be dying.'

On a different subject, you were responsible for setting up the Gay Humanist Group. Tell me about that.

BARRY Mary Whitehouse got up somewhere and said that what was wrong with this country is that it's being attacked by a secular homosexual lobby. I thought, What a very good idea! There were some gays in the secular movement but no secular homosexual lobby going out and telling her she was speaking clap-trap. She invented it by giving me and Brian an idea.

BRIAN I'd become involved with the National Secular Society as well and we were both writing for their magazine the *Free Thinker*. Barry liked the idea of a gay organization along the same sort of lines but I was totally opposed. He and five others agreed to have a meeting to see if they would or wouldn't set up a gay humanist group. On the day of the meeting he got flu and was too ill to go and, in what is typical humanist fashion, I went along to put his point of view across as well as my own. I ended up convincing myself that they were right and became a founding member, too. It was set up to opppose religious attacks on gays – most of the attacks on homosexuality were justified by people quoting the Bible. There was a gay Christian group then, but we felt it was necessary for somebody to say you don't have to fight these people on their home ground – one biblical quote with another biblical quote. It was time that someone said, 'We don't care what it says in the Bible. Come up with something else.'

BARRY   We had an international response! Enquiries from all over the world, even America.

Do you think that the reason you felt comfortable about being gay in the seventies when others were still closeted was because of the support you gave each other in your relationship?

BRIAN   Going on the streets on a gay march was quite something for me, and then coming out at work.

BARRY   We have always been regarded as a couple by the people in our workplace. Brian worked for a Japanese company and, although nothing was ever said as such, we would entertain his bosses.

BRIAN   Two sets of other couples started the Gay Humanist Movement with us – they are all still together.

Barry, is it you who instigates the closeness in the relationship?

BARRY   Am I the more emotional? Yes, I think I am. Brian does not give out much in the way of emotion and sometimes it irks me because he will get depressed and find himself unable to talk about what the problem is – although his bouts of depression were far worse when I first met him than they are now.

Brian, is it you who fights for the right of each of you to be independent?

BRIAN   Probably. I find it difficult to share emotion because of my upbringing. I was brought up in one of those left-over Victorian families. My mother was forty by the time she had me and she still had Victorian values. I don't ever remember having been hugged or kissed when I was a child. I remember being very embarrassed when my cousin's little girl was told to kiss me goodnight – I didn't know how to cope with that because nobody had ever kissed me before.

BARRY   Deep down, I'm still very insecure about a lot of things. I walked out of the psychiatrist's office having just been told I was the most normal homosexual man that he had ever met and I thought, The rest of my life begins here. Suddenly I was in the relationship with Richard. That lasted eight years, there was the three-year overlap and I've been with Brian for a further sixteen years. I have never been alone.

At each gay developmental stage we have a different task to learn. Although Barry's original relationship with Richard lasted eight years they never dealt with the gender-identity issues of the 'Nesting' stage, and got stuck on the ladder of gay coupledom. As the issues were not settled, the relationship floundered and collapsed.

In the shock period after Brian was diagnosed as HIV positive, he and Barry were unable to access their Collaborating skills. Even though they have started organizations together, they each retreated then into their own ways of coping. It was when they joined the support group together that they re-established Collaborating and dealt with their feelings about HIV. They are still using their skills by working together in the Aids Continuum organization.

STAGE 5 OF A GAY RELATIONSHIP
Adapting

Barry and Brian have entered the fifth developmental stage: I have called it 'Adapting' because it is more about coping with what life throws at a couple than internal changes within the relationship. It starts around fifteen years into the relationship and continues for about ten. By now each partner has given up any fantasy of how the other partner might be and tends to think, He's always been like this and probably always will be. Even his bad habits have stopped being irritants and become endearing. When someone stops trying to change us and accepts us the way we are, we feel appreciated and therefore more secure. Each partner has lost the fear that something could go drastically wrong between them; the threats are coming from outside. Brian and Barry feel that Brian's health is the only thing likely to separate them, it never occurred to them that the internal dynamics of their relationship would be affected by the diagnosis. Couples at this stage may feel contented; friendship and companionship are important. The journey from being two individuals to becoming a couple is complete: now the words used to describe possessions are 'ours' rather than 'mine' and 'we' rather than 'I'.

There is a darker side: the acceptance of each other can mean that a couple do not deal well with any underlying conflict and the unexpected life crises that occur. If you feel, 'That's how he has always been and nothing will change him', it is not that you avoid conflicts but that you do not even attempt to resolve them. The security can mean that the couple take each other for granted and because they expect their partner always to be there they may become less expressive and less likely to show affection. They become amiable flatmates rather than the two men who loved each other so deeply. Although I felt great love in the room while I interviewed Barry and Brian, when I listened to their taped conversation none of the warmth came over in the words they chose. Out of the strength of the security may spring the weaknesses; we need to be forever watchful. It is important to refuel the relationship after the 'Collaborating' stage where all the energy has been flowing outwards. Make certain that you show your affection, keep telling him that you love him. Even if your sex life is waning, try to sleep together so that cuddles and closeness flow between you.

During the 'Adapting' stage people often reach forty. It is now generally accepted that men go through a mid-life crisis, but this does not have to come at forty. It can come at any time when we stop and take stock of our lives. For some gays that can be in their late twenties or early thirties when the novelty of the scene wears off. When we are young we think that we are immortal and although intellectually we know we are going to die some day we do not emotionally believe it. When it dawns on us that our time on earth is limited, we consider what we have already done and what we still want to do. Gay men have fewer problems than heterosexual men at the mid-life crisis, because they are more likely to be in touch with their feelings. It is at this point that heterosexuals confront the gender issues that we dealt with much earlier in our lives. (Straight men try to get in touch with the nurturing side of their personalities just as their wives are exploring the assertive side of theirs.) Gay couples are more likely to have used their collaborating years to achieve their ambitions and explore new avenues which are not open to heterosexual men, who have to maintain high earnings to support their wives and children. For gay men the sadness can be more about sagging muscles and hair in the comb each morning – we live in a community which places much value on sex appeal and youth. Although those in relationships are less likely to feel so desperate about the passing years, they are not immune. Some people try and stave off middle age by re-creating youth (Barry's motorcycle is a good example) while others will compulsively trick to prove that they are still desirable. The mid-life crisis is just one of the issues that the couple have to face during the 'Adapting' stage. The only solution is to come to terms with the passing years and embrace the benefits.

We can no longer take secure employment for granted. The latest recession has affected all classes, and while in previous slumps companies 'let go' their factory workers and general office staff, this time the axe has fallen on senior management. The further up in a company, and the more successful someone is, the more likely that their job is a major source of identity.

Other couples find their lives changed when an elderly parent needs to move in with them. Most gay couples will have lived alone and, unlike straights who have children, have not learnt to share their partner. If there is a strong mother/son relationship, or if the son-in-law develops a close friendship with his mother-in-law, the other will feel left out. The elderly parent may also inhibit the couple's sexual desire.

One partner may develop a serious health problem – HIV and diabetes are just two examples – which may result in both learning just how important the other is. If they have been in a rut, the illness may jolt them out of taking each other for granted.

The skills needed for the 'Adapting' stage are flexibility and the ability to manage change – hopefully, the knowledge and trust they have already achieved will help the couple. It is remarkable how partners' in-built communication system allows them to pace problems so that they are not both in crisis at the same time: while Barry fell apart after the HIV diagnosis, Brian was functioning normally, ensuring that together they were not overwhelmed. But the psychological links between a well-established couple may be so strong that one may start to exhibit the feelings or symptoms you would have expected from the other – again, Brian and Barry illustrate this. Where one partner finds it difficult to express his feelings, their other half will pick up the unspoken cues and express them on their behalf – if one does not become angry the other will. This allows one partner to experience the anger second-hand without having to admit that he, too, is angry. To become properly balanced individuals, one has to stop pushing his feelings on to the other, while his partner has to stop accepting them. It is only when each person is clear about which feelings belong to him and which to his partner that the relationship problems can be understood and resolved.

If your relationship has to cope with a crisis it is of crucial importance that you continue to communicate with each other. Many of Barry and Brian's problems were caused because they did not confide in each other. We feel that our partner has enough to worry about without adding our own fears. There is also a natural tendency to withdraw into ourselves when we are overburdened. However, unless you continue to confide in each other, both of you may feel unsupported and alone. This is why tragedies, like the death of a child, can split up a couple rather than bind them together. As men we always think we have to solve the problem – but how can you solve a problem like HIV or a serious illness? Therefore we say nothing – but our partner will probably feel better if we listen and acknowledge how they feel. Often that is all that is needed. Remember that the 'supported' should try to give their partner an opportunity to offload too.

Does HIV cause Aids?

Although this is not within the brief of the book, I feel it important to comment on Barry and Brian's views. The world's experts on Aids seem to be falling into two camps: the non-believers and believers that HIV is the cause of Aids. Although the medical establishment, most doctors, nurses and health educationalists, feel the case is proven, a significant number of leading scientists do not. Recently 450 put their names to an open letter calling for a reappraisal of the conventional wisdom. It is felt by some that non-believers are dangerous because if people doubt HIV's role in Aids they may stop having safer sex and more lives will be lost.

Many believers feel that other contributing factors need to be present for the dormant HIV virus to attack the immune system. The non-believers give a wide range of alternative factors that could be the culprits: drug abuse (recreational and repeated use of prescription drugs), exposure to blood products, rectal exposure to semen, and auto-immune phenomena where the immune system becomes so confused that it starts to self-destruct. Repeated use of antibiotics to kill off sexually transmitted diseases could also be a factor, and countries where they are available without prescription tend to have higher rates of Aids deaths. Some scientists believe that sperm in the rectum may also suppress the immume system. Condoms and safer sex will help in both cases. We should think carefully about the abuse of poppers and other recreational drugs: if you are high you are less likely to use safer sex – but, more importantly, we do not know the long-term effects of using these drugs. Some researchers are again questioning whether poppers can harm the immune system.

The simple truth is that science can never be 100 per

cent sure about anything. Harry Rubin is a professor of molecular and cell biology at the University of California. He sums up the dilemma: 'It is not proven that Aids is caused by HIV infection, nor is it proven that it plays no role whatever in the syndrome.' While the debate rages, our lives need to go on. It is vital we continue to practise safer sex.

HIV positive people are under immense stress. Michael Ellner, a medical hypnotherapist, says, 'I have seen the constant terror, and the programming to get sick and die.' Those who are positive need to counteract this programming and choose to live. The alternative view that there is no link between HIV and Aids offers new hope. But no one, whether they know their HIV status or not, should expose themselves to infection and should continue always to practise safer sex. To scientists it is an academic debate; to us it is a matter of life and death.

'Trust me, I'm a doctor' is a seductive phrase. If you are HIV positive you must think carefully about the treatments you are offered. If a doctor suggests putting you on one of the experimental drugs, make certain that you give yourself time to discuss all the implications with your loved ones before you make your decision. Ring one of the Aids organizations for the latest drugs update. It is a positive step to stop being a passive patient and decide what is best for you. Take control of your own treatment.

HIV and Couples

Even if you are in a stable relationship you should still be practising safer sex. It is a fantasy to believe that if two people love each other, they can trust each other enough to have unprotected penetrative sex together. This is a complete fallacy. Love is not a protector against sexually transmitted diseases. If you love someone you will want to protect them. Always wear a condom. This is important even if you are both HIV positive. There are varying strains of the virus and it can constantly mutate. This means that if you have unprotected sex you could infect someone with a disease they might not have ultimately got from the breakdown of their own immune system.

If one or both of you is infected, do not isolate yourselves. Use the support services that have been set up by the gay community and the local health authorities. Most important, do not cut off from each other. Share your fears and pain as much as you share your joys and triumphs.

11

GROWING OLD TOGETHER

Although the popular image of gay men is that their relationships never last, the reality is that many have lasted over thirty years. When these partnerships first started, homosexuality was illegal and the couple faced imprisonment if the true nature of their bond was discovered. First out of necessity and then out of habit these men have been discreet about their love. However, they have a lot to teach younger gay men – if only that gay love can survive and thrive over three decades.

David comes from a traditional East-End working-class family; he was twenty-one and a policeman when he met his lover. Harry was thirty-two, had been to a top public school and was a consultant surgeon. The difference between their lifestyles and experiences could not have been greater, and the fifties was a period of social rigidity. Harry is now sixty-six and has retired while David still works part-time. If you did not know their backgrounds you would be forgiven for thinking they had the same upbringing, as David speaks with the clear, rounded tones of an actor playing Shakespeare. They live in an elegantly crumbling home full of cats and dogs. They have been lovers for thirty-four years.

DAVID   We were introduced by accident. I went to a steam baths and met a chap, we got talking and I was subsequently invited back to his flat in Hampstead. Later, on 22 December 1959 at ten past four, he visited me at work and brought a friend along with him. It was Harry, but I did not notice him at the time. At that meeting I was invited over for the weekend to his flat, only to discover when I got there that he had been out and had picked up someone he preferred. I was met with the statement, 'You'll have to sleep with 'im', and I've been sleeping with him ever since.

Harry, what was David like in 1959?

HARRY   Absolutely gorgeous.

DAVID   Do you want me to leave, because you might not do me sufficient justice?

HARRY   He had a heavenly smile and he was tall, a beautiful figure, and a lovely warm generous person. I quite easily fell in love with him. At that time, I had a two-roomed flat in Hampstead, which I shared with a New Zealander – he was somebody who used to like going out and looking for other people but didn't like me doing the same. I wasn't comfortable there. I was extremely comfortable with David; we used to meet whenever we could. We searched for about three years and eventually found this place where we are now. We moved in with very, very little indeed. David had a suitcase which he didn't unpack for months. In fact, he still hasn't properly unpacked it! He thinks it's a temporary relationship.

DAVID   I gave us three months, because I couldn't understand how anyone would want to stay with me. I was terribly insecure in those days and painfully shy. It didn't help that on the first night we were here, Harry said he couldn't understand why the New Zealander had disliked me so much, because, after all, I was one of hundreds. If I'm one of hundreds, I thought, I don't stand much chance and kept my suitcase packed for months afterwards.

HARRY I knew he was someone with whom I could get along very well. I felt that was a positive foundation. I've never been somebody who wants to chop and change for pastures new. So I really felt that I'd been lucky enough to find the person I would like to spend the rest of my life with, more or less.

What experience had you had of gay sex?

HARRY I was a late developer, but David started having a very active sex life from the age of about nine. I was one of those people who was terribly normal, I thought at the time. I was head of this and captain of that. I did have some problems with my sexuality because I fancied other boys and I discussed it with my tutors, who said, 'It's just a phase you're going through.' By the time I was twenty-nine and still hadn't changed I got very fed up. I was referred by a medical colleague in the army to the only sane psychiatrist I ever met. I went to him with a hypothetical question: if an officer had this particular problem how would he deal with it? He said he would send them to someone in town. I went to London and saw this very effeminate guy, and he said, 'Yes, you're gay. Get on with it!' Starting at twenty-nine in London, at that time, was not easy. I formed attachments with a number of people, one of whom was the New Zealander. We both felt we were not what the other person wanted. My view on relationships had always been that you can't hold somebody by refusing to let them see someone else. I suppose it was a reflection of my own lack of self-esteem because I never felt I was adequate to make up my half of a partnership.

David, what made you think that Harry was somebody special for you?

DAVID I never sat down and thought, Is he special? I met him and he became all-important to me. In the early days, before we got totally entangled as a couple, I used to find any excuse to telephone him. He was always on my mind. I just totally fell in love with him. In those days I had just come out of the police force and was bumming around a bit. I never thought of doing anything that would interrupt me seeing Harry. I was very active, successful in my athletic and swimming career, but Harry became the focal point of everything I thought and did.

What was it like being gay then, late fifties/early sixties, when you could be sent to prison for being gay?

DAVID I remember my first experience, knowing it was wrong. I never considered having anything more than a one-night stand. I was always attracted to men older than me, simply because I was so shy that I couldn't become the dominant person and the only dominant people I met were older. I never thought about the consequences of it being illegal because it was always a quick one-night stand, finished, and I never saw them again.

HARRY We were obviously aware that it was illegal, with David in the police force and me in the medical profession. But sex is a terribly vital thing, everything else goes into the background. In those days you couldn't even look at somebody in the street without running the risk of a charge of importuning. Being able to do something in private, where nobody knew anything about it, we felt comfortable and very lucky. But always we conformed, in that we weren't outrageously behaved, we knew we had to fit in at work. It was in the army that things got terrible for me. The workload wasn't that great and the sports availability was there all the time, so one was incredibly physically fit and, with that, one's desires became untenable – especially as I was surrounded by all these gorgeous creatures. I was so lucky that I didn't make a pass at somebody. I remember one poor boy, who was a corporal on my ward, he was had up because he was seen with somebody. He said to me, 'You'll find out one day, sir, what it's like.' I didn't protest much – I suppose I wasn't hiding it that well. I just said, 'Perhaps I would.'

So you were part of the process that expelled him from the army?

HARRY   No, I wasn't, but if I had been I would have proceeded, because that's what I would have had to do.

DAVID   Harry hadn't accepted that he was gay.

HARRY   I had boys making passes at me. There was one boy who was the chef in the officer's mess. He used to be nicknamed Garth after the man with the tremendous figure in the cartoon *Jane* in the *Daily Mirror*. He used to come to my room and say he had a pain in his tummy and could I examine him. I *really* didn't realize what he wanted! I was so naïve, and because I didn't know what it was, I was able to say, 'No, I'm sorry.'

From what you're saying, gay life used to be very furtive, with almost underground contacts.

DAVID   It was never furtive for me, as I was fairly outstanding. I was six foot four at the age of sixteen and had an Olympic swimmer's body. I was aware from a young age that if I fancied someone I could have them. It never occurred to me that other people were gay, I was the only gay person but other people liked sex.

It seems a strange thing to join the police!

269

DAVID   I never joined, my father signed me up. We didn't get on. He was an army man and I was a little soldier at the age of six – my life had been planned out by him. You have to keep in mind that my whole family came from the docklands area – as it was then, not now. I had been to a school where I had no interest at all. I was the only pupil who did no homework in the entire time I was there. I refused to take the examinations. In those days I regarded myself as an unintelligent cabbage, only capable of sports at which I did excel. I was in the police force for four years: I was an exception, they tolerated me because of my size. In my uniform I was seven feet tall, with the helmet on. I may be gay but I am masculine. There were two other tall policemen and when the three of us were together there were never any fights or trouble. They used to send for me if crowds got out of hand. Because I represented the police force in four major sports, I could do no wrong. I think I could have turned out in drag and still have been tolerated.

Were you ever involved with arresting somebody for doing something that you did when you weren't in your uniform?

DAVID   No, because in those days in the East End it was far more tolerant than people realize, when you were trolling around, unless you were very blatant. The police used to laugh and joke about it, in the nicest possible way. I remember only one occasion when I could have been embarrassed. I was walking with one of my colleagues along Stratford high street when a very effeminate chap on the other side of the road screamed out, 'Coo-eee'. I know it's been used ever since as a music-hall joke, but it happened. I turned straight to my colleagues and said, 'Do you know him?' The answer I got was, 'No, but I wouldn't mind!' I was never questioned about my sexuality – it was assumed that I was girl mad. I used to say, 'I had sex three times last night,' but I never said with a man or a woman. They never questioned it, and I just let them assume that I meant women.

Is it the case that when society didn't talk about things gay, although people were aware of it they were more tolerant? Then when it all came out into the open, the ambivalence came too.

DAVID It became obvious that as long as heterosexual people were not embarrassed, it made no difference to them. The moment a gay person embarrassed a heterosexual, the heterosexual would become aggressive.

HARRY There wasn't hostility to you being gay because nobody knew you were gay.

DAVID Sexuality didn't matter because nobody talked about sex then. It was a forbidden subject on all fronts. It was only with the recent 'we want equality' forces that people feel they have to admit they're gay when they go for a job and demand equal treatment. We had equal treatment because it was never a question of are you gay or are you straight.

What was it like living together, because there were great differences between the two of you?

DAVID Worlds apart.

HARRY As a child, he was a difficult little sod, while I had conformed. I was a good little boy, good at lessons, good at sports. Head boy at my prep school, and then on to a public school on a scholarship. I went to Tunbridge, so that, if the worst came to the worst and war broke out, I could walk home! I fitted in well. I became head boy again and was captain of rugger.

DAVID I think the main difference between Harry and me was that he was upper-middle class, all be it on the bottom rung, whereas I was on the bottom rung of the bottom class. I hated it, I wasn't a snob, but I just hated being from that area. I was never ashamed of my family, ever, but we were lower working class, we never knew where our next meal was coming from. What attracted me to Harry was his intelligence – he was, by the way, stunningly good-looking. The teachers used to say, 'People from your class never get anywhere.' I had it instilled in me that I was an idiot. In those days, in the East End, you had to be one of the flock, you had to follow in your father's footsteps who followed in his father's footsteps. However, I was different. Although even then I didn't speak like the rest of them, I was still down there with the lower working class. When I met Harry it's not surprising that I kept my suitcase packed for months afterwards. We were not on the same intellectual level. He had a background which I would have loved to have had. One of tolerance and individuality, one which I could never get.

Were there misunderstandings between you because you had had such different experiences of the world?

HARRY   Not really. Initially David was fairly intolerant of a whole range of things. If he had a driver in front of him who was driving stupidly, he would really 'get out of his pram' and want to go and beat them up. I would say, 'It's not important!'

DAVID   I remember consciously trying to make myself sound more intelligent because I felt that with my limited education I had nothing to offer. I do remember, three weeks after we moved into the house here, realizing that I had been walking around it never leaving him alone and just talking, talking. Trying to prove, I think, that I was not as unintelligent as he might think I was. Finally, I thought, 'Oh shit, I've talked non-stop for three weeks,' and that was it – I clammed up. I remember feeling insecure, that I couldn't hold his affections because there was no substance to my own background.

HARRY I couldn't see any of these faults, if that's what they were supposed to be, and I still can't. What I do remember was that his East-End way of speaking would sometimes come out and I had to try delicately to correct his 'weres' and 'wases'. I tried desperately hard not to do it in a way that would make him upset. It didn't worry me but I realized it would worry him if we were in circumstances where somebody else would think, 'Oh-oh.'

DAVID But at the same time I never denied where I came from, just hated people forgetting.

HARRY We did go through a number of problems, early on, when we were here – other people staying in the house who had been friends of mine rather than friends of David, and they were quite difficult.

DAVID Let me interrupt here. Harry had met these friends comparatively recently on a gay level so they were all somewhat jealous. One actually said, 'I want you out because I want him.' None of my friends came across with me. I left them all behind. They weren't particularly gay friends, but I cut all ties. All the friends we had here were originally sexual partners of Harry, past lovers, and I never knew when one was trying to usurp me. Harry was unaware of all of this.

HARRY One of them did have a lot of mental problems. He became vicious. A lot of phone calls throughout the day, our telephone number was written up on cottage walls.

DAVID All over the country.

HARRY Ashby-de-la-Zouch, Leicester Square underground station, everywhere!

DAVID Always 'for a good time ring David', never Harry, and our telephone number. But this man also rang my mother and told her about me, making her very ill. She refused to meet Harry for five years, but being a good old-fashioned East-End lady, to her doctors are on a pedestal that reaches up to the clouds. She came here for the first time and asked 'What should I call him?' and I said, 'Harry,' and she said, 'But he's a doctor!'

HARRY Two things helped in my relationship. One was that I found out that his youngest sister wasn't an idiot but was deaf. The second was his mother discovered that I had been hop-picking, and East-Enders go hop-picking. She realized I was human, after all! Ever after that if David went home on his own, she always looked past him and said, 'Where's Harry? You haven't had a row, have you?'

DAVID 'And if you have, you go back and make it up.' She adored him.

If one of the secrets of gay life in the early sixties was blending into the background, with your age differences and class differences, the assumption would be that you were having sex, because what else could these people have in common?

HARRY Yes, and right to the very end, there were certain places where I couldn't take David as my partner: medical dinners, things like that.

DAVID But they all expected me to give you a lift. They all knew, but we did not embarrass them by turning up as a gay couple.

How did you feel driving home? Everybody knew of your existence but you were not allowed in for the lovely meal.

DAVID No, no, you've got it wrong. It was not a question of not *allowed*. I didn't want to, because if I turned up I would have been embarrassed. This feeling that I'm not intellectually up to Harry's circle stopped me.

What about the age difference? Did that cause problems?

HARRY   I don't think so. David's always been very grown up. When I was trying to be logical about my sex life, and had only been active for a while, I thought, This is silly, going round with lots of people, I have to settle down. I had four or five people I was particularly attached to, and I thought I'd better settle down with the person who was nearest my age, which was the New Zealander in Hampstead, but that didn't work out at all. I never thought of David as being a twenty-one-year-old, I just thought of him as being David. I never thought of him being younger than I was and never thought of myself as older than he was. It hasn't seemed to present much difficulty up to now. We've had similar likes, although I haven't been able to share some of his enthusiasms.

DAVID   I think the difference in our age was a lot less because my father was an army man and I was an adult from the age of ten.

Were you looking for a father substitute?

DAVID   No, not at all. Pre-teens I was already having sex. I knew that if I was caught I would get into trouble but not as much trouble as the man I was having sex with. I knew that there was a difference between furtive sex behind the cinema and a lover – and that's what I wanted, a lover. I wanted from sex someone who was experienced, fully developed, emotionally and physically, and it was always somebody older than me. I wanted them to show me what to do, I didn't want to take the lead. It had been one-night stands, very rarely in the bedroom and never an act of love. With Harry it all changed, it was certainly far more emotional. Right through our entire lives I can still go out with someone for sex, come home and still be in need of love. Sex with love is different from sex for sex purposes – there's tremendous emotional fulfilment with your partner.

HARRY   Always with David, whatever I do is the best. When I was having sex with other people I was always looking forward to getting back to David, not that I do it so much now.

So why did you bother?

DAVID   The thrill of the hunt.

HARRY   Somebody finds you attractive.

DAVID   Let's get this correct, there is not a man on this planet who would not go with somebody else if they were free to do so. If Harry and I were together and I got pleasure from someone else, then he's happy for me because I'm happy. Sex means nothing if it's entirely physical, it's like going to the cinema with a friend. It's a release, great fun, it does not have to be a betrayal. If you lie about it and don't tell them, that's the betrayal.

HARRY   We nearly got into a no-go situation with one boy David met and brought back.

DAVID   If it's the one I'm thinking of, it's the only hiccup in thirty-four years.

HARRY   I fell madly in love with this guy, who was madly in love with me, but I hadn't stopped loving David. I was really being greedy. I got into a terrible state, floods of tears. I didn't want to leave David and we couldn't possibly have had a *ménage-à-trois*. Eventually the boy said no, he had gone off me, and I went into more floods of tears. It was a very draining thing, but David was strong enough to sit it out. Thank goodness he did.

276

DAVID   I thought that all the time we came back and told each other about it, fine. The first time that he went out, or I found that he had gone out, and not told me about it, I knew there was some reason for him not telling me and that reason was he didn't want to hurt me – that relationship went deeper.

What's your sex life like now? Do you still make love to each other?

DAVID   Not a great deal, but it's superfluous. I couldn't imagine life without Harry. I'm still vaguely interested in going around but not much.

HARRY   We have always slept together.

DAVID   The comfort of our relationship is simply being together in bed. In our lives we're together an awful lot now, and it gets better.

HARRY   In the last few years we haven't been anywhere near as interested in outside sexual activities, particularly since Aids.

DAVID   I had been very ill, passing out and falling over, they had done every test and could think of nothing else, until finally they asked right at the end if I was homosexual, checked me for HIV and I was clear. Since then, when I've been back to hospital I always tell them at the outset that I'm gay. The last time was in front of fourteen students. I must admit that it took perhaps more courage then, in front of all those students. I knew I would have to have internal examinations, and before I started I said to the professor, 'I have to tell you that I'm gay, I've been with one partner for thirty years and very few in the last ten years outside the relationship.' When I looked round, I would think about half of the students were blushing – all the men, not the women.

How did you feel?

DAVID Good. It made no difference.

How has retirement changed your relationship?

DAVID Sexually, we matured. I still have a fairly high sexual drive, but not the intense I-must-have-sex feeling. I can now look and say, 'I fancy that.' Fifteen years ago I would think, 'I fancy that,' and go and try and get it. You go to any couple, gay or heterosexual, who've been together for thirty-four years, and ask, 'Do you still have sex?' If they say, 'Yes,' and if you ask, 'More than once every six months?' and they say 'Yes', you're talking to a pair of liars. They may have sex but it won't be with each other! When I was young, the only way that I could show Harry my feelings was sex, but now I'm experienced enough to know I don't have to keep on reassuring him and there are other ways I can show my love. Likewise I have accepted that Harry still loves me, but he doesn't have to show me by sex, which he used to have to do. The intensity of my feelings for Harry has never changed: originally sex was dominant on an equal level with companionship and everything. Now everything is still intense, but the sex side has mellowed out. Both of us physically can't keep up, but the emotional side if anything is getting more and more intense all the time. For me.

HARRY I would say the same sort of thing. Sexually not as active as we used to be. But my love for him is as great as ever and I don't think of anything without thinking of doing it with David.

Is there a difference as you come into the later part of your life together? Have you become closer, in comparison with your thirties and forties when you're out competing in the world? You've now folded back into a life here together.

HARRY My giving up work made a big difference. I don't go out every day, so that I look forward even more to being with David when he comes in from work. I listen to all his stories about what's happened.

DAVID   It has got better because Harry was always on emergency call. It made our social life difficult to plan. He was always relaxed but now he's so laid back that we're both enjoying it.

HARRY   We're never out of each other's sight.

DAVID   Our love is an accepted thing, it's a lovely feeling.

HARRY   We're just us. I'm constantly amazed by David's abilities. This boy from the East End has a very good voice. If only there had been some music training at his school he would have made a big success of singing. I did everything in my power to help and encourage him. I took him to the music critic of the *Sunday Times*, who said David had the third best voice he had ever had in his house but no control over it.

DAVID   He was the foremost music critic in the Western world. Harry doesn't know this, but he took me to one side and said, 'Yes, you have one of the three finest voices in Europe. But you have no musical background. If you decide to take it further it will disrupt your life.' Now, that meant I had to choose whether to go forward and disrupt my life, or have a domestically happy life.

HARRY   To a certain extent I was aware that with every successful person in stage and theatre it has to be 95 per cent of their lives. I couldn't cope with the idea of only having 5 per cent of David's life.

DAVID   And I couldn't cope with having only 5 per cent of my life with Harry. It was a conscious decision that I would not take it up professionally.

Have you become more like each other?

DAVID   Without any conscious effort, Harry has influenced me more than anyone else ever could have done. He was intelligent, sensitive, generous, everything that I would have liked to have been.

How has David influenced you, Harry?

DAVID   You can only have one person in the relationship with a very strong character, the other is a somewhat pliant character. I truly believe that.

HARRY   Which is the pliant one?

DAVID   *Me!*

HARRY   Not particularly pliant, he's more of the leader now. He's the one with his voice, who does all the talking, he's the one who makes a lot of the arrangements in our lives.

How do you both feel about death?

DAVID   Inevitable.

HARRY   I can't imagine how I would exist if David were to die, because my life has revolved around him. Death is something we're becoming increasingly aware of — so many of our friends have died. We are trying to make arrangements, as much as we can, because the house had to be in my name. When we moved here, it was practically impossible for two males to take out a mortgage. There was no choice. I had more money than David, I was the provider. But a few years ago when house prices were at their highest, if I had died David would have had to sell it.

DAVID   I'm not an official partner with Harry. Although he's left everything to me as a 'friend', unlike a husband or wife I will have to pay tax. Therefore I will almost certainly lose my home after all these years because I'm not officially his partner. It is becoming slightly worrying for me. Slightly, because Harry's family all live into their nineties and mine only into their fifties. I'm now fifty-five and the longest-lived member of my family is sixty-four. I intend to outlive them but if by chance Harry does die before me that is where I start to worry. I can't imagine living without Harry because he's an integral part of my life, and secondly everything is in his name and if I get whacked for tax then I will have to sell my home. It has been a worry – he can't even sign over half the house to me because I would have to pay tax, which I can't afford. I can't even accept half as a partnership arrangement. Our friends in Denmark are officially registered as a couple and don't have these problems.

HARRY   One of the things that has happened in recent years is one's ability to discuss that one is gay with other people, like the bank. As little as five years ago, I think it would have caused the other person embarrassment and I would have got embarrassed because of that.

Has the fact that both sets of your parents have died made you more aware of the issues around death?

HARRY   My parents died of old age. Mother died aged eighty-seven in a nursing home – we felt we couldn't look after both of them here but we did look after my father. David was an absolute angel looking after my father who was set in his ways.

DAVID   He was an old bastard. Delightful.

HARRY   He would correct David's English and he always had to have the same breakfast. Prunes. A fried breakfast and five prunes. If you gave him six he would leave one and if you gave him less he would complain.

DAVID   I was on shift work so I was able to care for him much more closely than Harry could because he was out all day.

HARRY   That put a great strain on our lives. I felt it might tend to separate David away because my father was becoming incontinent and emotionally upset because he was conscious of what was going on. It was heavy going but that sort of experience either drags you apart or brings you even closer together.

DAVID   It was a separate thing from our relationship. One of my favourite memories of our relationship was shortly after we moved in here when we used to go down every Sunday to visit his mother and father. It was the same routine: Harry would go out into the garden with his father and walk around discussing the flowers and I would sit with his mother. A charmer. We started talking about Harry and I'll put it in her words. 'Of course, we're very proud of our Harry, we're just a tiny bit disappointed that he never married and had a family.' With that she stretched across, patted my knee and said, 'But I know you make him happy.' She was in her seventies. It must have been difficult for her. They made me feel fully accepted – in many ways I was closer to Harry's father than I was to my own.

HARRY   For me, I think one of the nicest things that has happened is getting more and more accepted by your family. It's delightful with his sister . . .

DAVID   Hang on, let me explain. First of all I did not tell the family, the immediate family – my mother, father, and two sisters I kept in touch with – but the other aunts, cousins, who in an East End family are very close, I cut them all off because I didn't want any embarrassment for them. When my mother died, I thought, This is it, I couldn't care less now, I'm going to tell the family because my mother's death brought home to me for the first time, that one of these days I could die and leave Harry behind. I didn't want the usual family descending and taking over. I decided to tell my sister first. I asked if we could be alone so she sent the kids out and there was just her, myself and her dog. I remember finding it difficult to have this conversation. I turned my back on her and looked out of the window and said, 'I have something to say but I'm finding it difficult and a little embarrassing.' The dog started to bark like crazy, and I ummed and I ahhed. After what seemed an eternity, Vera said, 'Hold everything. This dog barks at two kinds of people, postmen and gays, and you're not a postman!' Subsequently we went to a wedding party and the dog was standing in the middle of about two hundred people and barking at one man. I looked at my sister and she said, 'Yesss!' So a dog told my family that I was gay. Obviously they had their inklings – you don't live with a man from the age of twenty-one to your fifties without them having the slightest suspicion – but it was never discussed. The subject was always skirted around. We have now started meeting up with the rest of my family and they have all accepted Harry as my partner.

What has been the biggest problem you've had to deal with?

DAVID Our problems have not been from heterosexuals – we've always been accepted by them – but from other gay people. I know of five occasions where people have tried to split us up, and I've had a number of people say to me, 'For goodness sake, leave him,' and they've all been interested in Harry. So the aggro we have had has been from gay people not heterosexuals.

STAGE 6 OF A GAY RELATIONSHIP
Repartnering

Harry and David have been together for over thirty years and have now reached the final stage in their relationship, 'Repartnering'. This last milestone in a gay relationship is normally reached after about twenty-five years. Couples find a new closeness and togetherness that almost harks back to the early days of bonding and limerence. It is almost as if they have come full circle and are as romantic as the couples just starting out. Although there is an echo of 'Blending' the feelings then were based on the couple's *expectations*. 'Repartnering' is based on *reality* and a *shared history*. After the years of forging a living and achieving in the outside world a new commitment to each other develops and the partners become more important to each other than anything else.

To test this, I asked Harry and David to draw a commitment graph. Time is along the bottom axis and levels of closeness plotted on the vertical axis. They both had a steep gradient at the beginning when they first met and fell in love. To represent their life together now, Harry drew a line which showed a continuously increasing closeness line. Since retirement, he has fully entered the 'Repartnering' stage of his life.

I found meeting David and Harry deeply reassuring. Like many gay men, I am concerned about growing older but this couple showed me that there are benefits.

As you become older you have more control over your life and yourself; you are wiser and, hopefully, more financially secure. You become less concerned with what other people think of you and begin to live more and more by your own values. For gay men this means we are far more willing to stand up for our rights and to stop ignoring society's subtle put-downs. Harry and David grew up when you could be imprisoned for loving another man, and it is not surprising that they have been reticent in telling everybody that they are a gay couple. Yet now they can talk to the bank, discuss their sexuality with a roomful of student doctors, and they confused the woman who came to collect their census form because when they explained the nature of their relationship she could not work out which box to tick. This added confidence in being gay is partly because society has become more open and accepting but mostly because Harry and David care less about embarrassing people. The one sad feeling I was left with was about how much of their lives they had spent trying not to embarrass straight people so that they did not become the target of heterosexual aggression and prejudice. They used the word 'embarrass' nine times in the interview. Straight people, though, sometimes need to be embarrassed because this is the only way to make them aware of the problems gay couples face. For example, gay couples should be allowed to register officially in Britain so they are not punished by our tax laws.

During 'Repartnering', the couple assume that they will stay together until one partner dies, which makes their time together even more precious. Remembering the past is important and the couple value their shared history: David and Harry tell the story of how they first met as if it were just yesterday. It is in marked contrast to the 'Collaborating' stage which allowed each half of the couple to develop a successful career and explore outside interests. 'Adapting' is mainly about coping with the slings and arrows of fate but if the couple overcome these they grow closer, foreshadowing the restoring of the relationship at the final stage. With 'Repartnering' the couple achieve a return on the investment they have put into the relationship and each other, with rich emotional rewards, while the merging of money and the success of their collaboration makes them financially secure.

Any problems at this stage of the relationship are often outside the couple's control, like health. Yet it is vital that you keep an open mind to continue to grow and learn. Flexibility is still vital to keep the relationship fresh. 'Repartnering' couples sometimes find it difficult to compromise and like a 'Blending' couple they are so close and so important to each other they may sometimes deliberately avoid conflict. It is important also to let go of the past and accept changes. For example, when we become adults it is no longer appropriate to stamp our feet when we become frustrated because this is child-like behaviour; in the same way we have to reassess and judge what is appropriate as we enter this stage of our lives.

A stereotypical view of an older gay man is the sexually frustrated queen, leading a lonely isolated life. I hope I've helped to dispel this myth. Harry and David not only have each other, they are still finding new sexual contacts. Although they do not want sex as often, they enjoy it more together because of the depth and emotion that is layered into their lovemaking. You do not cease to be attractive as you grow older – perhaps there are fewer men beating a path to your door, but as your needs are less, you require less choice. It is only when you feel ugly and unwanted and you start to project that message to others, that it becomes self-fulfilling. Harry and David have also unhooked all the issues that people place on sex, which make it a more difficult arena than it needs be. In the early days of their relationship, it was used as an expression and proof of their love; now they have other ways of communicating this. If you use sex to prove to yourself that you are desirable, lovable, successful, valuable, or whatever, you are more likely to be fazed by ageing, because you have unrealistic expectations of sex. There are better ways of feeling good about yourself.

David and Harry exemplify the good that springs from a gay relationship: with Harry's support the young East-End boy with no formal education rose to the top echelons of the London Ambulance Service.

Differences

Gay couples need to be twice as good as heterosexuals to survive, because they have to cope with all of society's pressures with few of the supports that straight couples take for granted. I was interested to discover from Harry and David how they dealt with the class and age difference.

Gays are often better at coping with such variations than their heterosexual counterparts. A man and a woman have to handle the polar difference of their sex, and extra issues of race, religion, age and class may overburden the relationship. Men and women frequently show contrasting attitudes to sex, careers and family, which they need to communicate to each other. Two men are less likely to have fundamentally different views on these important subjects, but it goes deeper than this: gay men are more tolerant of nonconformity. We have spent so much time and energy fighting for the right to be different *ourselves* that we are more likely to offer the same to other minority groups.

Although differences can become problems for any couple, conversely in a gay relationship they may be a source of strength. We need differences to help us grow in a relationship, and to make it more interesting: my partner is German, so I am learning a new language and finding out about another culture. In counselling heterosexual couples I often find that the couples who benefit most are those who in some way take on the values traditionally associated with the opposite sex. The women learn the 'male' value of independence and the men the 'female' value of interdependence. In a gay context, a younger man can gain from the experience of an older one and the older from his younger partner's curiosity and openness to new ideas. This is just one example of how differences can make us question ourselves and help us grow.

How do you cope with differences?

Most of the couples in the book are dealing with differences: class, age, cultural, regional differences. Although on the surface some couples seem similar, if you look deeper you discover otherwise. For example, Jamey and Bill (see Chapter 2) were brought up by families with opposite ideas about closeness.

If differences are significant, and gay people more attracted to them than heterosexuals, we need to know how to make them work for us rather than let them split us up.

(1) *Accept the differences*. You might have chosen your partner because of how different he is from you – either consciously or subconsciously, but a younger partner might want to go out more often; different races have alternative values about families. When problems arise, try not to lose sight of the reasons why you first fell in love.

(2) *Don't try to change your partner*. Coming from the East End is an important element of David's identity. It is one of the ways in which he defines who he is. Although he wishes he had had an upbringing more like Harry's, he never denies where he came from and hates people forgetting it. If you try to change your partner, he is likely to cling to his own values even tighter.

(3) *How big are the differences anyway?* Sometimes it

seems that one partner is much more advanced in one area than the other: David thought that Harry was the confident one, whereas in reality Harry also lacked self-esteem and thought that he was not adequate to make up half of a partnership. We choose people who are normally just a couple of rungs up the ladder from us, who are better at helping us climb than someone shouting instructions from the top. From where we are low down the ladder they might seem confident, but they have similar doubts. It is important to understand that an apparent gulf may not be as wide as it first appears.

(4) *When we feel accepted, changes are possible.* It is often only when the pressure relaxes that we decide it is safe to become different. You cannot nag or cajole somebody, they must choose for themselves. By accepting David as he was, Harry gave him the space to adapt and grow. With David's singing, Harry supported and helped him, never standing in his way. I wonder if David would have chosen not to pursue this career if Harry had attempted to discourage him.

Over time, couples in successful relationships become more like each other. A stranger would not notice that Harry and David came from different backgrounds. We take on board our partner's better characteristics, and knock off each other's rough corners. Often we integrate into our own personality the part of the other person that attracted us to them, and feel more balanced, whole and fulfilled.

Making a will

This is not just a topic for older gay couples but is relevant to everybody. Making a will is the only way to avoid the heartache of this letter to *Gay Times*:

My lover died unexpectedly at a tragically early age. We had lived together for nine wonderfully happy years. After going through the trauma of the funeral arrangements, I then found myself forced to make arrangements to sell the house we had lived in for the last four years. Because my lover had not made a will, her share of the house was to be sold at the request of a distant relative. I could not afford to buy out my lover's half-share, so I found myself having to leave the place that we called home. At first I was bewildered and shocked. But now, several months later, I find myself growing increasingly angry at the absurdity of the situation. And also the obvious discrimination against us because we were a same-sex couple. Had we been a boy/girl couple then I'm sure that I would have enjoyed the protection of the law and not been a victim of it.

Your will is the legal document that expresses how everything you own should be distributed on your death. If you fail to make a will, you will be 'intestate' and the State will decide for you who gets your property. Unfortunately the law does not recognize gay partnerships: you may have been together for twenty or thirty years but the man you leave behind will have no rights in your share. If you fail to make a will, your parents, brothers, sisters and even distant relatives will benefit, not your lover. Although it is possible to write a 'Home' will, it is full of pitfalls. The rules for ensuring that your will is valid and effective are strict and complicated. Terms that you or I feel are explicit have different meanings in law from everyday use. For example, you may write that you leave all your money to your partner. Which money do you mean? The money in your pocket, your bank account, or the insurance policy? If your home-made will fails, the intestacy rules apply. It is best to consult a solicitor or professional who specializes in wills and probate: some companies advertise in the gay press, and I recommend that you use their services as they have accumulated experience on the problems that can arise when a gay man dies. It is also of vital importance that you explain fully your circumstances and sexuality to the person who will be writing your will, or they will not be able to foresee all the possible complications. If you choose a company that advertises in the gay press, or has been recommended by your local gay switchboard, you will feel more comfortable discussing the true nature of the relationship between you and your partner.

You need to consider whether your will may be challenged by your family. Although you have no obligation to leave anything to your relatives, if you fail to make provision for someone who is financially dependent on you or has an interest in your assets they could challenge the will. Their success will depend in part on how long you and your partner have been together and whether your money and house are the fruit of the relationship, gathered by the sweat of your own brow, or whether the house or most of the money to buy it has been inherited from the family. If the latter applies and your partnership is relatively new, it may not be straightforward. You should talk through the implications of your will with your family, and anybody who may feel they have a right to object, so that you know their views in advance of visiting the solicitor. This allows you fully to brief your adviser and help them to draft a will that makes certain that the people you wish to inherit are not left with the burden of a court case.

If you fail to make a will, your family may take charge after your death. Your partner may even be excluded from the funeral service or not accorded his rightful place as principal mourner. Some clergymen disapprove of homosexual love and may express this at the funeral by leaving out references to the surviving partner or by coolness after the service. The Lesbian and Gay Bereavement Project report some horror stories, including one about a vicar who prayed that the deceased would be forgiven for his deviant lifestyle! If you choose not to have a religious ceremony the British Humanist Association will carry out your wishes. As humanists do not believe in an afterlife, their funeral services are conducted to comfort the living and to celebrate the life that has ended. Both are important in helping your loved ones' healing process. When you make your will, name your lover as your executor so that he can determine the manner of the funeral. You can also lay down the type of service you would like, and whether you wish to be buried or cremated.

The Lesbian and Gay Bereavement Project not only offers support to a gay person whose partner has died but also gives advice aimed at avoiding the problems I have outlined. They suggest that homes, whether owned or rented, should be in joint ownership or on joint agreements so that the surviving partner can continue to live there. They also advise you to have everything of value in both names, which includes building society and bank accounts so that in an emergency both of you can draw money. Otherwise all assets are tied up until the will has been granted probate, leaving the bereaved with no ready cash. If you wish to keep your money separate, you could each have a joint account with the understanding that you can only draw on the other's account under these special circumstances.

If you have to be admitted to hospital you should always name your lover as your next of kin, no matter how minor the operation or how short you expect the stay to be. This means that even if visiting is restricted to family, your partner will still be allowed at your bedside and will be consulted if decisions need to be made.

You should also discuss your will with an accountant to make certain that you minimize the tax paid on your estate.

Any life assurance or death-in-service insurance, plus pension policies, should be written in trust so that they fall outside your estate when you die. This leaves them free of inheritance tax liability and gives your partner some immediate funds to provide living expenses. If you are in a position similar to David and Harry's, where all the money is in one person's name, you should take advice on how to minimize the problems. As I have said before, the law does not recognize same-sex couples and afford them the same protection as married couples, and you cannot 'gift' your entire estate without incurring a tax bill on anything above the inheritance-tax threshold. In Britain, it is possible to make small annual gifts to your partner without incurring inheritance tax. You can also make 'lifetime transfers': the first band has no tax liability, and in the rest the tax is levied at a lower figure. However, to be fully effective you must survive for seven years after making the transfer. There is a sliding scale of reliefs within the seven-year period. The problem is we can never predict when we are going to die and the transfer is not effective with the 'matrimonial' home. Take advice!

We find a million excuses for not getting round to making our wills. It seems ghoulish to plan our own funeral and we hope subconsciously that by ignoring it, we can deny it. However, all gay people should make a will, particularly couples. Remember, it is the only way that *your* wishes have any effect after you are gone.

12

COMMUNICATION: THE TWELVE GOLDEN RULES

Good communication is one of the main ingredients of a successful relationship. First, I have outlined two syndromes which illustrate a specific failure of communication within a couple. The Twelve Golden Rules that follow will help resolve both these problems and any others you may experience in communicating with your partner.

The Babes in the Wood Syndrome

It goes without saying that we do not like to experience difficult or painful feelings, which is why humans will find ways to avoid them, most of which are subconscious. In the Babes in the Wood story, all the dangerous and unpleasant things are in the dark wood; the Babes are pure, innocent, and huddle together for comfort. In the story they are so similar that we do not know even their names. They are not so much a couple but a two-headed person. Couples in this syndrome blame all their problems on the outside world.

They never argue: it is not their partner's fault, but that of the in-laws, fate, the neighbours or a difficult job. It sounds convenient, but problems cannot be solved because they do not tackle the source. It is like treating a bunion with a throat lozenge. The couple's relationship will be full of suppressed feelings but none will ever be resolved because the partners are always so nice to each other. It is often a boring relationship: an interesting one, just like a film, play or book, needs conflict. *Gone With The Wind* would have been very dull if Rhett Butler and Scarlett O'Hara had sat at Tara sipping mint juleps and discussing what to give Melanie and Ashley when they came over to supper. We would have closed the book faster than Scarlett could say 'Fiddle-dee-dee'. Instead we are shown Rhett trying to dominate Scarlett, who will not admit to herself the depth of her true feelings for him. Scarlett thinks herself desperately in love with Ashley and is willing to betray her friend Melanie; many layers of *conflict* all set against the even greater conflict of the civil war.

Adam, in Chapter Eight, attributes to his ex-wife all the blame for the pain that he and his children have gone through. In his mind, she is the bad one and he the good. Admittedly, from his telling of the story, she has let the children down badly. However, a more balanced approach would look at why she needed the affair that split them up. Throwing her out of the house on the night he found her in bed with the other man is a good example of pushing out the conflict rather than dealing with it. Adam must take some of the responsibility for the clinging of his children, their anxious attachment. He could have allowed his ex-wife to stay long enough for her to explain to them why she was leaving. Adam should be accepting some of the bad feelings rather than blaming them all on his ex-wife. Until he owns some of the pain, it will be difficult for him to deal with his feelings and to move on.

The Babes in the Wood syndrome is a trap that is easier

for gay couples to fall into, because we need to huddle together for protection from the dark threats of homophobia and the way that society does not value our relationships. Although it is a common problem also for heterosexual couples, it is a real trap for gay couples because this is the way we often experience the world, and the resonance can often ensnare us.

The Tom and Jerry Syndrome

This is the opposite of Babes in the Wood. There is plenty of conflict but, like the cartoon cat and mouse, the partners chase each other in circles and nothing is resolved. They only stop or call a truce when they are too exhausted to continue fighting. Although both might feel that they are trying to deal with their problems or become closer, in reality they are as close as Tom and Jerry.

As I have explained, getting close to somebody is dangerous: it is only our nearest and dearest who can hurt us. Yet warmth and closeness is something we all crave. It is a contradiction: we need to be intimate but are frightened of being too intimate. In the Tom and Jerry syndrome the couple are for ever chasing each other – but in the cartoon Tom never catches Jerry!

The Twelve Golden Rules of Communication

(1) *Good listening*. It is important that your partner feels that you are *really* listening to what he is saying. Do you understand what he means? Ask for clarification if you're

not certain. Whatever you do, don't use the time when he's talking to rehearse your own answers. Sometimes, just being allowed to feel a certain way and having these feelings acknowledged by your partner is enough to defuse an issue.

(2) *Check it out*. All too often we jump to conclusions, assuming one thing when our partner meant something completely different. A heterosexual couple whom I counselled fought over family days out: the wife wanted to take a packed lunch and the husband wanted to eat in a restaurant. The husband accused the wife of being a cheapskate and never wanting to spend money. A huge row erupted about money. When I finally got him to 'check it out' and ask, '*Am I right in thinking* that the reason you don't want to eat in a restaurant is because you want to save money?', we discovered that she was against the restaurant because she had to expend so much energy in controlling their young children that she could not enjoy the meal. She preferred a packed lunch on the beach where the children could play and she could unwind. Once they had 'checked it out' they could communicate properly.

(3) *One issue at a time*. Several issues often get mixed up together. In the example above, the argument became not only about where to eat on a day out but also about attitudes to money. As both sides try to win an argument, each party tends to throw old grievances into the ring, and before long it is not clear *what* the argument is about. These arguments become so destructive because couples begin to think there is something fundamentally wrong with their relationship rather than with the way in which they argue. A disagreement over where to eat is solvable but one about that plus money, plus the mother-in-law, plus buying the new car without properly consulting is not.

(4) *Deal with it here and now*. If you deal with problems as they occur you are less likely to have left-over issues

ready to throw on to the bonfire of anger. The other advantage of sorting it out when it happens is that often you can still do something about it. If you do not wish to see the film your lover is suggesting, tell him before you arrive at the cinema rather than sulking afterwards over how little you enjoyed *Ninja 3 – The Domination*. If you feel his mother is running you down, deal with it before she leaves, or the two of you will be arguing about history. Too many couples shut their eyes to problems hoping they will go away – a recipe for disaster. Either all the minor irritations (pinches) build up into an explosion (crunches) or the couple learn to sidestep the issues and end up sidestepping the relationship. Unless you deal with the issues you will both feel misunderstood and ignored. The result is that you will grow apart. Deal with the pinches when they happen and you will have fewer crunches.

(5) *Don't put words or feelings on to the other person.* We might like to think we know what our partner is thinking and sometimes we feel our partner should be a mind reader: if he loved me he would know! I have yet to meet a couple who can manage this trick successfully on every subject. We are not always clear ourselves on what we want or why we want it, so what chance has our partner got? *Never* start a sentence with 'you say' or 'you think' or 'you feel'. This can sound like an accusation. Instead try 'I feel that you think . . .' If you are wrong, your partner can correct you and explain how he really thinks or feels.

(6) *Separate the person from the act.* We all hate criticism. It touches on our fear that we are unlovable and that we can lose the man we love. Criticism puts us on the defensive and then we break all the golden rules of communication. It feels less like criticism if you talk about the action that is making you annoyed rather than the person. Don't say, 'You make me so angry', instead 'What you did made me angry'! For example, 'When you left your shoes in

the middle of the room for me to trip over it made me angry.' Notice I mentioned one particular time, rather than saying, 'You *always* leave your shoes lying about.' I've always found it difficult to take criticism. However, I can accept it when I know *one* of my actions is being criticized rather than me as a person.

(7) *Be specific*. Rather than making general complaints – 'You're irresponsible with money' – be specific. Generalizations start arguments because we can always think of a time when the complainer purchased something frivolous. If you are specific – 'I wish you would learn to balance your cheque book' – it is easier for your partner to accept. He understands what small manageable changes he is being asked for.

(8) *Show your workings*. My maths teacher would not give any marks for writing down an answer, even if it was right, unless you showed your workings. '42' on its own means nothing: we had to explain how we arrived there. Culturally, men are often expected to have all the answers. We need to show the assumptions on which decisions have been based in case they are wrong, but often we do not like to show the confused thinking we employ to reach our conclusions. However, unless you show your 'workings', your actions will sometimes make little sense to your partner.

(9) *Be direct*. 'I want doesn't get' is a phrase we are often taught in childhood. Not only is it considered rude to ask for something, but we also run the risk of the request being rejected. Many people find it impossible to ask directly for what they want: instead of saying, 'I'm tired, would you mind cooking the meal tonight', they drop hints or bang around in the kitchen, hoping that their partner will get the message. Other couples use humour to try to explain what they want. Your partner may not notice hints or may misinterpret them.

(10) *Give compliments.* We often tell our partners what we dislike about their behaviour but assume that they already know about the many things we like. If you compliment your partner and thank him for the tasks he performs for you, it will be easier for him to hear any complaints without feeling you're always criticizing. How long is it since you complimented your lover? Now, how long is it since you complained?

(11) *Good communication is a joint responsibility.* If there is a problem, *tell* your partner, don't wait for him to *ask*. If you feel that something is troubling him, *ask*. Don't wait for him to *tell* you.

(12) *It's OK to argue.* A lot of couples feel that a good relationship is one without arguments. However, a low-conflict partnership is a poor partnership: it is only through conflict that we learn about the relationship, reconcile our differences and grow together. When a couple does not argue, tensions under the surface are never addressed, leaving simmering resentment that eats away at the relationship. Rows are only destructive if they fail to solve anything or if you keep on having the same fights about the same things. If this is the case, look at the pattern of your arguments and see if you need to incorporate any of the golden rules.

How to use the Twelve Golden Rules of Communication

Change is always difficult, which is why it is a good idea to incorporate the golden rules one at a time. Take them in manageable steps. Next time you have a row try out the first. If it works incorporate it into your behaviour and use it again. If it did not work, try playing back the argument in your head and finding out what went wrong. This will allow you to learn from the experience and become better equipped next time round. When you feel you have incorporated one rule move on to the next.

CONCLUSION: WHAT STRAIGHT COUPLES CAN LEARN FROM US

What keeps gay relationships together? There is no single answer. The ingredients for success change as couples move through each of the six gay-relationship stages and solve the different issues as they present themselves. In the early years, couples who have rewarding relationships demonstrate a high degree of compatibility with complementary skills and needs. In the later years a lack of possessiveness is required for both men to achieve their individual potential. Love on its own is never enough to sustain *any* relationship – gay or straight.

The lack of role models for gay couples means that when problems occur we often feel that something is intrinsically wrong with our relationship. My model of how gay partnerships change over time will help you recognize if this is so or whether your difficulties are similar to those faced by other couples at your developmental stage.

As a reminder, the six stages are:

(1) BLENDING: FIRST YEAR

The couple are deeply in love and have eyes only for each other. Limerence is at its height and the partners concentrate on their similarities. Each is frightened of upsetting the other and arguments are avoided. Problems can arise when one partner holds back and is frightened of following his feelings. It is feared when limerence wears off that the relationship is flawed.

(2) NESTING: SECOND AND THIRD YEAR

The couple are aware of their surroundings and begin to set up home together. They start to air their differences, normally about smaller domestic issues. Each has to learn to set aside the 'male gender' issues and form an equal partnership. Problems are caused by a power struggle where both men try to lead, or when they fail to negotiate between their different opinions.

(3) SELF-AFFIRMING: FOURTH AND FIFTH YEAR

Each partner reasserts his own individual personality and the couple begin to solve their more fundamental differences. Each develops separate interests outside the relationship, which may include outside sexual partners. Problems may occur either because the couple are frightened to voice their personal needs, or from outside sexual interests.

(4) COLLABORATING: SIXTH TO FOURTEENTH YEAR

This is a period of intense productivity for the couple. Some form business partnerships together while others use the security of the relationship to embark alone on major projects. Problems arise when the couple take each for granted or one partner feels left behind. Boredom may also be an issue.

(5) ADAPTING: FIFTEENTH TO TWENTY-FOURTH YEAR

During this period the couple have to adapt to the changes life throws at them, in contrast to the early stages where they are more inward-looking. Ageing parents and mid-life crises are two of the most common problems and, if successfully negotiated, the experience can begin to bring the couple closer together again. Difficulties may arise because the partners take each too much for granted.

(6) REPARTNERING: TWENTY-FIFTH YEAR UPWARDS

The couple recommit to each other and achieve the closeness and interdependency of their early times together. Problems may come from ill-health.

There is no such thing as a typical gay couple, so the timings of the stages are only approximate. Each couple will stay in a stage until they solve the inherent dilemmas or separate after failing to reach a workable compromise. Although all couples will move through this process, one partner can arrive at the next stage before the other, which may cause distress especially in the early years.

One of the myths about relationships is that couples who are about the same age have the best ones or, to put it another way, that where there is a significant age difference 'it can never last'. The experiences of the men in this book put this generalization to question. The average age difference is 6.7 years but 50 per cent of the couples have more than a ten-year gap. No matter what the ages of the couple or the gap they will progress through the first three stages in the same way. However, in the later three stages, if one partner is younger he will probably use the 'Collaborating' years more, while the older partner normally reaches 'Repartnering' before his younger lover. If both men are older when they start the relationship the fourth and fifth stages tend to be shorter.

The Differences between Gay and Heterosexual Couples

The most fundamental difference is that straights have plenty of role models for how to conduct their relationships. (I hope this book helps to redress the balance for us.) The development of a heterosexual relationship is dominated by child-rearing, leaving less room for husband and wife to concentrate on their individual development. When the gay model was shown to a group of heterosexual Relate counsellors, they saw much that they would wish for their own relationships. This may sound radical but perhaps heterosexuals have something to learn from gay couples.

One of the findings of my research has been the 'equality' of gay relationships: neither partner is dominant or submissive, leader or follower. Heterosexual women often complain about the lack of equality in their relationships. Many straight couples cannot achieve the gay couple's ability to support each other in projects away from the relationship. This can present a problem when their children are older and when the woman seeks to achieve something for herself. We are better at coping with differences than they are – be they age or cultural. Heterosexuals are busy fighting about the differences between men and women. Equality, lack of possessiveness and tolerance are three qualities that many heterosexuals could learn from gay couples.

Straight couples who worry about being accepted by their families are the exception to the rule. For gay couples it *is* the rule. This lack of acceptance by society and the myth that gay relationships do not last mean that a homosexual couple feel settled and trust in their relationship much later than a heterosexual couple would. It also takes longer for gay couples to integrate their finances. When a man marries a woman everything that was 'his' or 'hers' legally becomes 'theirs'. Although gay couples are emotionally faithful, far fewer gays than straights are sexually exclusive.

In every relationship, one partner is more responsible for the 'closeness' and the other for 'independence'. This allows them to form a fulfilling relationship, but to protect their own needs. In a marriage the woman has been traditionally responsible for the 'closeness' and the man for the 'independence'. In a gay relationship these needs are more balanced and under certain circumstances the couple might swap roles. The couples in this book have generally taken up one of these responsibilities each. Finally, in both straight and gay couples, the partners become more like each other as they grow together.

Why are there not more gay couples?

As we feel more comfortable about being openly gay and come completely out of the closet, we will have better and more rewarding relationships. Being a couple is a radical statement: it directly challenges straight society's idea that we are unhappy and destined for loneliness. I believe that we are no longer internalizing homophobia but are fighting it and therefore better able to love ourselves and, in turn, someone special. We are taking great strides forward.

Many gay men want a relationship but fail because they mix up looking for a sexual contact with the search for a long-term partner. Good sex does not predict a good relationship: too many gays are looking for a handsome face and good body, forgetting about personality. Most of the men in this book would not describe their partner as the 'ideal' they had been searching for, but they compromised and found somebody special rather than waiting for 'Mr Perfect', that mythical man out there who will fulfil all our needs. The reality is that there are lots of people we could have great relationships with if only we compromised. Compromise is a very useful talent to bring to a relationship.

The gay community needs to value couples more. Many of my couples report problems with other gays who try to undermine their relationship, normally through jealousy. Many report that their friends are surprised that they're still together. Some gays who are not in a relationship expect couples to live up to their fantasy of what a perfect gay relationship is like – and are dismissive when they fail to achieve it.

We need to fight for the recognition of gay partnerships

The law must recognize gay relationships and give us the same protection enjoyed by heterosexuals. While we have to make certain we have made a will, the worldly goods of a married man or woman who dies intestate are automatically given to their spouse. Our wills are more likely to be challenged than those of our heterosexual brothers and sisters. Worse, we have to pay inheritance tax, which a heterosexual spouse does not, and even a gay couple's home is subject to tax. With private pension schemes, our partners receive only a lump-sum payment when we die. Heterosexual men leave their wives a pension worth, potentially, much more. Many companies offer benefits to the spouses of their employees that are unavailable to employees with gay partners. When a business offers customers 'family membership' we should be allowed to benefit, too. If we meet somebody from another country and fall in love, we should have the same rights as heterosexuals and not have to face immigration problems.

We need to celebrate our partnerships. Ceremonies like Roy and Martin's are fine, but we should also be able to undergo a civil marriage at a register office if we wish. It is a matter of equality. A debate is currently taking place about giving common-law wives and husbands the same rights as married men and women. We have an even stronger case, because, after all, they have *decided* not to marry. We have not even been allowed to choose.

Whether it is official registration for our relationships or some form of 'marriage', gay couples' rights should be put on the agenda and become part of our fight for equality.

And finally

At the beginning of this book I asked whether it is possible for gay couples to be 'together for ever'. My research has shown that our relationships are thriving and doing better than I dared even to hope. Long-term gay partnerships have always existed but we are fortunate that it is now easier today than it has ever been. Together for ever? Yes – but it's up to you!

INDEX

Scott, 203–24, 227, 230, 231,
    235
Seabrook, Jeremy, 85
Sean, 94–113, 141, 172
secrecy, 45, 53, 231–2, 233
    over HIV/Aids, 254
    see also closetedness
Secular Society, National, 255
security, 82, 83, 225, 235, 258
    children's, 201
    commitment ceremonies and,
        161–2
    of employment, 260
    familiarity and, 84
    monogamy/non-monogamy
        and, 234
    and moving in together, 60
    see also insecurity
'see-saws' concerning money,
    113–15
self-acceptance, 55–9, 96, 121,
    150–52, 163–4, 165,
    269, 307
    bisexuality and, 39, 45,
        67–9, 74–8, 178,
        179–80
    sex and, 228–9
    see also coming out,
        conversion *and*
        insecurity
self-affirming stage, *see* stages
    in relationships
self-employment, 91, 105
self-esteem, 133
    consent laws and, 132–3
    money and, 112, 117
self-knowledge, 71–2
self-protection, 139

separateness, 224, 225
separating, *see* relationships,
    breakdown of
sex
    age and, 129, 130, 132–3,
        286
    anonymous, 28
    attitudes towards, 13, 14,
        15–16, 46–9, 95–6,
        227
    as barometer in relationship,
        233–4
    discussing with children, 186
    dominance/submission in,
        67, 268
    emotion and, 227, 228
    as escape from other issues,
        229
    expectations concerning, 231
    frequency of, 83, 229, 242,
        277
    group, *see* group sex
    as hobby, 228
    importance of gay identity,
        203
    as issue in counselling, 169
    issues around, 203, 227–36,
        286–7
    and length/stage of
        relationship, 242, 277,
        278
    level of need for, 36, 48–9,
        211–12, 220, 231, 278
    and love, 212–13, 220, 221,
        227, 230, 234, 276
    place in relationships,
        10–16, 48

rules over sex with others,
231–3
see also monogamy *and*
non-monogamy
safe, *see* safe sex
stress and, 231
talking about, 109–10, 111,
235–6
as 'using' people, 47
sexuality, explanations of,
186–7
Shawn, 203–24, 227, 230,
231, 235
shingles, 243, 251–2
Skynner, Robin, 25
social class, *see* class
social security, 110
social workers, 202
space, 89–90, 91, 113, 138,
140–1, 187–8, 221
sexual freedom and, 221–2
spenders/savers, 113–14
spiritualism, 156–7
stability, *see* security
stages in relationships, 2–3,
33, 35, 174–5, 302–4
adapting, 258–61, 285, 304
blending, 32–5, 84, 141–2,
194, 229, 284, 303
return to after crises,
216–17, 224
collaborating, 224–6, 257,
259, 285, 304, 305
nesting, 61–5, 81–5, 140,
257, 303
repartnering, 284–7, 304,
305

self-affirming, 119–20,
140–44, 165, 224, 303
timing/length of, 85, 141,
258, 284, 303–5
status, equalizing, 225
step-families, *see* children,
relationships with
stereotypes, 70
see also roles
Steve, 120–34, 137, 142
stress, 94, 194–5, 243, 251–2
and sexual desire, 231
and support from friends,
245, 248
see also crises
subconscious motivations,
24–6, 55, 82
support, 99–100, 144, 151–2,
168, 171, 261, 306
around HIV/Aids, 264
in collaborating stage, 219,
224
sex and, 233
support groups, 249, 257

taboos, 111
tax, 91
inheritance, 91, 280–81,
292–3, 308
teaching, 96
telephone dating, 29
Tennov, Dorothy, 33–4
terminology, 154, 172–3
therapy, 24, 25, 151–2, 164,
249
see also counselling
threesomes, 11, 208–9, 211,
232